3o Centuries Under the Sea

30 Centuries Under the Sea

FRÉDÉRIC DUMAS
translated by **Philip A. Facey**

CROWN PUBLISHERS, INC.   NEW YORK

Printed in the United States of America
Published simultaneously in Canada by General Publish-
ing Company Limited

LIBRARY OF CONGRESS CATALOGING IN PUBLICATION DATA

Dumas, Frédéric.
  Thirty centuries under the sea.

  Translation of Trente siècles sous la mer.
  Bibliography: p.
  1. Shipwrecks—Mediterranean Sea. 2. Underwater
archaeology. I. Title.
G525.D7713 1976   909′.09′822   76-13031
ISBN 0-517-51875-9

Designed by Laurie Zuckerman

Contents

1 *Les Magnons*   1
2 *The Port Cros Amphora*   4
3 *Mahdia*   6
4 *The Amphora Field at La Chrétienne*   16
5 *Grand Congloué*   21
6 *Antikythera*   48
7 *The* Panama   61
8 *The* Dramont   68
9 *The Wreck from the Bronze Age*   77
10 *The Tiles*   111
11 *The* Slava Rossii   113
12 *La Chrétienne A*   118
13 *The Baths*   132
14 *The Bowls*   136
15 *The Ingots*   139

16 *Shab Rumi*   143
17 *Medeon*   147
18 *The Bilge Pump*   152
19 *In the Maldive Islands*   168
20 *Ancient Ships*   172
21 *Amphoras*   179
22 *The Formation of a Wreck*   181
23 *The Preservation of Materials*   192
24 *Pillage*   199
25 *The Future of Underwater Archaeology*   204
    Bibliography   212
    Index   214

LES MAGNONS

IN THE SEA NEAR our house a string of islands forms the outer limit of the Bay of Sanary. The last of these islands, Les Magnons, extends for some distance under the water in a plateau of large rocks hollowed out by caves and marked with faults. Where the tallest rocks reach the surface, the water is very clear and not more than thirty to fifty feet deep.

The first time we put on water goggles, these rocks became transformed for us into a community of merous (groupers), and we were astonished to find these forty-pound fish living so close to the shore, in a place where our lines had never brought in anything but whitebait.

The merous would come out of their caves, station themselves below me and look up at me. I would see only their heads and, to either side, their large pectoral fins that looked like the wings on a popular image of Cupid; and, like Cupid, they breathed out in gusts.

With the advent of war and the Occupation, those of us who lived on the Riviera, where there was no agriculture, had to give

up exploring the sea and start searching for food. We took to going
out by families to pick the little silver-gray leaves from the wild
bushes that grew on the cliff which fronted our homes. Boiled,
rinsed, and boiled again, these leaves could pass in a pinch for a
wretched sort of spinach.

Whenever our little band of friends wanted to get together, I
would be asked for a merou and I'd get a boat to take me out to
Les Magnons. There the merous out for a swim would be linger-
ing among the rocks, and as I approached they would turn to gape
at me. If my presence disturbed them, they would quickly retreat
and resume their contemplation from a little further away. I
would then swim very gently, like a floating piece of deadwood,
and, taking advantage of their curiosity, kill them cleanly with an
arrow through the brain. At the time I sought only perfection in
my technique, without acknowledging its cruelty; besides, such
catches had the semblance of an adventure, and, when I got back,
they brought me a bit of transient glory.

On certain days large numbers of black pomfrets about as long
as an adolescent goldfish, with long forked tails, would be suspended in the water like flies in the air. Leaving the surface with
a *coup de reins*,[1] I would break through this floating veil, and the
pomfrets would scatter in staccato bursts, making shock waves
that transmitted their fright through the water. The merou,
alerted, would slither into his cave, swallowed up by the rock.
But then, his curiosity being stronger than his instinct for self-
preservation, he would turn in his lair and poke his nose out the
entrance, or perhaps through a window that afforded him a better
look; and his curiosity would be fatal.

I knew every one of those big, dog-eyed fish, and I enjoyed the
luxury of being able to choose the one that was best suited for the
number of people who would be present among us on any given
day. Everyone would bring his own ration of bread and oil, and
the rather ordinary but abundant fish seemed to us like a deli-
cacy. We invariably ate too much.

Since 1938 a common interest in underwater hunting had
formed the basis of my friendship with Philippe Tailliez and

---

[1] The maneuver called the *coup de reins* is described by Jacques Cousteau in
The Silent World as "the technique the whale uses to sound. For a floating man it
consists of bending from the waist and pointing the head and torso down. Then
the legs are thrown up in the air with a powerful snap and the diver plummets
straight down." (Tr.)

Jacques Cousteau, both of whom were naval officers. We were separated by the war, but in 1941 we came together again. Jacques decided to make a documentary film about underwater hunting and, in order to facilitate the filming of my maneuvers, he brought to Les Magnons what we called "the merou pump," a noisy little compressor that delivered a pitiful supply of air through a hose that was always too short.

Ten years later, when simple goggle diving had given way to scuba diving, the merous were abundant once again and, working among them, I came to know them better and to be one of their best friends.

Some of my friends have found at Les Magnons a number of whole amphoras camouflaged by clusters of posidonia,* aquatic plants with long green ribbons.

Today most of the merous have been killed off, the naïve, the hesitant, and the overly curious being the first to go. The rare survivors have become very timid, and, if you're lucky enough to see one, it's only thanks to the persistence of retinal images.

Much to my chagrin, I now see fragments of amphoras everywhere about this terrain that I have traversed so often, my arbalest in hand. Welded to one another by concretions, the fragments lie embedded in the rocks and fill the spaces between them, partly concealed by the green or maroon moss of the algae. I see remnants of lead pipe and tubular forms covered with concretions that break easily, giving off a black liquid, the residue from corroded iron. Under the water, even more than on land, you see only what you're looking for.

---

*A deciduous marine plant whose fallen leaves accumulate underwater and on beaches. They cover vast areas of the bottom of the Mediterranean.

2

The PORT CROS AMPHORA

I FOUND MY FIRST amphora in 1939. At that time undersea hunting was still a novelty, and I was fascinated by it. We would come out of the water naked and frozen, gather up some driftwood, and build a huge fire whose flames would curl the hairs on our legs and marble our skins with red blotches, creating an aroma of roasted pig flesh.

On the day that I found the amphora, I was hunting around Port Cros, a high, craggy island covered with pines and scrub right down to the shoreline. The water was so transparent that it was almost invisible, and I felt as if I could fall right through it to the bottom. Under a misty sky, I swam in the too pure, deserted water, following the contours of the rocky shore. As I entered a little bay where the bottom was all barren sand, I spied a rather bulky but intact amphora lying all by itself between two pieces of pottery. A *coup de reins* and I had it by the handles, but it was too heavy to bring up to the surface. Instead, I dragged it along the bottom, progressing slowly and surfacing at intervals for air. To my great relief, I was able to go the last few yards with my head above the water.

The amphora must have rubbed against the sand for a long time, and the constant abrasion had made a hole in its side that I could put my hand through.

The owner of the only hotel on the island was displeased to see the amphora carted off, but archaeological discoveries in the sea have yet to give rise to any legal problems. Since I had caught no fish, I was happy to have the amphora, but I had no idea of the significance of its being there under the water.

When, later on, Cousteau built a house at Sanary, I gave him the amphora and he put it on the mantel in his living room. There it remained until the time when we were exploring the wreck of a Roman ship at Grand Congloué with the aid of Lallemand, a stocky, exuberant amateur archaeologist from Marseille. On a visit to Cousteau one day, Lallemand saw my find and was astounded. I had discovered intact one of those Ionian amphoras made of whitish earth spangled with mica, of which he had until then seen only scattered fragments dug up in the ground under Marseille, at a depth where the layers of soil went back to the foundation of the city by the Greeks.

3

MAHDIA

AFTER WE COMPLETED our first film, Jacques Cousteau invented the aqualung, and in 1945 it occurred to him that we might share our new methods of diving with the French navy, of which he was a member. The Ministry wasn't too enthusiastic about the idea, but Jacques showed them the film of our work in wrecked ships and secured the necessary permission. That was the origin of what became the Undersea Research Group.

Philippe Tailliez, who was senior to Cousteau, was put in charge of the group as a whole, and Cousteau was given command of the *Elie Monnier*, a former German diving tender that I was to help him fetch at Cherbourg. Jacques had arranged for me to be engaged by the navy, despite the fact that I was just an ordinary civilian who had never had any rank in the army, where I served as a mule driver.

In 1948 Jacques organized a training cruise to Tunisia. He had succeeded in obtaining for his ship an official, though not very military, mission: to find the ancient Roman port of Carthage, under the direction of Father Poidebar, a learned Jesuit well

known in archaeological circles. Father Poidebar had been one of
the first to use aerial photography in the search for old ruins,
having used this technique in the course of his remarkable work
on the ports of ancient Tyre and Sidon.

Jacques was also planning to get on film some shots of men
fishing for tuna with a Tunisian madrague.

Our enthusiasm reached its height when he announced that we
would make some dives to explore a Roman galley discovered in
1907. The existence of this galley became known to archaeologists at that time as a result of their efforts to determine
the origin of certain Greek works of art that were circulating
clandestinely in Tunisia. The archaeologists found out that some
sponge divers fishing off Mahdia had found on the sea bottom a
collection of pillars arranged in tidy rows, together with a whole
assortment of Greek *objets d'art*. With the help of the French
navy the researchers were able, between 1908 and 1913, to bring
up from the sea enough statues, bronzes, marbles, and architectural elements to fill six rooms at the Bardo Museum in Tunis.

Jacques had consulted the reports made at the time, from
which he learned that about sixty pillars had been left in place
and that, what was disturbing to us, the helmet divers had penetrated the deck of the ship, dug into the mud below, and discovered still more trinkets.

I love to swim around over the dilapidated decks of modern
sunken ships, go down into their dark holds, where I'm afraid,
and wrench free their copper lamps. Already I could imagine
myself inside the Roman ship, groping around up to my elbows
in the mud, and the thought of all the wonders that I would touch
saddened me. I would have liked to possess them.

No sooner had we arrived in Tunis than we began to see marbles that were eroded partially, but less than is usually the case,
and bronzes that were magnificently preserved—or restored; but
we also saw some pieces of very pure art that stood out amid the
host of fraudulent copies. The specialists had given it as their
opinion, without committing themselves, that the ship had gone
down in 86 B.C., and they attributed its cargo to the pillage of
Athens by the Romans. They had even uncovered some parts of
the ship itself: leaden stocks from wooden anchors that had disintegrated, fragments of the hull all blackened and curled up, copper nails of various lengths, fishhooks, and ship's crockery. Would
I have enough faith in the efficacy of our new methods to dream

of the treasures that we would find left behind by the helmet divers?

On the twelfth of June we dropped anchor off Salammbô, where Father Poidebar had seen the Roman port of Carthage on aerial photographs. It was there that, dressed in his black cassock, he came aboard, striding purposefully as if to take possession of us. Aged, but still willful and energetic, he explained his theory to us, weaving into it his memories of other ancient ports. He expected of us that we should furnish the proof of the existence of the Roman port, which he was convinced was there.

I dove with Lieutenant Commander Alinat, whose competence and kindness were a delight to us all. He was always working or puttering around, without making a fuss about his gold stripes, the symbols of his rank, which he hardly ever wore anyway. And since he could do everything, we fell into the bad habit of leaving too much of the dirty work to him.

In the shallow, turbid water the posidonia, as they would, have formed on the bottom little mounds called "mattes," leaving only small areas of sand. Further on, still in shallow water, the bottom was covered with a green leafy plant that looked like cress. Some rather ordinary pebbles, tin cans, rusted oil drums, and broken goblets all shared the terrain with the familiar discarded tires, new guests of the sea that seem to be as durable as the amphoras.

At sea it's hard to judge distances, and it would be difficult to direct with the naked eye a systematic search by divers. Alinat took up his hydrographic circle, an instrument analogous to the sextant and used to fix the position of the ship. The first thing he had to do was to draft a map of the area in order to find the locations indicated by Father Poidebar's sketches and photographs.

Jacques made his usual round of visits, official and unofficial, a task for which he is very gifted. He always pretended to dislike such chores, but we knew better.

For three days, with Father Poidebar looking on and becoming more and more irritated, we conscientiously but unenthusiastically explored the turbid, monotonous bay. We sank our arms into the soft walls of the mattes and made soundings in the soil with a rod. Whenever we felt the rod strike an obstacle, we would start digging, but the obstacle invariably turned out to be a perfectly ordinary boulder. Indulging my passion for explosives, I dynamited a rocky table; the surface shuddered and collapsed, leaving a cone-shaped hollow in the bottom. We dove into the yellowish cloud stirred up by the explosion and brought up hardened clay covered with a thin layer of calcification.

We were all convinced that our search was futile, except for Father Poidebar, who kept muttering the same sentences and seemed to be harboring a grudge against us.

In the bay there was a layer of clear water near the surface through which one could see the peaks of the mattes, but their bases were hidden by the murky layer below. The depth at which this murky layer began varied from day to day and, the sides of the mattes being steep and very irregular, the view of the bay from the air must have been quite different from one day to the next, so that an observer might have seen all sorts of things—the face of Hitler or, with a little luck, even a Roman port.

If the port was indeed there, it had to be much further down in the soil; but we didn't have the equipment necessary to dig down far enough so that we would either find the port or be able to affirm that the priest, carried away in old age by the momentum of his active youth, had only dreamed that it was there.

We left Father Poidebar to his cherished illusions and went to make some films of tuna fishing. The fishermen would stretch an enormous net along the length of the shore, blocking the path of the migratory tuna. The big blue fish, looking in profile like aerial bombs, would swim into the net and, searching for a way out, wind up in the "death chamber," where the fishermen massacred them with long hooks, and the water ran thick and red with their blood.

On the twentieth of June we dropped anchor off Mahdia, at the point indicated in the official report of the first expedition. To get a ship into a position described by polar coordinates is a laborious task. Jacques and Alinat manipulated their hydrographic circles, but I couldn't help them. The depth of the water at this point was a hundred twenty-eight feet, and the shore in the distance was a thin, buff-colored line that just barely separated the sea from the sky. Without waiting for a ladder to be put out, we jumped over the side and soon arrived at a bottom that was sandy and corrugated by gently sloping dunes, with some meager vegetation and large, full-grown sponges scattered about. In the past we had almost always chosen to dive in places where the sea had some particular attraction to offer, like an unusual rock formation, an underwater cliff, or a wrecked ship; but here I saw a very ordinary bottom that seemed to be as vast as the sea itself, and I couldn't imagine finding a sunken galley in such a place.

For five days we searched by various methods: a sled towed through the water close to the bottom, divers armed with compasses, a "rake" of six divers side by side all in view of one another. We systematically explored an area eight hundred feet long and four hundred eighty feet wide, marked out on the bottom by rope lines and numbered buoys. But there was no ship, only a flat, monotonous sea bottom.

Jacques and Alinat plunged themselves into their calculations down in the mess, then went up to the bridge to manipulate the hydrographic circle, or train their binoculars on the coastline in search of "landmarks" that were never where they were supposed to be.

At the end of the fifth day we returned to Mahdia. There the streets, lined by white walls unbroken by windows or stores, would turn several times, only to finish in a dead end; and the children would follow us mockingly. Behind the walls, young but raucous voices wailed oriental songs. Everything was bathed in the light of a brilliant sun.

Father Poidebar, despite the fact that he had no interest in the galley, was kind enough to come by with some new information for us. Jacques and Alinat went back to their calculations. By this time the search for the galley had become a personal affair, and we were more concerned with simply solving the mystery of its location than with any treasures that it might contain. Down in the water, however, there was still nothing.

On the twenty-fifth, after we had discussed the problem at dinner, Jacques handed out some slips of paper and asked each one of us to write his opinion anonymously. When the opinions had been read, the choice fell upon that of Philippe Tailliez, who thought that we should search along the line of position indicated by the alignment of the Bordj, the ancient citadel of Mahdia, with a ruin that was shaped like a tooth. This was the only alignment about which we could say with certainty that the landmarks had withstood the ravages of time.

We resumed operations, this time with the motor launch dragging a heavy weight along the bottom and a diver holding on to the towline at whatever distance from the bottom gave him the greatest visibility. In turbid waters this method was inefficient because the diver had to stay close to the bottom and could explore only a narrow strip of terrain; but here, where the water was clear, he could station himself fairly high and get a good view. The diver could concentrate on his search, leaving the navigation to those on the surface.

Tailliez was the first to go down, and before long he broke the surface, gesticulating wildly. He had seen a column. I went down the weighted line hand over hand, and soon it started into motion as the launch got underway again. The water lashed my face and ran insistently along the length of my body. In the distance a large fish loitered about above the sand. Fish always seem to me to be loitering. I'm probably just misled by the way they hold themselves suspended in the water, as if they were perfectly idle.

Out of the blue up ahead appeared a single small column, followed by a longer one overgrown with sponges. The presence of these clearly defined shapes made it easier for me to judge distances, enlarging, in effect, my field of vision. I was nevertheless still hesitant to let go of the towrope. The bottom became barren once again in the hazy water and I couldn't distinguish anything. As I reproached myself bitterly for not having stopped to look around, I passed by a shiny tin can and the trail of an anchor in the sand, signs that we had been in the vicinity before, which was hardly encouraging. But then a vague, dark mass suddenly came into focus. It was the galley!

My hand let go of the towrope and I immediately ceased to feel the water massaging my body as it passed. I swam about freely, feasting my eyes on the outlines of the wreck, an exhilarating sight after the disheartening monotony of the plain I had just surveyed. Below me, enormous columns lay side by side, supporting others whose bulk had been reduced by erosion. In the bluish light nothing had any color, but you could still perceive the soft, occasionally repugnant texture of the round or corollaceous sponges and other animal excrescences. The merous came out of their caves opaque, but became diaphanous as they swam over the sand and approached me without fear. All along the periphery of the wreck the water, richer in oxygen, had given the marine life a vigor that was extraordinary for this barren ground, making it an oasis in the vague shape of a boat. Since there were no statues about, I gathered up some remnants of spongy wood and some nails swollen by the amalgamation of sand with their corroding copper.

Jacques served champagne and ordered the ship to full dress with the action pennant aloft.

The next day I went down with Alinat to sketch out the dimensions of the wreck. It was seventy feet long and forty feet wide. Some capitals and column bases had escaped from the hold and lay half buried in the sand, riddled with more holes than a Swiss cheese. When I dug around them, I found the marble of the buried portion to be perfectly smooth, which explains why statues in museums display parts that have been corroded by the sea and others that are intact, having been protected by the soil. A few yards beyond one end of the ship, the tips of two large leaden anchor stocks could just barely be seen protruding from the earth. The anchors had not been let out, which meant that the ship had not been moored before it went down. Near the anchors, among the first of the columns, I spied a large piece of wood that was surprisingly well preserved. As I ran my hand along it under the mud of the bottom, I found that it followed the axis of the ship, between the masses of marble.

For five days, nine divers went down as often as the laws of diving—i.e., the decompression tables—would permit. When a diver's time below was up, those on the surface would fire a rifle into the sea. The diver would be alerted by the sound wave, which traveled rapidly in the water, while the bullet itself, creating a foamy wake, hardly went a yard before it became inert and sank to the bottom. Each diver left with a specific task to perform, but it was hard to keep from being distracted. As members of the group we were obliged to work in the interests of science, while as individuals we were looking for statuary. Little by little our disdain for the old helmeted sponge divers gave way to admiration.

The cargo boom brought up columns and heavy blocks of marble that made the ship list, and when they broke the surface they had more colors than a parrot. Those who had never witnessed this spectacle before always get ecstatic, and the literature on the subject abounds with enthusiastic epithets that have become clichés. Shortly, however, the colors faded away, the marble got black and sticky, and gave off a persistent, frightful odor. With a hammer I broke up one slender column that was riddled with holes made by date mussels, delicious shellfish that have the shape and color of dates, and which we found hidden in regular cells with polished walls. My colleagues, claiming that the column was Pentelic marble, pretended to be scandalized that I had broken it up.

Alinat was always coming up with new ideas, which he insisted on trying out himself, usually with whatever materials he could find at hand. One afternoon he attached the hose from a compressed air supply to the nozzle of a powerful water gun, with the intention of creating an ascending column of air that would carry off the mud raised by the stream of water when it was directed at something that we wanted to disengage from the bottom. In its first trial, we used it to tunnel out under the stock of an anchor, so that I could get a rope around it and the anchor could be hauled up. The water gun stirred up a tremendous cloud of mud and the air sent a considerable volume spiraling to the surface, but we were still engulfed by darkness. The gun shook violently and escaped from my grasp to dance about in the water. I took off in pursuit, catching hold of it about halfway along its length. It lashed back furiously under the reaction from the water jet, flinging me upward in a spiral path. Then it occurred to me to bend the hose and point the jet upwards, so that the water gun, subdued at last, took me back down to the galley. Later on, Alinat's idea would be abandoned in favor of the suction hose.

Rather than wrestle with the bucking water gun, I preferred to dig with my hands. Crouched on the bottom, I would sink my arms down through the surface layer of dense, glutinous mud and, as if I were reaching under a rug, grope around in the gravel below, where I would find pieces of wood and fragments of pottery and marble. Under the gravel there was a layer of soil that was hard, like packed earth, and I couldn't hope to find anything there. Driven by the desire to feel the sweet, smooth lines of a piece of sculpture, I dug until my hands were raw and shredded. But we had decided to dig a trench around the wreck, and I was obliged to take up the water gun again. Feeling around in the mud, I found two large copper nails, but in the darkness I had no idea where to put them, so I used them to dig with. When I got tired and swam out of the muddy cloud on my way to the surface, the nails were shining like gold.

Jacques was making his first color film, in which each of us had the opportunity to play a role. This passion for making films contributed greatly to the success of Cousteau's work. Unlike the rest of us, he wasn't haunted by statuary; he wanted visual documentation of our activities. The theme of his film was the contrast between the drab, blue, shadowless appearance of the bottom under natural light, and the vivid colors that materialized when the same area was illuminated by a battery of electric lights.

In the sea a diver's body is weightless, and we didn't have the leverage we needed to do our digging. I tried to solve this problem by diving with a forty-pound lead weight of the kind used by helmet divers. There was no danger involved in making a rapid descent, because my ears would adjust by themselves to the changes in pressure. As soon as I let go of the ladder, I went down like a plane in a nosedive, then leveled off and glided the rest of the way to the galley. The weight was very practical until I got to the bottom, because the minute I put it down, I lost it.

As I lay wallowing in the mud my hand came in contact with something round, of a rough texture, that I thought at first might be the bottom of a large earthenware jar. But I could tell from the feel of it that it was made of stone. The sides flared out into hard soil that I couldn't penetrate with my hand. By this time I was running out of air, and I went rapidly up to the surface. I asked Jacques to take leave of his camera for a minute in order to have a look at what I had found, for he was the only one who had the authority to decide whether it was worth our while to dig for it. He was intrigued himself and agreed that the thing should be brought up. As I excavated with the water gun, my hands were stung by tiny flying pebbles. Feeling a cavity form itself under the object, I got a grip on it and wrenched free a stone for grinding flour, such as I would see much later on all the ancient ships. The merous, who were pale when we first arrived, changed their color to match that of the swirls of mud we stirred up. I now felt very tender toward these big fish.

That evening I experienced a throbbing pain in my left shoulder, which had been fractured during the Occupation. It was "the bends," an excess of nitrogen in the body that occurs when a diver comes up too fast from the bottom. My colleagues threw me into the decompression chamber and set the dial at four atmospheres. The pain went away, but boredom set in. The pressure was decreased by stages for an hour, after which I was liberated from the chamber and from the pain as well. It came back during the night, however, and lasted for several days.

Often at the end of a stint underwater, I would head for the big piece of wood that went down between the columns and fascinated me so much. I saw there the keel, with the garboards still in the rabbets, or, as we would say today, with the first range of hull planks still in their grooves; but the whole structure seemed to me to be too complex to be analyzed at the end of a dive some hundred thirty feet down. Under a thin layer of mud, the columns rested on wood that had flattened out under the enormous weight. It wasn't a deck, because I could feel the ribs of the hull with my hands, which meant that there was nothing underneath. The sponge divers knew this and had misled the archaeologists. I got this impression from my hands, more than my eyes, and in the course of forays that were much too brief. At a hundred thirty feet there was just enough time for each diver to carry out a plan of action that was established in advance and rehearsed many times in his mind. When this was done, we were exhausted. I was therefore hardly in a position to contradict my colleagues when they talked as if the columns were resting on a deck.

As the days passed, the mud we raised drifted down to settle on the columns again, and the excavation took on a gray, dirty, lifeless appearance that somewhat diminished the tenderness we felt for this great commercial vessel that had sailed on the highest seas.

We no longer called the wreck a galley. A galley was a ship of war, rather than commerce; it was long and narrow, having been built for speed, and although it did have sails, it was propelled by large numbers of oars while in combat, or when, in the course of a journey, there was no wind.

On July 1, in the evening, we regretfully left Mahdia. Pressed for time, as usual, we went off without a single objet d'art, but we did have our memories and some truly valuable ideas.

4

The AMPHORA FIELD at LA CHRÉTIENNE

THE FOLLOWING YEAR, 1949, Jacques was assigned to the clearance of mines in Languedoc, where he revolutionized its technique. Houot replaced him on the *Elie Monnier,* and Tailliez relinquished command of the Undersea Research Group to Rossignol.

After Mahdia I had a longing to see other ancient wrecks. I was particularly attracted by the "amphora field" discovered not long before by Broussard and Dénéréaz of the Undersea Mountain-climbing Club of Cannes.

On the eleventh of August, taking advantage of an official mission of the *Elie Monnier* in Antibes, I lured my new colleagues off toward the lighthouse of La Chrétienne at Anthéor.

I went into the water in the company of Devilla, the ship's doctor, who was kind, humane, and not very military; he also had an athletic physique that often came in handy. We struggled against the current above a rocky ridge that rose sharply from the bottom and arrived, swimming underwater now, above a small patch of sand where there lay several broken amphoras only recently dug up. Where the sand ended, a large porous rock covered with strange concretions broke through a field of long posidonia, concealing the amphoras that were embedded there over a distance of about a hundred feet and at a depth of sixty feet.

In the afternoon we brought the ship to the site, and everyone dove for pottery.

For some time I had wanted to dig with the aid of a *suceuse* (suction hose), so that I could really excavate this seabed that I had surveyed so often with my eyes. I put together a rather simple device that consisted of a large hose made of heavy reinforced rubber through which compressed air from a smaller hose attached at the mouth could be sent up to the surface. As the air ascended, the bubbles would get larger and larger, creating a vacuum that drew in the water. A schoolboy would say that the water, made lighter by the air in the hose, rose in accordance with the principle of communicating vessels. In any case, there was suction at the mouth of the hose, and in deep water the *suceuse* would gobble up everything in sight. Devilla and I were assisted by Hodges, a young Royal Navy officer who had joined our mission as an observer. Employing all our strength, the three of us dragged the enormous, recalcitrant hose to the amphoras, raising in the process a cloud of white mud that must have reminded Hodges of the fogs in London. I traveled the last few yards with the hose held between my legs, so that I could pull myself along the rocks with my hands. Finally, half-exhausted and driven mad by the turbid water that was full of moving silhouettes, I opened the pet cock. The *suceuse* came to life with a gurgle and then began to purr. It sucked up all the mud from the water around us, so that at last we could see. The mouth of the hose bit into the soil, carving out a funnel-shaped hole, and the sand ran slowly down the sides to be swallowed up, together with large concretions, algae, and jar handles that looked like shinbones. As large as it was, however, the *suceuse* could be blocked, and I had to stop Hodges as he was feeding it an object that was simply too big. Now the amphoras emerging from the sand became more and more numerous; they were also getting cleaner, and before long we would find specimens that were almost like new. Small fish that came to forage near the *suceuse* would suddenly disappear, swallowed up. While my colleagues hauled up the amphoras that we dug out, I relished the excitement of manipulating this powerful new tool.

During the evening meal, on our way back to Toulon, we discussed the amphora field. Drawing on my experience at Mahdia, I maintained that there was a ship hidden underneath it. Although they didn't exactly contradict me, my associates had reservations about my thesis and looked for another explanation.

When we returned to La Chrétienne in September, the appearance of the site had changed, an indication that other divers had been at work there. The hole we had made was concealed by the bellies of abandoned amphoras, which, just to amuse myself, I piled neatly in a narrow, rocky fault that stood nearby. Later on I would recognize this "wall of amphoras" in an underwater photograph published in a learned journal.

Our excavation was now a rather vaguely defined depression that fed the *suceuse* bits and pieces of pottery. The larger fragments would block the mouth of the hose and would have to be removed by hand; others would just clear the mouth only to get stuck higher up, causing the *suceuse* to fill with air and send me dancing helplessly toward the surface. This was amusing to see, but we lost a great deal of time just trying to unclog the hose. We finally uncovered the necks of the second layer of amphoras, which were arranged in a more orderly fashion and only slightly inclined. The water nearest the bottom was thick with whitish mud that there was no current to carry off, so we had to dispose of it with the *suceuse*. The amphoras were full of sand and defied our most strenuous efforts to remove them. When I tried prying them loose with a crowbar, I broke the neck of one that had conserved its seal, and my hand went plunging into water inside that was still cold from the last mistral. The broken amphora gave me an idea, however unsophisticated. I asked Podevin, the quartermaster, who had just completed a course of training in deep-sea diving, to go down with a pickaxe and break up a certain centrally located amphora that I described for him. He wore a regular copper-helmeted diving suit that kept him from getting cold. The suit was fitted with a communications system, and as we listened to him work we would hear the sound of the pick, followed each time by a long silence. Podevin had to wait for the mud to settle before striking again, and that took forever. I never would have believed that an amphora could be so hard to break.

The small cavity created by Podevin allowed us to salvage a few more unbroken specimens.

We cleaned the amphoras on the main deck, delighted to be in the sun again. Some of them still had in their necks a grayish-lime seal bearing an inscription in an unknown tongue, written twice in large letters arranged in a circle. We would learn later that the seals were inscribed with the name of the importer of the wine, M(ARCUS) (ET) C(AIUS) LASS(IUS), and that the language was Oscan, which was still in use in the area around Naples during the first half of the first century B.C.

The amphoras were all of the Italian type, with cylindrical bodies, high necks, and straight handles. We flushed them out with a fire hose and found a muddy sand full of half-eaten shellfish left behind, no doubt, by a family of octopuses. Inside those amphoras that were still corked, there was no sand, just moldy water.

A few days later, after we had fixed a metal bar across the mouth of the *suceuse* in order to prevent it from picking up things that were too large, the sea covered our site with a blanket of dead posidonia, and their long red ribbons wound themselves around the bar. I expected the worst, but it turned out that attrition from the constant flow of sand caused the plants to disappear without my intervention. On the other hand, putting a bit in the mouth of the *suceuse* had made it so tame that it just nibbled at the mud. We had to remove the bar.

Our captain was fond of giving amphoras as gifts, and, since he was always making new friends, we returned to La Chrétienne the following summer, much to my delight.

In the struggle against this magma of sand and pottery, I was pitted against two thousand years of work done by the sea. I wanted to know the limits of its power to dissimulate. The enigma of all those amphoras piled up systematically in the soil whetted my appetite for digging, and I therefore maintained that we would find more intact amphoras by tunneling straight down than we would if we enlarged the area of excavation.

One team after another went down to grope about in the dark and work in a haphazard manner. The *suceuse* was constantly getting clogged up by posidonia roots, shards of pottery, and concretions. I was preoccupied with getting to the bottom of the mystery and spent my time removing the larger pieces of debris; my colleagues inspected the amphoras, working them loose and taking them to the surface if they proved to be intact, and leaving them to me if they were broken.

The next day I won Devilla over to my cause, and he went

down in the first team with Bézaudin, one of our best divers. I
kept track of their progress by leaning over the gunwale to observe the rhythm and location of their air bubbles. Before long
the *suceuse* began to spit out muddy water, and I knew they were
hard at work.

Then the bubbles suddenly got much larger, and the two men
emerged from the sea waving and shouting excitedly: "The hull!
Like new!" The second team, already on the ladder, went down
to continue the work, while I remained on board to savor the
delights of anticipation. When at last it was my turn to dive, I
found the bottom of the trench carpeted with sand. I beat about
in the water with my hand, the sand dispersed, and I could see
the hull. I had to think of the three layers of amphoras that we had
removed, and stare at the slanted walls of the trench, where the
serried rows of pottery held back the sand, to convince myself
that the clear wooden planks were real. I went to work with the
suceuse, uncovering first a rib and then the hull itself. The boards
that I saw were part of the *vaigrage,* or interior floor of the ship. It
seemed to me that the wood wasn't very strong for the kind of
cargo it had to carry.

What a difference there was between Mahdia and La
Chrétienne! At Mahdia the wreck lay three miles off the shore, on
a flat, deserted bottom, with its keel barely submerged in a shallow bed of mud; at La Chrétienne the ship was close to the shore
and buried about six feet down, in sand formed from the detritus
of the intense marine life and from dust that came with the rain.
Why had the last layer of amphoras not been displaced by the
shifting sands? My life seems to me to be a particular phase of the
march of time, but in the sea the bottom is always rising, and one
day the last amphoras will disappear.

5

GRAND CONGLOUÉ

AFTER THE DEPARTURE of Cousteau and Tailliez, the spirit of adventure that had animated the Undersea Research Group began little by little to disappear; and since our paper work, which we had neglected in the excitement of our early days, was mounting up, things necessarily settled into a certain routine.

In 1950 a benefactor had offered to buy Cousteau a ship, the *Calypso*, that had once been an American minesweeper. Jacques was given an extended leave by the navy and created a nonprofit organization to operate *Calypso*.

My own contract with the navy being quite flexible, I was allowed to take several months of unpaid leave in order to accompany him on this new venture. Without waiting for even the most elementary refittings of *Calypso* to be completed, Cousteau set sail for the Red Sea with a handful of scientists who wanted to learn about diving and to collect some tiny specimens. While we were there, I discovered the joys of coral reefs.

When we got back, Jacques petitioned the government for a subsidy that would enable him to continue his work.

Looking for something to do in the interim, he consulted with me about the possibility of undertaking the excavation of an ancient wreck.

Although we didn't actually appreciate the magnitude of such an undertaking, we did suspect that we would need the kind of help that only a large industrial port would be able to offer. We considered going to La Chrétienne, but that was in an isolated resort area, and the site was overrun with posidonia whose roots would stop up our *suceuse*. Moreover, it was now 1952 and the wreck had been thoroughly pillaged.

Then I thought of the old Greek helmet diver who, six years before, had told us that he was out harvesting coral with a hammer one day, when he saw on the bottom what he thought were cannons, and which proved on closer inspection to be earthenware jars; but the old man couldn't find the location where he had been working on our charts of the sea around Marseilles, and his own descriptions were too vague for our purposes.

In 1950 another diver from Marseilles, Christianini, had been brought to our headquarters in Toulon in an ambulance, half-paralyzed with "the bends." We put him in our decompression chamber, which kept the paralysis from spreading, but it was too late to cure him. He had to spend long months in the hospital, and if he is able to walk today it is only because, undaunted by his misfortune, he refused to believe that his lifeless limbs would never serve him again. Christianini had told me once about some rocks way down in the sea where he had found coral of a kind that he was never to see again. I was particularly interested in a dive he had made at Grand Congloué, on which he had seen, just beyond a rock with a hollow arch, the amphoras described to us by the old helmet diver.

We were attracted by the proximity to Marseilles and the area around it, which was full of all kinds of sunken ships; if the wreck at Grand Congloué fell short of our expectations, we could choose another one.

A few small discoveries I had made on land had brought me into contact with the very learned Professor Benoit, Director of Antiquities for Provence. A rather smallish man with a dark complexion and white, unkempt hair, Benoit was outspoken and could sometimes be quite brusque. Cousteau commissioned me to speak to him about our project, adding that I shouldn't hesitate to bluff a little. It would be up to Benoit to ask for the financial assistance that we hoped to get from the French government.

The subsidy came through, and Jacques gave September 27 as the terminal date for the project.

Calypso arrived in Marseilles on the fifteenth of August.[1] Jacques always liked to get underway on a holiday, just to show his contempt for the obstacles that time would stubbornly put in the way of his feverish pursuit of a goal. Besides, we could usually catch up on our rest when the weather was bad.

The very next day, we dropped anchor at Grand Congloué, an imposing mass of white rock bordered by steep cliffs. Jacques, Benoit, and I set out with several divers in the light metal motor launch that was our favorite ship's boat. As the first winds of the mistral rippled the surface of the water, I went over the side in the vicinity of a rocky spur that widened into a small shelf, the only approachable point on the island. At the foot of a steep incline a dark patch far off in the murky depths of the water came into focus; it was a needle of rock that showed clear blue light through a hole in the base—a well-rounded arch fringed with violaceous gorgonians. The water became clear and very cold, yet there was nothing but sand as far as the eye could see. Perplexed by this unexpected development, I began systematically to inspect the area in front of the arch, swimming over the sand in increasingly larger semicircular paths; but the rapid descent must have taken me below a hundred sixty feet, because I was beginning to be overcome by a torpor that took the sting out of my disappointment. I was too confused to analyze the situation and devise a new course of action, so I went back up to the surface.

Benoit sat motionless in an attitude of resignation and said nothing, but, watching him out of the corners of our eyes, we could see that he was displeased. The mistral had grown colder, and the water, bluer now than before, was marbled through with foamy whitecaps; we had to move the motor launch to take shelter behind the rock spur. A good twenty minutes had passed since we had lost sight of Cousteau's air bubbles. Although I had been diving for ten years, I still couldn't suppress the anxiety I felt

---

[1] The Feast of the Assumption, a legal holiday in France. (Tr.)

whenever one of my fellow divers was alone on the bottom, where we couldn't help him at all.

Then a white, shimmering form suddenly appeared beneath the launch and a barrage of bubbles broke the surface, followed by Cousteau's hand, which held out red, yellow, and mauve cups brought up from the depths. We all exploded with joy, and Benoit was exultant. Here we were looking for amphoras, and Jacques had brought up Campanian pottery! Everyone wanted to get a look at the cups, but Benoit took immediate possession, exclaiming repeatedly, "Marvelous, marvelous! Second century B.C.!" Jacques had seen all sorts of pottery in the area, and numerous amphoras. All the ancient wrecks discovered before that time had been from the first century B.C. The spell had been broken.

I knew that I was going to go down again, yet the chill of the water was still in my body, and I had to forget it for an instant before I could jump. I swam around the spur, and descended the length of a bare, white vertical wall to a mossy landing; then I sank down again through a school of silvery fish whose movements caused intermittent flashes of light. Blue gorgonians growing thick on the side of the cliff created a nocturnal aura that was soon dispelled by light emanating from a sand dune, from which protruded the necks of a well-ordered collection of amphoras. Long Italian specimens had tumbled down the slopes to mingle with ones that were shorter and rounder. The transparency of the water made it possible to get an idea of the size of the area where the pottery lay, by measuring it against the cliff nearby. As I poked about in the piles of crockery between the necks of the amphoras, I became more and more excited; each shape changed dimensions, every dimension took on a different shape, and my mind boggled at the complexity of such a jumble. It was too complicated to sort out at a hundred thirty feet; besides, I was frozen.

At lunch we used up our excess energy by talking all at once, while Benoit sat there beaming; but, the mistral having grown still stronger, we ran the risk of seeing our anchor let go, and we had to get the ship underway.

We were assisted on our project by François Junier, who was in charge of the maintenance of beacons and lighthouses in Marseilles. A gentle, affable man, Junier never got angry at the sea. Putting his modest fleet at our disposal, he moored three anchor buoys to the island and fastened some iron rings to the cliff, so that we would be able to station *Calypso* over the wreck and keep it there during a mild mistral or an east wind.

The bad weather persisted, the waves pitching *Calypso* to and fro as they dashed against the spur, which was supposed to shelter us. We dove three times a day into water that was as cold as it was in winter, and came out after fifteen minutes livid, with swollen hands and chattering teeth, in spite of our foam rubber diving suits. It took us an hour to get warm again. Every time we went down, the wreck seemed to be larger, so one night Jacques and I measured it with some string. It was sixty-four feet long and twenty-six feet wide, but we had no idea how far down it was in the sand.

Some of the other divers spoke in their reports about a ten-ton boulder on the site. Since Jacques had seen amphoras higher up on the slope and I had seen them further down, we concluded that the boulder must have tumbled down onto the wreck. We would have to ask our friend Junier to get rid of it for us.

With our black footfins alone showing above the cloud of white mud that the current carried off too slowly, we groped around on the bottom and brought up corroded crockery, together with those amphoras that were easiest to extract. We piled everything into a large wire-mesh basket that was hauled up to the afterdeck of *Calypso* by the Lombardini, our little motor winch that started up under protest and emitted huge puffs of smoke like a man lighting his pipe.

Lallemand and I were always on the lookout for amphoras bearing violets, blackish creatures that had the shape and appearance of a potato left in the bin too long. We would cut them open along the length and, with a thumb, detach from its nacreous shell the yellow, gelatinous, purple-veined pulp, which we would then gobble up with obvious relish. The look of disgust that this performance always produced in our audience was part of the charm associated with eating violets.

As the work continued, one diver after another went down to the bottom, to be called back to the surface after fifteen minutes by two rounds fired from the "shooting clock," which was the nickname given to my German rifle found in the woods at Sanary toward the end of the war.

Raud, our boatswain, the only member of the crew who was a

seaman by trade, had his work cut out for him. Full of good humor, he was always running up forward to ease off on the steel cable, or back aft to haul in on a hawser, or else jumping into the dinghy.

Raud was besieged with requests for rope, and was forever breaking out a new coil for some emergency; but since he didn't have time to wind any up again, there was rope all over the place. The afterdeck became a veritable spider's web where, with the amphoras swaying back and forth in response to the movements of the ship, rolling and crashing against our diving gear, there was hardly room to put your feet. You would also be jostled by divers fresh from the sea, or by others who, loaded down with equipment, were staggering toward the ladder.

Benoit and Lallemand kept a notebook stained with white mud, in which they recorded all our finds. We helped them clear the deck, so that we would have a path to walk through, and to flush out the amphoras with a fire hose. Lallemand, bent over the thick stream that belched forth from the amphoras and covered him up to the shoulders with mud, would roar triumphantly over a shriveled scrap of leaden hull plate, an olive pit, or a fragment of pottery with its handsome black varnish. One day he came up with two bronze fishhooks. On the afterdeck awash with his sand, mud, shells, and dirty water, Lallemand would get knocked about as the cargo basket came up from below loaded to the brim, and every tug by the motor winch would bring a whipping rain from the tautened lift-rope. One time, just as a load of streaming amphoras broke the surface, the rope parted and the basket sank majestically to the bottom, leaving a broad white wake in the blue sea. Raud got chewed out.

In the time that had elapsed since our arrival, the school of bogues that habitually hovered over the wreck had grown larger, leaving us just barely enough room to pass through them.

On the worksite, which was covered with sand stirred up by each diver in his turn, a squat, spiny fish peaceably kept station among the amphoras; although his color down below was pale, it was bright red on the surface. I can attest from personal experience that the first dorsal spine of this fish is quite venomous.

Other fish—sardines, mullets—were also established on the site and would swim around our ankles to feed on the worms that we turned up with our digging. The only thing that disturbed them was a line put in the water by Ahnen, our cook; every once in a while there would be a flash of light and we would see one of them winging his way toward the frying pan.

At night in the ship's mess, which was full of ancient crockery, the archaeologists would be busy taking measurements, making drawings, and comparing their specimens. They had arranged their finds according to height, and now the series was nearing completion on the shelves of the library, where unbroken specimens were taking the place of ones that had been found smashed. Every new addition occasioned generous applause. On the pottery we brought up now there was not so much erosion as at first, with patches of black varnish being visible between the loosely adhering calcareous concretions. The various bowls, salad plates, and cups without handles resembled those made today, but were more elegant; the chalices, scent bottles, and rouge pots were reminiscent of Greek artifacts we had seen in museums. The plates rested on tiny bases that made them so unstable that we couldn't imagine the Romans cutting their steaks on them. We especially liked the fish plates, which had a well in the center designed to catch the juice, or, perhaps, to contain some special sauce. Each piece of this black crockery was discreetly decorated with a rosette, palmette, or marguerite printed in the center, a few modest rings, and some light strokes of the fingernail; all of which gave it a rather sober elegance. It was manufactured near Naples, in a region called Campania, part of Magna Graecia, and exported by the Romans to all the port cities of the Mediterranean, whence it made its way to the hinterlands.

A fragment of Greek pottery that we found among the Roman one day sent Benoit into ecstasy; after that he used to go around saying, "That's not Greek, it's Roman," to the point where we became annoyed and took to imitating him in chorus once his back was turned. A few sly wits even accused Benoit of saying that if we continued to dig, we would eventually get to a layer of Greek pottery.

For several days we took nothing to Marseilles; but then we were informed one morning that two city trucks and a team of volunteer helpers would be waiting for us at night on the Quai des Belges, across from the Canebière. We had to get some amphoras.

In the hope of bringing them up more rapidly, I rigged up a "phalanx" consisting of eleven light lines attached at intervals along the length of a large rope. I took one end of the rope down to the bottom and tied it to an amphora that had already been extracted from the sand. I then tugged gently on the rope in order to get some slack, dug out another amphora, and secured it to the first line. I chose amphoras that wouldn't get stuck, or arranged them so that they could be easily hauled up, being careful all the while to keep the rope taut lest it become entangled. I was running out of breath. The guardian fish, seeing the water grow more and more opaque, had left in disgust. When I had finally secured the last amphora, I gave two sharp pulls on the rope. On the surface, Jacques had hold of the other end of the rope, by which he could sense and interpret my slightest movement. The rope stiffened like a fakir's, the last amphora bounded up into its ascent, and the next one quickly followed suit. I just had time to free part of the rope that had caught on the neck of an amphora before the third one took off. I wound myself like a snake along the length of the rope in order to launch each amphora on its way to become part of the long string that disappeared into the cloudy sky. Something banged against the steel air bottles strapped on my back, making them ring—an amphora had gotten loose; but eleven had come up, and my new method seemed to work well enough. Another diver went down. After fifteen minutes he came back up, looking very satisfied. When the first amphora came out of the water, however, its neck broke, the belly fell on the second amphora, breaking that, and so on. All we had left was half an amphora and one neck. I didn't pursue the matter any further.

Labat, our chief volunteer, who had an almost mystic passion for the water, proposed that we raise amphoras by filling them with compressed air. This method, curious as it was, didn't appear to me to be very productive, but Jacques was intrigued by its originality and gave Labat a chance to try it out. As soon as we had eaten, Labat went into the water with a compressed-air hose that had a copper nozzle at the end. For a quarter of an hour a rapid stream of air came up to the surface. Labat's supporters looked a bit dejected, and the others envisioned an easy victory. Then an inverted amphora suddenly burst from the sea, settled on its side and bobbed about at the mercy of the waves. With that, everyone became enthusiastic. Labat had put air into two amphoras, but one had broken on the way up. They seemed to take off all at once. Despite this success, it was decided that we would revert to using the wire-mesh basket.

We arrived back in Marseilles with a hundred fifty amphoras and about two hundred pieces of Campanian pottery. As Jacques maneuvered in order to get the ship into position next to the pier, which was crowded with people, Raud sent over the messenger, a long, light line, one end of which is braided around a lead ball. I always suspected Raud of aiming his messenger at some woman's dog or man's hat, because every time he threw it there was trouble. The trucks were there with their volunteers, who invaded the afterdeck to shoulder the amphoras and weave their way through the crowd like a procession of ants.

The *Calypso* was moored at the stern by two steel cables made fast at ground level to bollards which stood in the middle of the pier. During the course of the evening more than one stroller come to admire the ship tripped over one of the cables and went sprawling; there was, of course, a puddle of water there to receive him.

Beuchat, an old friend who was a pioneer in underwater hunting and photography, brought us a new member of our crew in the person of Albert Falco, known as Bébert. Bébert was an experienced seaman and could help Raud on the ship; but he was also a first-rate diver who could swim like a fish, which was all the more important since Raud, like the good Breton that he was, never went into the water.

We also had a number of volunteer divers who worked with us whenever they could, coming and going according to their own schedules. These men always needed a certain amount of time to familiarize themselves with our rather special worksite. Once on the bottom, groping around in the mud raised by the previous diver, they would get carried away by the profusion of artifacts scattered about and, forgetting our instructions, would just look for some novelty that might start a flurry of excitement among their colleagues on the surface.

It was now almost the end of August. Amphoras by the hundreds were heaped up in a shed back at the Borély Museum, and, in the little room where Professor Benoit worked at his task of classification, piles of crockery fouled the air. Despite all this, however, we were still very far from victory in our struggle to excavate the ancient wreck. It was way down in the sea, and the water clouded up with the slightest movement of one's hand. A fine layer of dust veiled the gorgonians that grew on the cliff. The amphoras lay hidden under a muddy sand strewn with old news-papers, scraps of rope, tin cans, and garbage. We had undertaken to remove the cargo from this huge ship without any knowledge of the most elementary principles of archaeology. Our method of hauling up whatever lay at hand wasn't getting us anywhere; we would have to concentrate our efforts on digging a hole that would uncover the wood of the hull and give us some idea of what we were doing. We were more interested in the ship itself than in its cargo, but we wondered if the sand had protected it from the shipworms that could devour a docked vessel in a matter of months. Digging such a hole would make the work of discharg-ing the cargo much easier.

I marked the limits of the hole with four buoys whose floats would rise above the clouds of mud.

A few days later I went down before anyone else in order to have the opportunity to work in clear water—but there was no hole! Furious, I dug with my hands and extracted a few frag-ments of pottery; then, instinctively, like all the others, I backed away from the cloud in order to see. We would definitely have to get a *suceuse.*

Out of the morning fog a ship came toward us. It was the *Fresnel,* a hardy vessel rigged for heavy lifting, sent to the site by Junier to remove some large rocks that we had girded with steel slings the day before. The *Fresnel* was commanded by Jeres, a huge man of Spanish descent who, with a thunderous laugh, took great pleasure in his own strength and in that of his ship.

After the two ships had completed the customary exchange of salutations, Jeres asked Jacques how much the largest boulder weighed. "Two tons? No problem," he replied, his eyes shining. Needing a strong man to dive with me, I chose Galerne. We followed the big winch-hook all the way down until it came to rest in the sand about twenty feet from the boulder. Galerne took hold of the hook, then lost his balance, stirring up the inevitable mud cloud to envelop Cousteau, who had accompanied us with his camera, in total darkness. Jacques was furious.

I steadied Galerne with my hand and helped him to lodge the hook in the sling; then I gave a few tugs on the light rope that was our means of communication with those on the surface. The boulder stirred under my feet, hesitated, and then rose ever so little, only to come crashing down again onto the amphoras. It was enormous. There was a second brief stirring, then nothing. We went up to the surface and found ourselves face to face with an angry Jeres, who shouted, "That thing weighs at least twelve tons! My motor was giving off sparks."

The fog eventually lifted and the weather was now ideal. Schools of small fish came up to forage, breaking the smooth surface of the water like bits of gravel falling from the sky.

Jeres had plenty of equipment at his disposal, and after attaching a large pulley block to the winch he was able to raise the boulder, which the *Fresnel* then took off to be deposited at a safe distance from the excavation. We were reluctant to admit that we had been mistaken about the size of the rock, so we teased Jeres about the capacity of his winch; but there were smiles all around, and no hard feelings.

Jeres removed two smaller rocks from the site, and this time, since he had been careful to bring the right equipment, it was his turn to do the teasing.

We eventually got our *suceuse,* but, being too flexible, it flattened out, coughed, gasped, and had spasms. The air traveled through it like a mouse in a boa constrictor—without doing any work. Jacques persuaded the navy to lend him a hose that was heavier. With that, we were through fooling around. We were ready to dig a trench and see how the two types of amphora were arranged. At the height of the incline there was an orderly array of long Italian amphoras, so the situation there was quite clear. The limits of this layer, however, were somewhat vague, at least in our own minds, because we kept coming across small groups of the more bulbous Greco-Italian type. On the sides of the incline there was total chaos, the two types having been thrown together at random when the hull gave way under the weight of its cargo. Although we were at that stage finding more of the long amphoras, we anticipated that we would encounter the round ones further down.

I went down with another diver and at sixty feet the water turned brutally cold; but I felt the shock only very briefly before it was dispelled by the anesthetic effect of the lower depths.[1] The

[1] See pages 207–208.

suceuse devoured everything—sand, pebbles blown off the island by storms, pieces of amphoras, concretions that had tumbled
down from the littoral plateau formed by erosion at the point
where the sea meets the air, and spondyles, massive spiny oysters
that it was not unusual to find on wrecks close to the shore. What
an appetite! The two of us looked at each other in amazement. As
the compressed air roared away, pebbles would first slide toward
the hose, then leap forward to be snapped up and rattle around in
the copper nozzle. The sand settled around the periphery of our
funnel-shaped hole, ran down the sides toward me, and con-
verged to form a sort of whitish tongue that palpitated before the
mouth of the *suceuse*. I had never worked with a *suceuse* so far
down in the sea; this one was so powerful that, had I put it on my
thigh, I think it would have torn off the skin.

All of a sudden a cup jumped up and got stuck in the nozzle; I
couldn't disengage it, but under the constant barrage of pellets it
finally disintegrated and went up the pipe. The thought of Benoit
up there on the surface made me laugh, in spite of the water.
Then some large pebbles lodged in the nozzle and I had to strike
it against some amphoras to get it clear.

We were relieved by the next team and went up again, delighted with the performance of our new tool.

But Benoit was not amused. He stood by the wire-mesh basket
moaning and groaning as the *suceuse* disgorged debris and newly
broken crockery, in a stream that was thick with sand. With a look
of sadness he turned in his hand a small triangle of shiny black
pottery—he had given up trying to fit such fragments together
again. "It's a disaster," he said.

Full of the nervous enthusiasm that always follows a deep descent, I began to describe to Benoit how the *suceuse* disposed of
the piles of dishes, grazing on the large plates and smashing the
cups to bits. Raud, who resented the cumbersome and useless
crockery and the amphoras that soiled his deck, was overjoyed.
To him Benoit's despair was sweet.

Lallemand rushed over to the basket and, getting himself soak-
ing wet in the process, fished out of the torrent a single black cup
that had somehow survived the journey up the hose in perfect
condition.

This distracted Benoit momentarily; but then Labat and Médan, still wet and frozen from their stint below, asked permission
to use a hammer to break up the crockery that was blocking the

suceuse. We all crowded around Benoit to console him, pointing out that there was a great abundance of dishes on the site.

The question of breaking up the crockery was put to a vote, and everyone but Benoit was for it. Alongside *Calypso* there was spread out in the blue water a vaporous mud that the current gradually made thinner and thinner.

The turmoil created by the *suceuse* didn't seen to frighten the octopuses that lurked in the necks of the amphoras, crowded together and unable to hide themselves in this village in ruins. I thought to myself that the octopuses must have been happy indeed when, two thousand years ago, they saw coming down out of the sky, under its flaming mainsail, this prefabricated palace with its spacious private rooms whose narrow entrances put the octopuses safely out of the reach of the big merous, who would suck them in and swallow them. Awarding this modern hotel the maximum number of stars, the octopuses dined there on shellfish and decorated the place with bric-a-brac that they picked up, like magpies, in the course of their travels. And so it happened that we would sometimes find in the amphoras things left behind by occupants who were not so ancient.

That morning an octopus came to uncoil his numerous, undulating tentacles at the edge of the hole we were digging with the *suceuse.* I extended my hand and wiggled my fingers to attract him; then I guided him gently towards the nozzle, and he disappeared like a puff of smoke. It seems that he came out the other end flailing vigorously in a fit of ill temper.

Once the *suceuse* was idle, Lallemand would sift through the contents of the basket, where he would find crumpled pieces of hull plate and sinkers, both Roman and those lost by Sunday fishermen, some of which were themselves very old. Occasionally he would give a start at the sight of a small shiny object, only to have it turn out to be rifle shot. He would also find newly minted coins fed into the *suceuse* by a mischievous diver, much in the way that one gives peanuts to an elephant in the zoo.

The pieces of crockery that emptied into the basket were arriving in progressively better states of preservation. As for the black varnish . . .

With the excitability characteristic of those who live along the shores of the Mediterranean, Lallemand let his imagination be carried away by each piece of debris and tried, a bit prematurely, to reconstruct the events that led to the sinking of the ship.

At dinner that night he took from his pocket a tiny black object that he fondled as if it were a precious stone; it was actually a pine seed found inside one of the amphoras. When an Italian crew gutted the wreck at Albenga with a dredge, they brought up amphoras that were full of these delectable pine almonds. Lallemand also had a rather poorly conserved fragment of a wine stopper. At La Chrétienne many of the amphoras still had their stoppers, but here they didn't, although it was clear that they had been corked. I wondered if it were not the case that at a certain depth, the pressure of the water broke the lime seal and cork stopper; for it seemed to me that the shallower the water, the more corks were found in place.

The success of Lallemand's presentation fell somewhat short of his expectations, due to the fact that, with the east wind blowing stronger and stronger, he had to compete for our attention with the entertainment provided throughout the meal by the rolling of the ship. As everything slid from side to side and the bottles oscillated dangerously, each member of the crew revealed his true character by holding down whatever he judged to be most valuable. The chief steward did a fancy dance on the mess deck to balance the platter perched on his hand. Taking issue with Jacques, who claimed that being a sailor is the best job in the world, I exaggerated a bit and cursed life on the sea in the strongest terms. A sailor's idea of paradise, I said, is a nice, comfortable bar where he can sit and watch other, less fortunate, members of his profession who have been condemned to sail forever, under the worst possible conditions and without a single night ashore, on the infinite, turbulent waters of the Infernal Sea.

The duty section relieved the watch and, as I lay reflecting on the mysteries surrounding the wreck, I was lulled into sleep by the motion of the ship.

Awakened by the sound of near and distant shouting, I climbed out of my bunk. The afterdeck, illumined by the blinding glare of a floodlight, was swarming with people in an atmosphere of tension. In the choppy water, the motor launch, manned by three dark figures, bounded about in the night. With the menacing reef of Petit Congloué to leeward, Jacques coolly gave commands for a maneuver that I didn't understand at all. To help out, I tried to put the afterdeck in some kind of order; somebody might need some line, and it was all either in use or hopelessly tangled up. Little by little, I began to see what had happened. The after hawsers had parted, and the ship had pivoted around the northwest mooring buoy; the *suceuse* was wrapped around the rope to the southwest buoy, keeping our stern to windward. The sea raged around us. The dinghy was bilged, while on the motor launch they were trying to lash the *suceuse* to one of the buoys; but the sea was too rough. Trapped under the stern there was a steel cable that would get caught in the propellers if we had to get underway. From the bridge, someone was following the action with a floodlight, whose glare was harsh and blinding. With the calm that he always maintained under such circumstances, Jacques gave the order to cut the lines to the *suceuse*, and it disappeared into the night.

Down in the mess, where he had taken refuge, Benoit was desolate. "This is horrendous," he said.

Meanwhile, the wind continued to howl.

With one eye on me, Jacques discussed the possibility of a quick dive to free the cable trapped under the stern. This brought back unpleasant memories of a stormy night in Corsica when, under the heaving stern of *Calypso*, I struggled warily with a cable caught in the screws. But this time Bébert managed to reach the cable with a boathook and shake it free. With that, there was a collective sigh of relief—we were in control of the situation. Anyone who has ever been a sailor will understand the joy that reigned on board the ship. Although it was by then three o'clock in the morning, we all sat down to a healthy snack and made jokes about the events of what we had already christened "the tragic night." Since Benoit had retired, we got to telling stories about the destructive habits of the *suceuse* and laughing about all the broken crockery. Each recitation of a calamity was greeted with the same refrain: "Ah, if Benoit only knew that!" We learned later that Benoit's children had heard our chant and were serving it up to him at the dinner table.

Perhaps it's only an illusion, but it seems to me that in the south of France—whether it concerns the heat, cold, dryness, or even, sometimes, the rain—they say the same thing every year: "It's never been so bad."

A few days after this incident, Jacques decided that, despite the mistral, we would remain on station overnight. We were just finishing our dinner when Raud poked his head through a porthole and shouted, "We're drifting!" Everyone rushed out into the passageway. Off the stern, the frothy waves battered the rocky shore, and the spur passed by under the harsh glare of the flood-light. We were dragging the mooring buoy. Jacques raced the engines to keep the ship away from the rock. Before long the bow skirted the rock spur, and we were behind the island, still dragging the buoy. With the wind, which was stronger now, threatening to dash us against the cliff, we had to cast the whole anchor chain into the sea.

When the good weather returned, we were unable to find the buoy. The *Fresnel* came out to place another one "big enough for a battleship," according to Jeres. "This time it'll be your stempost that breaks," he added. Little did he suspect that he would soon have to come out and moor another one even heavier. While the new buoy was being moored, we dove to retrieve our anchor chain, which we thought was probably keeping the old buoy underwater. Robert, also known as Picassou, or simply Pic, furnished me with the pulley block I would need to haul up the chain. Pic was a baker and pastrycook from Marseilles who earned a rather meager living in the sea. Malville descended with a hawser strung out from the island to secure the chain.

The mistral had brought up to the surface the colder water from the depths. We found the buoy at a hundred feet, crushed by the pressure and resting on a hillock covered with posidonia. The chain, stiff as an iron bar, formed a bridge over a fault. Upset by this unforeseen development, I looked for Pic, but he was already too far below me to hear my call. The slope at the base of the island was steep, and I rejoined Pic around two hundred feet. On our way back up toward the buoy, we met Malville with his hawser. By this time we were beginning to experience the stupor that comes with working at such a depth, and, gasping for breath, we dragged the hawser along without realizing that it had folded back on itself to form a loop. The gorgonians on the cliff empurpled our hands, and something got caught in the loop. After descending and ascending once again, we were almost totally out of breath, but the hawser wouldn't budge. I signaled that we should give up and move on to the buoy. Pic still had the pulley block, which, although it was useless, we expended considerable effort to put into place. I was just about to pronounce the whole operation a failure, when I looked around me and saw another hawser dangling from the cliff. Pic had disappeared, but I enlisted Malville to help me secure the hawser to the chain so that the *Fresnel* could haul it up.

When we got back to the ship everyone was still laughing at Pic, who had sprung up out of the water like a popped cork, belching lustily. Through a leak in his mask he had swallowed water and compressed air until he couldn't stand it any longer. As he came back up, he was doubled over with pain from the expansion of the air in his stomach.

Impressed by the tenacity with which we struggled against the sea—it isn't true that the Mediterranean is calm—the citizens of Marseilles outdid themselves in their eagerness to help us. The city virtually adopted us, and their generosity and encouragement made it possible for us to continue in defiance of the inclement weather. If there was damage to the ship or work to be done, the damage was repaired, the work completed. The Chamber of Commerce gave us a radio transmitter, so that we could join their network, and the departmental council awarded us a subsidy of one million *anciens francs* and ten tons of diesel fuel. Down at City Hall they agreed to lend us Davso, a streetsweeper recommended to us by some friends as an excellent diver and highly skilled mechanic. A regular, full-time diver has the superiority of the professional and is worth ten visiting divers. Although he was originally supposed to be with us only for the duration of our project, Davso eventually became a permanent member of our crew.

It was now mid-September, and under its skin of sand, with its many wrinkles and depressions, the old wreck looked limp and flaccid, like a punctured balloon. The minor wounds caused by the *suceuse* in the process of digging for pottery were quickly scarred over by rivulets of sand. Still virtually unscathed, the enormous ship continued to thwart us. Some of the more recent amphoras posed problems for Benoit when he attempted to date them. Since they no longer came up covered with concretions, the cachet imprinted on the necks of the Italian specimens before firing was now quite legible. Benoit had succeeded in identifying one such inscription that consisted of the letters SES followed by an anchor or trident. It was not the mark of the potter, but that of the importer of the wine, Marcus Sestius, an Italian from the Naples area established in Delos at the beginning of the second century B.C. After being naturalized as an honorary citizen of Delos, which was a center of commerce comparable to our twentieth-century Marseilles, the wealthy shipper became Marcos Sestios. These facts explained the presence on the ship of the amphoras and fragment of sculptured pottery from Greece. Our wrecked ship showed the importance of the wine trade with Gaul and the power of merchants like Sestios, who had already invented the monopoly by concentrating in their hands vineyards, the manufacture of amphoras, and fleets of ships that plowed the Mediterranean. The ports of call on the long route between Delos and the spot where the ship went down promised to provide us with some exciting discoveries.

For the divers on *Calypso,* amphoras and varnished crockery were just part of the impersonal mass of cargo marked for exportation, to which we preferred a crudely fashioned lard pot or a few pieces of cookware still bearing traces from the wood fire. Items like that came from the ship's galley, and conjured up in our minds images of the Roman sailors who handled them every day. The familiar appearance of such pottery moved me to dig in search of other evidence of life on the ship, and I was tempted to put the stones and remnants of amphoras off to one side. I cursed the water for preventing me from throwing them any distance. It annoyed me that I couldn't make a choice, but had to deposit all the remnants in the basket, one by one, so that they wouldn't accumulate on the worksite.

For reasons of security, *Calypso* was usually stationed away from the rock at night, which gave us amateurs the opportunity to throw the detritus, piece by piece, into the sea—a satisfying gesture that we never tired of repeating. We would put aside for Benoit the butts and necks of amphoras, because he had to count them and take note of their markings.

Many of the divers who made the pilgrimage to Grand Congloué never realized how much work Benoit actually did. He liked to decipher and explain the markings of the amphoras and the graffiti on the Campanian pottery, analyzing and classifying the various forms; and we were amazed at his competence. Benoit could occasionally be abrasive, for he was just as fanatical as we were, but the way he rejoiced over a newly discovered piece of pottery gave us support and encouragement. If we sometimes made fun of him, it was just a sailor's way of amusing himself.

With the end of September the days grew shorter, and the

setting sun, casting the shadow of the big rock into the water over the wreck, signaled the advent of winter. Under the sea we didn't feel any difference, but we were more reluctant to go in. Many of the divers, their leaves having expired, were forced to go; some of them wanted to come back at Christmastime.

Our practice of moving the ship every night was causing us to lose a great deal of time. After every move we had to reinstall the *suceuse,* but it never fell in the right place; so the first diver would start in to work where he found the hose and then, instinctively, move it off toward clearer water. And every time the ship lurched, the *suceuse* would knock the diver off balance and drag him away from his work. Jacques therefore decided to suspend the *suceuse* from a long boom that would jut out from the island. At an official banquet he had charmed the general in command of the local corps of engineers. We put out to sea with a team of engineers who were to install a fifty-five-foot crane mast that had been lent to us by a lumberyard. Although they were a bit discommoded by the trip to the site, the soldiers perked right up when it came to mounting the assault on the island, where they deployed a wealth of materials and instruments. They mixed up cement and put up iron bars and girders, until our arid little island began to take on a civilized, albeit military, appearance.

By nightfall the windlass platform was finished; they had also built a sort of pier consisting of a huge beam suspended on chains, to which we could tie up the ship's boats.

The engineers preferred to camp on the island, rather than brave *Calypso's* pitch and roll.

During the night, however, there was rain, followed by a violent mistral, and we had to haul anchor to take shelter elsewhere.

Around noon, Jacques decided to return to Marseilles. With the wind raging and the sea around us full of foamy whitecaps, *Calypso* approached the island. On the surface of the water, iridescent spindrifts whistled through the hollows in the rocks. With gestures and mimicry we persuaded the engineers, who had been lolling in the sun, to jump into the motor launch, which brought them on board a little wet, but happy to have conducted themselves like sailors. On the way back, however, they had to squat on the afterdeck like marines on a landing ship, and their *esprit de corps* was somewhat dampened.

Once the stormy weather—which we called "engineers' weather"—had subsided, the crane mast was hoisted into place.

We attached a weight to its cable, and I went into the water to see where it would fall. After passing the little platform, the cable hugged the cliff, well short of the wreck. Beyond the last amphoras a clump of seaweed attracted my attention, because seaweed doesn't grow on the sand. I gave it a pull, and out of a cloud of mud came a marble basin that was eroded and too flat to be a mortar for grinding garlic. I tried to swim away with it, but it was too heavy and I couldn't get off the ground. I walked along the bottom, then climbed up on the cable. There, however, I became conscious again of the weight of my charge, and, afraid of falling into the void below, I released it.

Jacques wasn't surprised to hear the bad news. We thought of various schemes which would allow us to use the *suceuse* anyway, but all of these stopgap solutions involved too many problems. Once again, we had to call on our friends in Marseilles, whose patience seemed to be limitless. Selecting a seventy-five-foot mast, the longest they had, we made it even longer by attaching a steel tube that had rings to hold the cables.

The journey of this mammoth pole through streets that were narrow and crowded would have been worth getting on film. Lashing the pole to the side of *Calypso* was easy enough, but at Grand Congloué, in the absence of the engineers, we had to divide ourselves between the island and the ship. Concerned that the installation on the island might not bear up under the weight of the new mast, we posted a lookout on the height of the cliff, to give warning if the rock to which we had secured the cable gave way under the strain from the winch. Given the circumstances, it seemed to me that the lookout was purely ornamental.

Slowly, and with creaking sounds that were painful to our ears, the mast curved more and more inward, until it finally decided to rise. This time the cable fell right on the wreck; we would have been totally demoralized if it hadn't.

Calypso was in need of repairs, and Jacques wanted to use it for other work anyway, so he decided to equip the island with a comfortable Quonset hut that would have electricity and compressed air. A team of "Robinson Crusoes" would stay there and continue the work.

A mason built an iron ladder into the cliff, under the slight incline that overlooked the wreck. This was the only habitable spot on the island, and it even had a small patch of soil, with a few tufts of thick grass nurtured by the humid Mediterranean nights. With some dynamite I carved out the foundation for the future "Cité radieuse," as it had already been christened by the divers from Marseilles, who were still awed by the building Le Corbusier had put up in their midst.

My leave having expired, I resumed my work with the Undersea Research Group, but I spent my weekends, weather permitting, at Grand Congloué. There the remaining few divers, under the direction of Bébert, were quietly discharging the upper part of the wreck, just as I would have wanted to do. The foot of the cliff under the sand was bare and white, except for the spots where the leaden hull plate had been crushed against the rock. The *suceuse* now rose way up in the air before descending again along the length of the crane mast to pass the rock spur and empty into a fault, where the accumulation of sand could be sifted. You would hear the grating of the sand inside the hose and the rattling of the rubble in the elbows; then the hose would quiver painfully, and, between gasps, vomit spasmodically until it finally fell motionless, thoroughly blocked. We ultimately had to suppress the length of hose that ran down the mast, leaving the *suceuse* to discharge directly into a basket suspended from the tip.

The muddy water brought up by the hose would spread out on the surface and be carried off by the slightest current. The sand, shells, and concretions, being cleansed as they fell, rained down on us very slowly, like snow, without clouding up the water. The entire wreck was hidden under a carpet of white that we tore with the *suceuse*. The platform had become a sort of factory where, after emerging from the winter water, we would roast to our heart's content between some infrared lamps.

Some of the other divers claimed that there was a lead-plated deck under the amphoras, but it was probably just a portion of the hull that bent inward as the ship sank. Protruding from the sand in the middle of the worksite, there was a large lead pipe, which we believed to be connected to the bilge pump.

On March first, Bébert showed me, near the cliff, the ends of some blackened ribs that had been eaten through by shipworms—he had had a glimpse of the keel.

I had come to the island that day on the *Hou Hop*, but by

evening the sea had risen so much that there was no place for them to tie up. I was, nevertheless, determined to get back to Marseilles.

At the moment when the *Hou Hop*, buffeted by the waves, drew alongside the cliff, I didn't quite have the courage to jump onto the wet deck from such a height. But sometimes we do things in spite of ourselves, and when the ship made a second pass I found myself on the deck, with an excruciating pain in my heel. Actually, it was more than just a pain, it was a sensation that was positively frightening. During the trip back I was in constant agony, but I tried to convince myself that my injury wasn't serious. When, at the pier, I tried to put some weight on my weakened heel, it gave way and I cried out in pain. Semiconscious, I was taken out to Sanary by friends. We had invited some people for dinner, but I became nauseated and had to finish the meal stretched out on the floor. Afterward, we spent a long time listening to records.

The surgeon informed me that I had a fractured calcaneus. He apparently thought that anyone who could be a professional diver had to have a certain amount of courage, for he advised me that this was the kind of injury that I shouldn't wish on my worst enemy. It took me a long time to get over the tendency to bitterly and uselessly reproach myself for not having stayed on the island.

There was now no longer any question of my going to Nairobi, where I was supposed to recover a large quantity of World War II munitions from the bottom of a lake infested with crocodiles.

At the end of June, with the plaster cast at last removed from my foot, and my leg shrunken to half its normal size, I resumed diving at Grand Congloué.

A vast expanse of the deck, or the between decks—without, of course, a trace of plating—covered several layers of Greco-Italian amphoras that had been stowed directly beneath the Italian. We still came across scattered veins of crockery, but it was not perfectly preserved, and I was amazed that the sea should have eroded and concreted the upper part of the cargo while sparing the lower.

The following year the project was under the direction of another member of the crew, Girault. He had replaced the old, flexible *suceuse* that had caused so much trouble with a rigid, vertical hose having a flexible trunk at the lower end. The *suceuse* discharged through an elbow at the upper end into a barrel drilled with numerous holes. Another important innovation was a device for removing obstructions from the hose. This consisted of a cylindrical weight that could be sent down the hose on the end of a cable controlled from the island. When the weight was brought all the way up again, it sealed the opening through which it entered the hose and was manipulated.

On a double-planked piece of the hull that had come to rest on the edge of our huge funnel, I saw three pieces of wood running parallel to one another. When I dug out around them with the *suceuse,* I came to the ribs to which these boards were attached as stringers, reinforcing the hull from the inside. As the funnel grew larger, the ribs ran down toward their central part, called the *varangue,* which was still under the sand on the axis of the ship.

As a result of our efforts, there was now a rather impressive excavation that went down a hundred fifty feet; but there was still a great deal of pottery further down in the sand. How much, we will never know. Too many teams of divers worked the site between 1952 and 1960, before eventually abandoning it to looters, who were even then able to find something of value.

The ship that foundered at Grand Congloué had been carrying a rather diverse lot of cargo, taken on along the course of an extended route. By what is almost surely a conservative estimate, the vessel was about a hundred feet long and was transporting around three thousand amphoras.

We found about thirty Greek amphoras of the type made in Rhodes, which were shaped like a child's top and had a rim around the mouth. Some of them displayed a mark on the handle that enabled Miss Grace, the distinguished American expert on amphoras, to fix their origin between 220 and 180 B.C. In this group there were also variants deriving from certain tiny islands near Turkey that were known at the time for the quality of their wine.

Two of the amphoras were of the Punic type, perhaps from southern Italy.

The greater part of the cargo was made up of Italian and Greco-Italian amphoras. The latter, rounded and elegant in form, were manufactured just about everywhere in the Mediterranean regions. We brought up more than four hundred, of two different sizes. The large ones had a capacity of about four and a half gallons, and the small ones two and a half. None of them had any distinguishing mark.

The Italian amphoras, which were tall, with a cylindrical belly, long neck, and straight handles, could hold about nine gallons. Judging from the number recovered, which was more than a thousand, this was the predominant type; but the Greco-Italian amphoras were buried further down in the sand, and it's possible that many of them were never found.

Benoit separated the Italian amphoras into two groups that varied slightly in shape and bore different markings.

The great majority carried the insignia of Marcus Sestius: S E S, followed by an anchor or trident. Amphoras belonging to the Sestii, who were well known in the south of Italy, have been found almost everywhere in Western Europe and, in the sea, on wrecks other than ours.

Another group of seventeen amphoras were stamped D A V ATEC. According to Benoit's interpretation, D stood for Decimus, and A for one of the following family names, all of which were known in Campania: AV(fidius), AU(relius), AV(ianus), AV(illius), or AV(illianus). The excessive use of abbreviations isn't peculiar to modern times. ATEC(chnos) would be the Greek surname given to the slave attached to the domain, vine grower, or potter.

It seemed certain to us that all the amphoras, which had been found full of muddy sand, had contained wine, although analysis failed to reveal any trace of it.

We found only very few opercula. One of the Italian amphoras had retained an operculum with four cachets. We had seen a few like that at La Chrétienne. An operculum in one of the amphoras belonging to Marcus Sestius bore the following still legible inscription: L.TITI.CF.

More than six thousand pieces of Campanian pottery had been recovered at Grand Congloué. We were continually finding it among the amphoras, without being able to say how it had been arranged. Often there would be piles of unbroken crockery mixed in with broken amphoras. I noticed the same thing on a sunken ship at the Ile du Levant, where whole lots of magnificent Campanian pottery, including a number of large platters, had remained intact among the shards of amphoras. I surmised that the material in which the crockery was packed was strong enough to protect it, even when the ship sank and many of the amphoras got broken on the way to their final resting place.

When all the crockery had been classified, there were twenty-five different forms and an assortment of sizes totaling eleven. Production on such a massive scale led us to think that the crockery was made in a factory. Among the items were a great variety of cups, both with and without handles, dinner plates, fish platters, lamps, flasks, pitchers, vases, and urns. We especially fancied the little receptacles that were shaped like teapots, with a lion's head for a spout. Benoit called them guttus, and informed us that they were used to fill oil lamps.

Some of the pottery had been marked with a pointed instrument after firing. Benoit's opinion was that these marks had been made by the wine merchant after he sampled the contents, or by customs officers after inspection. Some of the goblets displayed an inscription in Greek, also added after firing, that was an invocation to Hygeia, the goddess of health. Included in this collection, which was the most important up to that date, was a broad sampling of common pottery: cups, mortars, plates, tureens, small pots, goblets without handles, single-handled flasks, small pitchers, storage jars, urns, and pans with their covers.

Back when we first began digging, Bébert brought up a heavy lead ring ten inches in diameter, fitted with a tenon pierced with two holes. This kind of ring was also made out of stone. Later, in Crete, I saw one that was brand-new. It seems that they were used then, as they are now, to free lines or other fishing gear, or even anchors.

By the time we stopped work on the project, we had accumulated roughly a hundred smaller rings, most of which had a diameter of about three inches. Some of them had a tenon attached, while others did not. Although it seems unlikely that both these types served the same purpose, they were both designated as brail rings, it being supposed, without proof, that they were sewn to the sail to guide the movement of the lines when, during bad weather, the sail was gathered in.

Lead, which was easy to melt and resisted corrosion, was widely employed on ancient ships. All the pipes were made of lead, and on some ships the hull was plated with sheets of lead

fastened by small copper nails with large heads, driven in quin-
cuncially, about two inches apart. The practice of plating hulls
with lead seems to have persisted until the sixteenth century.

Among the leaden objects we found at Grand Congloué were
sinkers, triangular net weights, plummets, and some melting pots
with holes in the bottom, whose function is still a mystery. And
what could have been the purpose of the two square boxes, four-
teen inches long and three and a half deep, made of lead-plated
wood drilled with holes?

Only one leaden anchor stock was recovered at Grand Congloué. After having used anchors made from stone, the ancients
turned to wooden anchors with stocks of stone, lead, or lead-
plated wood. On some of these anchors there was a piece of lead
with three rectangular holes, that joined the flukes to the shank.
Occasionally the tips of the flukes were made of lead. We would
also sometimes find, next to the leaden stock, a rather high,
square, lead collar that was like a box without a top or bottom and
had a hole through the side. It seems logical to assume that this
collar was placed toward the end of the shaft, but there is nothing
to prevent one from concluding that it protected the heel. Anchors of this type have yet to be the object of any serious study.

There are also in the sea Roman anchors made of iron, but the
date of their first appearance remains to be determined. The exploration of the floor under Lake Nemi showed that there existed
simultaneously wooden anchors with lead stocks, iron anchors,
and a transitional model made of iron sheathed in wood. This last
type doesn't seem to have had any particular advantage, and was
probably introduced as a concession to the sailor's preference for
what was traditional, just as, in our own time, plastics were mod-
estly disguised as other materials until we dared to admit what
they were.

Caesar admired the iron anchors with chains that he saw on the
ships of the Veneti in Brittany. The Romans were still securing
their anchors with rope, which could be one reason why they lost
so many.

All these leaden objects that we brought up from the sea and
the purpose of which we didn't always understand, the copper
nails of all sizes, and the few pieces of wood that we examined
will eventually be of value, in the sense that they will serve as
points of comparison for more systematic excavations that will
explain their place and function. An artifact doesn't have the

same significance when it is thought to be unique and due to chance as it does when later research shows that it was in regular use. The great abundance of pottery found at Grand Congloué will make it possible to assign more precise dates to sites on land, from the examination of potsherds.

The ship went down where it did purely by chance, and the relationship between the soil and the man-made object was not intentional, as it would be for a temple, a city, or even a tomb. We could not, therefore, be guided by that. As we went about extracting crockery, amphoras, and pieces of the ship from the sand, we had no previous experience to inspire us, or help us divine the outlines of the wreck under the soil. I realized too late that our persistent digging of funnels and vaguely defined trenches could only lead to confusion. We should have made little soundings around the wreck in order to determine its limits, and then dug a huge trench all around it, beyond the furthest point where the amphoras had tumbled down. The *suceuse* would have worked better in the natural soil, and could have been wielded even by those who were inexpert. The sand would have run by itself into this peripheral trench, which would have been constantly emptied, and we could have hurried it along with the water gun. The mountain of pottery would have emerged from the soil untouched, and we could have photographed and measured it, gaining some understanding of the disarray before modifying its structure; then we could have extracted it, analyzing in the process the relationships between the various components.

In order to make a convincing argument, you have to have artifacts, evidence. If we hadn't opened up this sunken ship, would anyone have been willing to undertake the task on a scientific basis? Even after our demonstration of the importance of ancient wrecks, it is still difficult to get science on the move. A project that lacks potential for financial gain is hard to get started, and is bound to be short of funds for a long time, if not forever.

Certain journalists, taking their cue from a few archaeologists, have condemned us for our mistakes at Grand Congloué. But to us the essential thing was to get the project underway, and you can't do that by just sitting around and thinking about it.

6

ANTIKYTHERA

DURING THE DAY, the island of Grand Congloué was austere and majestic, but at night it was just gloomy. The first winter there was a long ordeal for those who endured it. Jacques sensed the weariness and mounting tension among the divers due to their lengthy seclusion, so in August 1953 he took us on board *Calypso* to Greece, to look for traces of Marcos Sestios.

We were accompanied by Harold Edgerton, a scientist from the Massachusetts Institute of Technology who had conceived and built our deepwater automatic cameras. I liked Edgerton because he had the simplicity and gentility that you very often find in people who are really worth knowing. We called him familiarly, but not without respect and affection, "Papa Flash."

Louis Malle also came along to acquaint himself with *Calypso*. He was to return later on to direct us in the filming of *The Silent World*. We got underway with a full crew of happy-go-lucky men.

In the vicinity of Cape Corse we sighted a family of orcs, with their dorsal fins long and thin like scythes, idling on the surface of a still and shining sea. They were only the first of the many cetaceans that we saw in the area.

At night we sailed past under the steep slopes of Stromboli, which was crowned by a dense fiery cloud.

The next day we entered the Strait of Messina, where ancient sailors accused Scylla and Charybdis of lying in wait to swamp their ships. By Charybdis, on the Sicilian side of the strait, the strong surface currents created smooth, flat expanses of water, with eddies that sucked in the air, to whip it around and spew it out again. We weren't tempted to dive there, which was just as well because the sea was said to be too deep. The other rock, Scylla, linked by a narrow strip of land to a little white village dwarfed by the mountain, seemed peaceful enough to us; still, its bad reputation made it worth a dive. Once below, we found ourselves surrounded by fish, just as in the good old days on the Riviera, but there wasn't the least trace of any wreck, ancient or modern.

The islands of Kythera and Antikythera lie on a line across the maritime route, between the Aegean Sea and the Mediterranean. We planned to make some dives at Antikythera to explore the famous sister of the wreck at Mahdia. In 1901 a team of sponge divers had found quite a few statues there.

Because of the wind, we were forced to take shelter at Kythera. After considerable discussion with the local authorities, we were permitted to visit the island without being examined by a doctor. Once there, we were befriended by a young boy who spoke broken English, whom we called John. John introduced us to two fishermen who claimed to have knowledge of a sunken city, which is something every diver dreams about; so we were quickly back in the sea again. One thing that bothered us was that on our chart of the sea the location in question was described as being the site of "ancient Kythera." We swam around among dense rocks with bare, indefinite shapes that had been strangely eroded. Standing there in the sand, they presented a perfectly natural picture of vague walls, canopies, and round open areas.

The next day we took our faithful friend John and steamed off to Antikythera, where we dropped anchor off Port Potamos, a village of little white, cubical houses built on soil that was full of yellowed rocks and devoid of vegetation. There we were met by five policemen dressed in green, of whose torrent of words I understood nothing, except that we lacked the proper authorization from Athens. Eventually it was arranged that the officers would come along on *Calypso* together with two fishermen who were familiar with the wreck, which lay behind a low promontory at the foot of a cliff about sixty feet deep. After our search for the sunken city and so many other disappointments during the course of our years as divers, we were surprised at being led so quickly to a site that had been explored fifty years before. I went down alone, under the pretext of verifying the location. The water was so transparent that I felt as if it might let me fall right down the cliff, which extended vertically to a group of fallen boulders a hundred sixty feet below. Although I saw no trace of the wreck, I was sure that it was there. The excavation in 1901 was still the most important event in the history of the island, and it was unlikely that the fishermen, who lived by tradition, could have forgotten the location, especially when they had the cliff to go by, and not just some remote landmarks or a certain distance out to sea. Once past the fallen boulders, I followed the gentle slope of the sand toward a dark, isolated expanse that proved to be a small platform marked by scattered posidonia. After that, at two hundred feet, I came to the edge of another cliff, where I instinctively hesitated before leaning over to look into the void below. At the foot of this cliff, which was thick with large blue gorgonians, there was more sand, this time extending into the distance as far as the eye could see. My experience at Mahdia had taught me to respect sponge divers, so I turned back. Then I spotted a tuft of long algae in the sand, gave it an idle pull, and came up with a fragment from an amphora. Moving from tuft to tuft, I extracted an earthenware decanter with a handle, then another, both of which I left in place as markers. In the sand further on I found nothing. I swam off along the foot of the cliff, came back, then left again. For some inexplicable reason I felt that the terrain around me was not in its natural, unspoiled state. I thought I sensed the presence of the wreck right there, parallel to the shore, about a hundred feet down, because beyond that all the evidence suggested that the soil had never been disturbed. On my way back to where I had left the decanters, two mossy boulders caught my eye, way down among the fallen rocks. I overturned the smaller one, which was surprisingly light, thoroughly eroded, and more like a sponge than a statue, although it did have a shape that resembled a torso.

Back on the surface I told Jacques I was certain the wreck was there, warning him all the while that he wouldn't see much.

Jacques was disappointed by his dive, and asked me where I had seen the sunken ship. He had done some digging and found debris piled up like tiles, but he hadn't noticed the boulders shaped like statues that I had seen. Bébert, however, did see them.

John had been listening to our conversation very intently and apparently understood a bit of French, for he proceeded to inform us that back when the statues were being brought up, the helmet divers, annoyed at the demands of their boss, had dynamited the cliff and caused an enormous rock to tumble down. The reference to explosives didn't surprise us, because we had often seen Greeks use dynamite to catch fish. "The big rock," John continued, "fell on the wreck, and that's the platform you've been talking about. Underneath, there's a bronze horse and statues of women and children."

I must say that John's story left us cold. We were accustomed to such tales. Usually it was a golden virgin.

By that time the police were reassured, and we took them back to Port Potamos. Then we returned to the wreck, where I dove with Girault. Digging here and there like rabbits, we unearthed quite a bit of pottery. I brought up one of the decanters, which Lallemand called an olpe.

When Jacques and Bébert came up from their stint below, they were convinced that the rock accused of concealing statues of women and children had always been there.

Toward evening the deep water seem black and uninviting, but I decided to make one more quick dive, just to look around. In the soft light, which still penetrated the water, the rocks had taken on a disturbingly somber appearance and the sand had become more luminous. I surveyed the landscape. When I reached the second cliff, the familiar sight of our anchor chain stretched out on the sand gave me the courage to float on down. The anchor had come to rest at two hundred sixty feet, next to the butt of an olpe and the neck of an amphora, both of which had fallen there in our time. Feeling the effects of a heavy narcosis, I used the chain to guide me as I made my way back to the ship. The ascent cleared my mind, and now I knew that the wreck lay entirely in the sand that bordered the fallen rocks. Some of the other divers discovered, about a thousand feet away, a second wreck with amphoras still intact.

That night my shoulder was so sore that it felt as if I had fractured it, and, although I took aspirin and a sedative, I couldn't sleep at all. At five o'clock, up on deck, Saout, our captain, said it had just come over the radio that the city of Zante had been destroyed by an earthquake on the very night when we were passing through a violent storm off its shores. Despite the fact that I had lost the use of one arm, I went to dive on the second wreck, leaving Jacques and Bébert to explore the bottom along the coast toward Port Potamos.

The warm, limpid water helped relieve the fatigue I felt after my sleepless night. Floating about lazily at a hundred thirty feet, I noticed that the terrain around me lacked the austerity that was usual at that depth; it was even rather pleasant, not at all unlike the kind of scenery you would see on land. It reminded me of the hillsides in Provence, where nature, left to itself, had succeeded in preserving an appearance of civilization. I had completely forgotten the pain in my shoulder. On the wreck, which had never been explored before, the huge, bulky amphoras, shaped like primitive barrels, were overrun by posidonia and thick concretions.

On my way back up the slope, I came across the leaden collar brace from an ancient anchor. A few yards away, I found the thinly concealed stock, which was also made of lead. When I scratched it with my knife, it became shiny right away.

Back aboard the motor launch, my shoulder felt as if someone had stuck a knife into it, and it began to throb again. The gaseous bubbles that were the cause of the pain had decreased in volume with the increased pressure below, but I hadn't been down long enough to eliminate them. As I came up, they grew larger again and renewed their attack. After a few days the pain subsided, then disappeared altogether.

The two minor decompression accidents of my long career have both taken place after dives on ancient wrecks. Most of the divers stricken with paralysis who have been brought to our decompression chamber at the Undersea Research Group have eventually confessed to fishing for amphoras. Several divers have lost their lives working on archaeological projects. After the tomb of Tutankhamen was opened, some superstitious individuals remarked that all the scientists who had worked on the project died from unnatural causes. I wouldn't go so far as to say the same about ancient wrecks, but it is true that such ships, with their air of mystery and promise of lost treasures, fascinate the average diver and cause him to lose the sangfroid that is so necessary in underwater operations. The work of digging out the amphoras by hand, wrenching them free, and handling them when they're full of sand, in the darkness of the mud cloud, leaves a diver short of breath; and the fear of exhausting his air supply leads him into hasty efforts that are dangerous and excessive. Many novices, when they see hundreds of amphoras just lying around, get greedy and forget the laws of diving, assuming, of course, that they know them.

We returned to the wreck at Antikythera a few days later, to poke around a little with a portable *suceuse* made from a light sheet-metal pipe. Diving two at a time, my colleagues dug up shards and bellies of amphoras. When I went into the water to relieve the last divers, who were a hundred sixty feet below me, they looked tiny and the cliff dropped off at an increasingly dizzy rate.

Digging in the sand here and there, I uncovered only scattered debris. At the bottom of my last funnel, about two yards from the rocks, the pipe ran right into the hull of the sunken ship, which was perfectly preserved under a foot and a half of sand. There was no *vaigrage* at that point. If only I had had more time!

The slopes around the reef-island of Pori were gradual enough so that one could dive wearing just a pair of goggles. Bébert had been in the water only a short time when he came back up and took me aside. He had informed Jacques that they had seen at least five hundred ingots of lead weighing more than two hundred pounds each, but had been unable to lift them. We rushed to get on our gear, already full of talk about the improvements we would be able to make on *Calypso*.

On the barren rock, in full view among the sea urchins, there were bluish balls and ingots that bore a strange resemblance to lead. I tried in vain to lift one of the ingots, then turned to a ball, which I couldn't budge either, although it wasn't that heavy. It had become welded to the rock. I finally managed to detach a ball from a stock of them piled up in a fault. It was light in my hand and gave off a stream of black rust. On one of the ingots Jacques wrote the word IRON; then he saw some sheets of copper plating under a rock. A navy sailing ship must have crashed against the reef and jettisoned its ballast and munitions, after which, being considerably lightened, it was probably carried off by the wind. We were naïve to think that all those sponge divers would leave fifty tons of lead lying around in their midst.

At last we arrived in Delos, a city built from marble that seemed out of place amid the reddish-brown rocks that covered the rest of the desolate island.

When we visited the ruins, all my companions walked slowly, with their eyes glued to the ground. Shocked by their lack of curiosity, I drew nearer and realized that they were gathering up little coins that were no bigger than lentils. Philippe Cousteau showed me one that was comparatively large. He was just bending down to pick up another one that was even larger when one of the guards came along and made him put them all back; meanwhile, everyone else discreetly moved away. After that, they raised their eyes from the ground to admire Delos, or to make sure that the guard had gone away. The streets were narrow and bordered closely on either side by houses that had on the ground floor mosaics of geometric figures, decorated objects, and, finally, two arched dolphins gamboling about with a tiny rider on their backs. Then we saw a trident between two interfacing S's, and we knew that we had entered the villa of Marcos Sestios. After the racing dolphins, the row of white, arrogant lions, and all the underpinnings of a pleasure resort spread out in the sun, I expected to find some expression of emotion visible in the courtyard; but it was quite bare and impersonal.

Exploring the sea around the island from our two motor launches, we brought back an earthenware basin, some amphora necks, a strange leaden anchor stock, a cup reminiscent of those at Grand Congloué, and a lead pipe that still bore some fragments of wood. Bébert had seen seven column shafts made of black stone. He led me to an area where there was a thin layer of sand and the sun still created the dancing latticework patterns of light that drive filmmakers to despair. The few scattered pieces of amphoras on the site were not enough to convince me that there was a wreck nearby. The portable *suceuse* didn't exactly devour the soil, but it did make a dent in it, and, even if all it dug up was sand, I couldn't complain. As Bébert crouched down over the pipe to keep it vertical, he was enveloped in the thick, opaque fog at the top, which made him look as if he were trying to light a recalcitrant wood stove.

It took considerable force and ingenuity to hoist one of the column shafts into the motor launch. When we got back to *Calypso*, however, we discovered that our "column" was actually the hardened contents of a barrel of cement.

In Athens, at the museum, we were pleased to note that great bronzes come from the sea. The *Zeus,* or *Poseidon,* which is said to go back to 460 B.C., was raised in 1928 from the roads off Cape Artemision. The *Jockey,* although executed two hundred years later, was found on the same wreck. And in 1925, the *Youth* from Marathon, created during the fourth century B.C., was brought up in a fisherman's net from a depth of two hundred thirty feet.

On one of the pedestals in the museum was a plaque that read "*Youth* from Antikythera, 340 B.C.," but the statue wasn't in its place, so we asked if we might see it. It had been sent to the restoration laboratory where, as a special favor, we were permitted to enter. The head of the statue, with its short, curly hair, lay in a basket while the statuary surgeon cleaned the large stone eyes. On the torso, which rested on the workbench, you could see miscellaneous sutures and bands that had been riveted to the interior to reinforce it. The new director hadn't liked the pose given to the *Youth* by those who had first restored it. The bronzes from Mahdia also came from the sea. The only important bronze that did not was the *Charioteer,* which had been hastily stashed in a sewer in Delphi at the moment when enemy soldiers were climbing up the slopes through the olive trees to massacre the inhabitants, smash the sexual organs on the marble statues, and melt the bronzes to make swords.

In the time that has elapsed since our stay in Athens, the land has scored another point against the sea, in Piraeus, where, after some men digging a ditch struck a bronze hand with their picks, three statues—a Pallas Athena, a Minerva, and an archaic Apollo—were unearthed. I was fortunate enough to get a look at them while they were still lying in stretchers, looking, with their patina of green oxide, longer and more lifelike than they would once they were ensconced in a museum. The statues had been buried under the ashes of a wharf that was part of the port destroyed by fire around 86 B.C. This is about the time when the ships at Mahdia and Antikythera went down, which means that the bronzes were probably scheduled to go by sea to Rome.

The sea got its revenge when the sponge trawlers from Bodrum, the ancient Halicarnassus, caught in their net the upper half of a large bronze statue of the goddess Demeter, from the fifth century B.C. And it triumphed again when some friends of mine from Agde found, in the bed of the Hérault, which empties into the sea, a bronze *Youth* of Hellenistic inspiration. The statue was missing a leg, but they groped around for days in the muddy water and, believe it or not, found it, a good distance away.

Having just arrived from Antikythera, we wanted to see something more than the dismembered *Youth,* so we asked where the marble statues were hidden. Once again by special dispensation, we were led into a vast courtyard, a morgue for ancient statuary where mutilated bodies with deeply pitted skins, atrophied flesh, and festering tumors stood propped against the wall or lay strewn about in heaps. Two large horses, martyred as well, stood on the stumps of their legs. One of them, the head of which had also been salvaged and stored elsewhere, sported withers that looked as if they were fresh from the hands of the sculptor; the other, which had retained its head, was a pitiful sight. A Venus with a hideously eroded front faced the wall in order to show its immaculate posterior instead. Here and there a breast or a knee had fortuitously escaped the generalized decrepitude. It's unfortunate that museums aren't organized with a bit more imagination. A collection of these damaged marbles displayed in the middle of a large gallery would be certain to arouse the public.

The condition of these statues taught me something new. I had been trying to analyze the wreck from which they had been salvaged without any idea of how it had looked before it was excavated. Now I realized that the sculptures couldn't have been buried under the soil, but must have been just lying on top of it. Those that had been touching the sand, or that had penetrated it slightly as the ship rotted away, showed parts that remained unscathed. The others, the ones that had been kept up in the water, or that had landed on the fallen rocks, had been thoroughly eroded. If there was any marble left it was only because the accumulation of sand produced by the marine life and by debris from the cliff had eventually brought the corrosion to a halt. The horse with the well-preserved withers had been resting in the sand on its back, which is why its body was not equally well preserved. Any statues still in the sand are undoubtedly in good condition.

In 1969 I went through the museum again and came across the two horses together with a few of the other statues exhibited erect and in isolation, like their terrestrial counterparts. They still bore witness to the awful majesty of the sea, but the effect of sheer numbers was lost.

A complete excavation of the Antikythera site would bring to light a good many interesting little items, like the other half of the famous astronomical clock, which was a bronze mechanism with a complicated system of gears and a number of dials inscribed with the names of the months and the signs of the zodiac. With the dials at the proper setting, the clock would describe the annual movements of the sun and give the dates of the rising and setting of the most important stars. This block of oxidized bronze, which sat in a crate for more than fifty years, was the subject of a recent study by Derek Price. It seems too delicate to have been a shipboard instrument of navigation, and was probably a part of the booty taken from Greece by the Romans. The scholarly analysis of the Antikythera pottery, also undertaken only recently, has yet to be concluded. At the beginning of this century archaeologists were looking for objets d'art, and they ignored ordinary pottery, either whole or in fragments, that was unworthy of being exhibited in a museum. No one ever asked himself if there was a ship under the statues at Antikythera. And at Mahdia, where the helmet divers led everyone to believe they had penetrated the main deck and explored the interior of a ship in a good state of preservation, the indifference of the archaeologists is astonishing.

After examining the pottery recovered at Antikythera, the experts concluded that the ship must have gone down during the first half of the first century B.C. At that time the *Youth* was already more than two hundred fifty years old, which makes it comparable for us to a work from the era of Louis XIV. The archaic Apollo from Piraeus, packed in with bronzes that were clearly of more recent origin, was then five hundred years old, like a statue from the Renaissance today. The Romans excelled in urbanism and monumental architecture, but they had no talent for sculpture. Excavations in Italy have provided evidence of their infatuation with Greek statues, especially those that came from an era when Greek art was in full flower, and which were, for the Romans, antiques. Even in the best of times creative geniuses are few, so wealthy Romans often had to content themselves with copies of famous works. The wrecks at Mahdia and Antikythera demonstrate the importance for shippers of the traffic in works of art, whether old originals or copies, and prove that many of the copies found in Italy came from studios in Greece.

On the way back we did some diving near Naxos, on a reef consisting of a large rock perched on an underwater hill. A strong current that brought algae and clear water carried me along above a monotonous seabed toward the remains of a sunken freighter. When a wrecked ship comes to rest in the sea, its various structural components form a high relief on the bottom, and the vessel itself presents a picture of vast unavailable resources; it remains sufficiently familiar, however, to retain the aura of catastrophe that is relieved, even on barren soil, by flights of fish, animal excrescences, and rich algae. More than anything else in the sea, the sunken ship gives the diver an awareness of the degree to which he can conquer space. As he swims along the length of the masts, he realizes the kind of flight he has always dreamed of, without having to fear the inevitable fall. He glides over slanted decks and descends into passageways by traversing with a single swift movement steep ladders to which sailors of yore had to cling fast against the rolling of the ship.

I advanced slowly, struggling against the current as it swirled about around the freestanding boiler plates. The bow section of the ship, which was in better condition, rested on the highest rock, leaving a space under the hull from which a troop of fish made their exit. I swam into this tunnel to get away from the current and discovered, under the freighter, some broken amphoras from an ancient wreck.

At the end of August, we entered the narrows guarded by the little fortified town of Navarino. In 1827, in this circular roadstead framed by tiered mountains and protected from the high seas by the bare, white, towering cliff of the island of Sphacteria, a fleet of twenty-six English, French, and Russian vessels—ships of the line, frigates, corvettes, and brigs—annihilated more than a hundred Turco-Egyptian ships that were pillaging Greece. Under the heavy smoke from the fire ships and other vessels in flames, and from the guns, whose salvos sometimes landed on allies, this massacre was the prelude to the liberation of Greece from Turkish dominion.

In the reports of the various admirals are descriptions of Turco-Egyptian ships exploding in the water like set pieces or hurtling in flames against Sphacteria.

Ever since it became possible to explore the bottom of the sea, the accounts of naval battles, from Salamis to Trafalgar, have taken on an added interest. At Navarino we would be looking for the treasures carted off by the Turks, as well as bronze cannons— the *Grande Sultane,* one of the ships that was captured, boasted fifty-four of them. And I would get a chance to see how the record of a mass liquidation of ships had been preserved by the sea.

We went into town to see what we could find out and were accosted by an idle man speaking broken English. He took us to the home of a fisherman who said he would guide us to the most promising wrecks. On a small ship like *Calypso,* there's no place to sit outside of the mess, and since standing up for any length of time gives you pins and needles in your legs, taking a walk becomes as much a necessity as a pleasure. When we got back to the fisherman's house, he wasn't there, so a young boy served as our guide.

Under sixty feet of murky water, with about a yard of visibility, Bébert and I skimmed along the surface of a smooth mud, each of us at the head of a cloud raised by his foot fins, expecting at any moment to stumble onto the twisted hull of a treasure ship.

We eventually got bored and went back up to the surface to swim toward Sphacteria. The water there seemed to be almost transparent. Beginning at twenty feet, the steep, rocky slope was obscured under the most incredible heap of rotted timber that anyone could ever imagine—huge beams, joists, splinters, and debris. Nails sheathed in wood jutted out from beneath the algae. I picked up several enormous beams that were surprisingly light and riddled with white tunnels hollowed out by shipworms. I made a game of sending these beams crashing down the cliff in spirals of mud. A fold in the rock attracted my attention. I fanned it with my hand, which stirred up mud that was first black, then white, and full of rusty bits of iron. With such an abundance of wood lying around, I had hopes of finding some hulls further down. As the fog slowly cast its shadow over the water, I sank down without seeing anything resembling a ship, or even any logical disorder, and without being able to tell whether the chaos was due to the steep incline or the work of helmet divers. At a hundred thirty feet the last rocks protruded from the magma into the gloomy twilight, beyond which was a barren, sandy plain where there wasn't a single sign of life.

I wove my way back up the cliff, hundreds of yards of which looked like an abandoned timberland.

At this point Jacques decided that we had spent enough time hunting for sunken treasures, and he ordered *Calypso* made ready for sea.

We next undertook to explore, by relays of divers whose bubbles we followed with the motor launch, Sicilian waters between Cape Passero, the southernmost point of the island, and Cape Murro di Porco, near Syracuse. On this gentle slope the diver saw a narrow strip of a vast accessible territory. We went on ahead in the launch to get an estimate of the relative distribution of the artifacts. During the course of the day, over a distance of three miles, we found all sorts of things: a tiny leaden anchor stock with collar brace; other leaden parts of anchors that we couldn't identify; cut stones of different shapes; whole Carthaginian amphoras with large, flat lips; various amphora shards from all along the route; and a large, flat stone with four pierced lobes and a wide round hole in the middle. A scientific exploration of the waters around Sicily would add a great deal to our knowledge of the sea.

7

The PANAMA

IN ADDITION TO CARRYING out specific tasks assigned to us by the navy, we often made training cruises, the nature of which was determined in large part by our need for diversion. We particularly liked sunken ships, with their souvenirs and their lobsters.

Tailliez now had command of a ship, but he was still very much interested in the Undersea Research Group and came to visit us quite regularly. One of his friends was a fisherman from Toulon who had been netting old pieces of wood with large copper nails, at a location which he called "the Panama." An English frigate was supposed to have sunk there in 1811. Generations of fishermen scan the shallow water with their glass-bottomed buckets, and dredge the deeper waters with their nets, which sometimes bring up pottery or pieces of sunken ships, and with their trawls, which bring them up even more frequently. Although they don't know the bottom of the sea as well as the sponge divers, the fishermen could direct us to many an old or ancient wreck. But they don't trust us.

In November 1963, Tailliez succeeded in persuading his friend to come aboard the *Elie Monnier* and show him where the *Panama* was. After many disappointments we no longer trusted oral descriptions and much preferred to have the fisherman take us to the site himself. When he said, "It's here," we would take bearings on the coast, sail around in a little circle, and discreetly approach the spot again. If he was still sure, we would moor a buoy.

The divers brought up a copper bar twenty inches long and sheathed in a length of wood preserved by the oxide.

Their reports were far from conclusive. One of them had seen pieces of grillwork lying flat on the ground, some metal bars, and various corroded objects. Another had found sheets of copper hull plate. Everyone gave a different description of the bottom, and they began to wonder if there was more than one wreck.

A month later I went to the site myself on the *Elie Monnier*. The ultrasonic depth finder indicated a depth of a hundred eighty feet and drew on its chart a barely visible fault about a yard high. Ortolan, in command of the ship, dropped the anchor and sent two divers down to make sure that the weighted line fell in view of the wreck. In deep water, even a highly skilled sea captain doesn't always succeed, with the first try, in mooring his ship in such a way that it will end up, once it is stationary, directly above a given point. The anchor chain has to be quite a bit longer than the distance to the bottom, because the wind and the current often push in different directions, and their irregularities combine to force the ship into unexpected positions. At such a depth, therefore, we would descend along a weighted line, which we would try to find again at the end of the dive, in order to be certain that our ascent would be made in accordance with the decompression tables. If there was a sunken ship nearby, we would use certain parts of it as reference points to guide us back to the lifeline. When there was no wreck in sight, however, our fear of getting lost kept us from going very far, with the result that we often saw nothing.

The divers came back up to report that we were directly over the wreck and that there was a large assortment of relics in plain view.

I went into the water in a state of great excitement. I had to go down slowly, however, because I had only recently recovered from a cold, and it had left one of my ears sensitive to the penetration of compressed air. The human ear is the only one of our organs that adapts poorly to diving, and it is often a source of trouble, sometimes to such an extent that it is impossible for a person to operate in deep water at all.

The water is still warm at that time of the year, but since it had rained quite a bit during the fall it was fairly cloudy. I traveled down the lifeline hand over hand, pausing for a moment to clear my ear. After I passed through the cold, transparent layer, the water became less cloudy, and I was near the bottom. The visibility was good, but it was late in the day and the sun was obscured by a rainy sky. I swam along over a pile of colorless debris, then chose two iron girders that lay across the hull of the ship as my reference points. Although I hadn't planned to do any fishing, I had a net on my belt and there were lobsters about, thrashing the water with their antennae. While I had no desire to harvest them, I was curious, considering that they had no shelter, to see how easy it would be to trap them. I made a pass at one, but he got away. This annoyed me, so I went into contortions in order to get into a better position. Soon my net was full, but the water had turned yellow and I had to move away to see. Looking around, I realized that I had no idea where I was, so I stopped right there. Then I noticed a black shape covered with mud that stood fast against the currents—the chain from the *Elie Monnier*. I found the iron girders again and started off along the axis of the wreck, which was wide and flat. On the ground to one side there were pieces of hull plate with fragments of wood still attached. There were also some vague forms that were so encrusted with marine life that it was impossible to identify them. After passing several times by what appeared to be the same capstan head, I came upon a huge windlass lying flat on the bottom. Beyond that the ship narrowed to meet the stempost, or rather the "forefoot," which is the part of the stempost that curves to join with the keel. I was pleased to see the bow section, because it could tell me what had happened to the ship since it had sunk. Plated with copper, the bow jutted out above a depression in the soil and listed slightly to port. The thick sides of the hull formed a triangular relief full of big copper nails that had fallen there as the wood rotted. Retracing my path, I swam over two heavy, mud-colored chains that formed a V, passed by some hawsepipes lying flat on the ground, and came to the windlass again. Lying on the port side were some long pieces of debris that could have been part of the ship's rigging. The impression I had gathered from viewing the bow proved to be correct—the entire ship listed to port. Toward the after part of the ship, there was another long object that looked like a mast, but at the broken end I could see that it had lamina of cork, which was not in use at the time when the ship was supposed to have been built. While undergoing stage decompression on the weighted line, I tried to sort out what I had seen and reviewed all the fleeting impressions that I was bringing back from my tour below. The wreck formed a plateau thirty to fifty feet wide and more than two hundred feet long, which ended rather abruptly on the barren plain. Although I had seen hardly anything except mud, I sensed the presence of the ship there, rotted and flattened out. Among the things I actually had seen was a large collection of pipes—too many, in fact, for a sailing ship operating in 1811.

As I climbed up on deck, I proudly announced that the wreck was a wooden ship plated with copper, and that it was resting on the port side. Then I noticed that there was water running out of my rubber diving suit through a hole in the leg, and I remembered feeling a slight chill just as I was placing one last lobster into the net, which I was holding between my knees. When you're a hundred eighty feet below the surface you don't really feel the cold, and it's easier to swim with a little water in your drysuit, which fits very tightly over an undergarment of wool.

The next divers discovered a spent torpedo, which was the long object I had seen and, under the stupefying influence of the deep water, taken for a mast. The fact of the matter was that we were right in the middle of the torpedo firing range. Ortolan had examined the links of the chain, which were studded and a foot long. Bézaudin brought up a porthole, a heavy piece of bronze with a small glass lens, one face of which was smooth, flat, and shiny, while the other was convex and unpolished, a design that was probably intended to prevent the sun from setting fires inside the ship. At last we had found an identifiable object that was an authentic relic of the old navy. Seeing it on the deck, I remembered having passed over such things resting on the bottom, without recognizing them. I shouldn't have gathered up those lobsters. My guess was that the porthole had been on the starboard side, and had wound up in the soil when the rotted hull collapsed.

Now we were quite excited about the sunken ship and we

wanted to know how old it was, whether it was English or French, why there were all those pipes with bolted couplings, and why we hadn't seen any cannons.

A retired admiral who knew everything about sailing ships told Ortolan that our porthole had illuminated the between decks under the gun emplacements, at water level, and that the presence of such a large studded chain was evidence that the ship was a first-rate man-of-war with eighty guns, built between 1840 and 1850.

More excited than ever, we returned to the site. I had buoys placed every thirty feet along the axis of the wreck. Each buoy carried, at ten feet from the bottom, a number that would tell us where we were as we swam about in the turbid water and enable us to record the location of any identifiable object. The eighth buoy marked the stern, making the string of buoys two hundred twenty feet long, which is the size of an average sailing vessel.

In order to get a better idea of the situation, I followed the outlines of the ship in the gray light. I passed by the capstan, for there was in reality only one, and saw its chains stretching out into the distance. The ship had been riding at anchor—a bad sign. In certain places the massive hull section supported the soil of the plateau, which was supported in turn by a sloping bank of mud. Probing the soil, I found it muddy—the whole wreck was full of mud held in place by rotted wood. By the after section, which was rounded and well preserved, our burrowing anchor had unearthed a truncated sternpost. But there were no cannons, nor even the slightest suggestion that there might be some under the mud. We did, however, come up with another porthole, which was encrusted with limestone turned green by the copper. I scraped away at it mechanically and uncovered an inscription, II AV T, which I took to be an abbreviation for *numéro deux, avant tribord* (No. 2, starboard bow). The ship was French! Turning to the first porthole, I found it marked VI T (No. 6, starboard). I was quite proud of this discovery, because it confirmed what I had been saying all along.

The next day, in the hope of finding some cannons, I went down to dig in the center of the wreck with the portable *suceuse*. But when I turned it on, the mouth just stuck to the mud and nothing happened. The mud didn't run at all, being hard to the touch like clay. When I tried striking the soil with the *suceuse*, it punched out circular clods and got stopped up. It was hopeless, but, then, what could I expect? I was discouraged by the depth and extent of the wreck.

When we got back to Toulon, another expert contacted by Ortolan informed us that the ship we had been diving on was indeed the *Panama*. Ordered on February 1, 1841, as the eleventh in a series of twelve paddle-wheel frigates, the *Panama* was launched in 1843, with the following characteristics: length at the waterline, 228 feet; breadth at the waterline, 40 feet; depth, 21 feet; displacement, 1,873 tons. Decommissioned in 1871, it was converted into a pontoon and served for twenty-four years as a barracks for sailors in transit. In July 1895, the *Panama* was declared surplus and priced for sale at 17,000 francs. Before being relinquished, however, it was condemned to be used as a practice target by the torpedo boat *Dragonne*, which had been fitted for the occasion with a 55mm "close range" gun. The navy must have suspected that the *Panama* wouldn't survive the ordeal, because they stuffed it full of large, empty barrels to keep it afloat.

On November 3, 1896, seamen attached to the Toulon Port Administration, acting on orders from higher up, moored the ship in the Vignettes roadstead, a mile and a half southwest of the lower battery on Cape Brun.

That night the *Dragonne* fired only twenty-eight of the thirty rounds that the technicians had called for, because after the twenty-first the *Panama* showed signs of weakening. Then the wind began to blow and the sea got rough, so they called it a day.

The next morning found the *Panama* resting on the bottom; it had sunk by itself during the night. The old warrior had perished under arms, but ingloriously, like a lamb being led to slaughter.

Fifty-seven years later, what had once been an enormous mass of copper-plated oak with thick walls fortified by copper bars was nothing but a little plateau of mud and a few concreted protrusions. And it had probably been that way for a very long time— which is the one thing that I had until then failed to understand about ancient wrecks. I had been surprised to find the pottery at Grand Congloué corroded on the surface of the wreck but intact in the sand; and to see the lower part of a ship well preserved when most of the rest of it had rotted away. I didn't appreciate the significance of such phenomena, because I had always thought that deterioration in the sea took place by stages, over a period of several centuries. Any evidence to the contrary I simply dismissed as another of those mysteries that surround life in the sea.

Now, however, I understood. The upper parts of a ship, rotted and gnawed by shipworms, cave in rather quickly, forming a layer of mud that protects the lower parts. Within a very short time the wreck is reduced to just a low, flat mound, which will be its stable, definitive condition.

8

The *DRAMONT*

IN 1959 I HAD AN unexpected opportunity to test, on a wreck that reposed on a homogeneous bottom, certain theories that I had begun to formulate.

The wreck of the *Dramont*, so called because of its proximity to the cape of the same name, was discovered in 1956 by Santamaria, an experienced diver who immediately, but discreetly, began to investigate the buried remains. When he found it, the wreck was just a huge mass projecting from the sand in the shape of a ship, a solid body of amphoras welded together by a thick, almost continuous layer of concretions.

The part that had not been swallowed up by the sand was searched by the Undersea Exploration Club of Saint-Raphaël. The amphoras they recovered displayed a great variety of markings and belonged to several types, the coexistence of which presented a problem for the archaeologists. The fact that this same problem was encountered at Grand Congloué leads one to think that sunken ships will continue for some time to provide data that will be useful in the classification of amphoras. The *Dramont*, a ship from the first century B.C., was pillaged several times and is even said to have been dynamited.

Professor Benoit had obtained a modest grant from the Centre National de la Recherche Scientifique and from the Direction de l'Architecture, for the purpose of making a partial excavation of this wreck, which was full of amphoras with different markings and appeared to be exceptionally well preserved.

I anticipated that a considerable portion of the hull would prove to be in relatively good condition, so I proposed that a trench be dug across the wreck to give us access to a whole section of it. This approach had never been used before.

Cousteau lent Benoit the second ship of his little fleet, the *Espadon*, a former trawler sixty feet long and thirteen feet wide. He also offered the assistance of the Office Français de Recherches Sous-marines, which he had created at Marseilles in conjunction with the foremost experts on the problems of diving and undersea operations.

On August 9, after conferring with Benoit at Saint-Raphaël, we proceeded to the worksite, which was about a hundred yards from a reef that came right up to the surface of the water, so that the sea crashed against it in the stormy weather. This reef was part of the rocky base of the Ile d'Or, and we suspected it of having caused the wreck of our Roman ship as well as that of others, like the one with the marble blocks. In subsequent years, four ancient wrecks were discovered around the reef, the most distant being about half a mile off toward the destination of the east wind.

We went into the water near the reef, in an area that was full of large, mossy boulders cut by deep faults. As we followed the slope we arrived at a final cliff that was known locally as a *tombant*. *Tombants* are quite familiar to divers and fishermen, for whom they have a slight air of mystery. We have often found at the foot of such a cliff an antique anchor whose rope had broken after rubbing against the crest. Beyond the cliff a few meager tufts of posidonia in the sand formed a sparse prairie that ended at a hundred fifteen feet, which is where the wreck began. The axis of the sunken ship followed the slope of the sand, with the result that the further end was a hundred thirty feet down. The site was a hundred feet long and thirty feet wide. No longer the enchanting spectacle described by Santamaria, it was now a vast junkyard, a chaotic, dull gray heap of broken amphoras. A small block of these jars fused to one another was all that remained to commemorate the lost beauty of the wreck.

Since the site was relatively well protected, we would be able to continue working even under a moderately strong wind. The mistral, which had given us so much trouble at Grand Congloué, was rare in these parts, and the *Espadon* could stay on station for several days at a time. But we decided that we would rather return each night to Saint-Raphaël, which was only half an hour away. To install the *suceuse* each morning and take it up again at night would have caused us to lose time, so I suggested that we leave it in place in the water, to be supported by a large anchor buoy that would be unaffected by subsurface waves. I wanted to remove the layer of displaced, broken amphoras, so that we could start in to work on fresh soil where everything would be *in situ,* as the archaeologists say.

The *Espadon* arrived on the fifteenth of August. In order to provide a fixed mooring for the ship, we girded two rocks with a steel cable that had a crow's-foot at the end. On the other side we moored two anchors weighted with half a ton of pig iron and spaced three hundred feet apart. Between the crow's-foot and the two anchors, the ship could be kept over the site under any conditions.

After removing about two hundred fifty broken amphoras, which we placed in seven piles around the wreck, we drew a line across the site at the center of the visible portion of the ship, to mark the path of the trench we planned to dig. The trench would pass close to the solid block of amphoras, which we intended to preserve as a memorial, and it was against this block that, with an anchorage of pig iron, we installed a *suceuse* having an inside diameter of four and a half inches.

Because my time was taken up with the Undersea Research Group, I couldn't get to the site as often as I wanted to. And Cousteau, who had been named director of the Oceanographic Museum in Monaco, had to ask our friend Alinat to fill in for him. Alinat, with whom I got along very well, visited the site from time to time, and that, together with precise reports from divers, enabled me to follow and direct the operations. The permanent divers on the project were all professionals from Cousteau's team, but every day there were visiting divers who did a good share of the work.

In the beginning the water was very clear, the visibility was good, and we were able to work effectively. But as we continued to dig, the mud rose faster and higher, forming a cloud that kept getting larger. The strong current that the local divers had promised for the site never came that year. Only the first diver into the water in the morning, or after the break for lunch, could really see what he was doing. We had to do all the heavy work in zero visibility. Meanwhile, we were running out of time and, although we had planned only a partial excavation, we didn't have the funds or technical personnel that we needed to do the job right. But at least we knew where we were going; we felt that we were in control of the situation, and that we were doing much better than we had done at Grand Congloué.

Clouds of mud have plagued me on almost every archaeological project. I think we will eventually see the day when artificial currents will be created by means of watertight fans placed on the bottom.

We went into the water in two-man teams, one man to handle the *suceuse* and the other to remove the pottery. The thin, fine mud that went up the pipe with the other materials would spread out in a film on the surface and be carried off by the slightest current. As they did at Grand Congloué, the shells, concretions, and sand would drift back down to the site without clouding the water. Fortunately for us, they were well dispersed.

A school of quite edible mullets became regular visitors to the trench, where they would busily rummage about as if to help us; we also enjoyed the company of a family of beautiful white fish. I'm always amazed to see how quickly the fish adjust to our presence, taking salutary fright or becoming our friends, according to our attitude.

Toward the end of August, patches of the hull began to appear at the bottom of the trench; the wood was soft and delicate, which meant that the divers had to be careful with the *suceuse*. Although the condition of the first layer of amphoras had encouraged us to think that the entire cargo might be just as orderly, that was not the case, and we found a number of tumbled, broken jars. But we didn't have time to look for an explanation. On one side of the trench you could see very clearly how the amphoras had been stored in the hold in three vertical, imbricated layers, just as they had been at La Chrétienne and on many another wreck. The whole cargo had sunk down and spread out when the hull collapsed. Most of the amphoras were leaning or lying toward the south, which must have been the way the ship was inclined.

Alinat and I were particularly interested in the architecture of the ship, and we searched in vain for the keel. One day I thought I had seen it, but it was only a stringer. The stringers were an inch and a half thick and ten inches wide, whereas the *vaigrage,* or interior floor, was made from boards an inch and a quarter thick, all of which had, at some point along the length between the ribs, broken under the weight of the amphoras. We eventually uncovered another stringer, but there was still no keel. The ribs, all identical and well preserved, ranged in height from 3⅛ to 3½ inches, and in width from 4¾ to 6¼ inches, while the space between them was only slightly greater than their width. The combined thickness of the double-planked hull was 2¾ inches. Each layer of planking had wooden tongues that fitted into the grooves of the layer below and were cottered with a wooden peg, according to the method of construction that was traditional at that time. We found no trace of leaden plating. It has yet to be explained why some ancient ships had this plating while others did not.

It was hard to examine the hull at the bottom of the trench because the slightest movement made the water turbid and caused the sand to run down the sides, in spite of the fact that we had been forced to give them a gentle slope. We had already noticed at La Chrétienne and at Grand Congloué that the sand runs down into an excavation from a considerable distance, and continues to run until it has found its level. A hole in the sand spontaneously assumes the shape of a funnel.

About half a mile from where we were working, on the leeward side of the red, rocky slopes of Cape Dramont, a bend in the coastline forms the little port of Le Poussail. The forest of pines that borders the coast in the harbor provided shelter for the multicolored tents of a vast international camping ground, from which hordes of pink, chubby little divers from Germany, Belgium, and Switzerland set out in feverish pursuit of nautical souvenirs. They were especially fond of archaeological items, and the wrecks in the vicinity were the victims of regularly scheduled clandestine explorations.

Every day toward evening we would see them coming in little groups, swimming along behind the inflatable mattresses that carried their diving gear. They would land on the Ile d'Or and sit all in a row by the edge of the water, waiting patiently for the *Espadon* to leave so that they could exploit the site for their own purposes. Others, more afraid of the police than of diving in the dark, came during the night, often leaving behind a watertight lamp or other instrument for us to find the next day. In the hope of discouraging such activity, I left instructions to the effect that, every evening, all intact amphoras should be removed from the site. Despite all the nocturnal incursions, we still brought up a large number of amphoras, which we would empty out on the fantail. In the muddy sand that they disgorged, there were numerous shells as well as pieces of charcoal, which had probably been added to help preserve the wine.

One day, disgusted with the mud that hung in the water and masked the whole worksite, I took off in the direction of the wreck with the blocks of marble. Before the dark area by the *tombant,* three rectangular blocks loomed enormous in the blue green water. In front of the blocks there were two long pieces of wood lying flush with the soil. I dispersed the sand that covered the wood and saw that it was a remnant of hull planking with the traditional tongue-and-groove joints. There was no pottery. If the ship had been carrying amphoras, there would have been some shards, regardless of how thoroughly it might have been pillaged.

Even when the weather was good, the *Espadon* never ceased to roll in its mooring over the wreck. It was a hard, fast roll that rattled your bones and cramped all your muscles, so much so, in fact, that we thought we would never get used to it. By the end of the day we were completely exhausted and only too glad to get our feet on solid ground. When the sea was rough, of course, this perpetual roll was even worse, a fact that deterred many a timorous soul from coming aboard for a visit.

The trench was now almost eight yards long. It was quite broad at the top, but only three feet wide down at the bottom, where the hull was plainly visible. Although we had definitely cut across the axis of the ship, we had yet to find any trace of the keel. The lower part of the hull was flattened out on one side, while it rose slightly on the other. There was no significant difference between the frames and no keelson.

In accordance with our established plan, we took a handsaw and cut away a twenty-inch section of the hull, so that we could continue to dig and disengage the part we were working on.

Much to our surprise, we found several more amphoras under the hull. Had they fallen from the sinking ship and landed on the bottom ahead of it, or had they escaped through a breach in the hull before it was permanently flattened out? In order to find out what had happened, we would have had to excavate the entire site and record the location of every amphora and every fragment, which we had neither the time nor the means to do.

At one point we saw under the hull a heavy piece of white wood that had been partly destroyed by shipworms. We thought it might be the keel, although it didn't really look like one.

Qn September 19 I arrived in Saint-Raphaël just as the *Espadon* was returning to port, after rough seas had forced the divers out of the water. Alinat appeared, then Benoit. It seems that the heavy piece of wood was a garboard strake, which, as the first plank of the hull, is thicker than all the rest and grooved to join with the keel. The keel had been reduced to a spongy pulp that any movement in the water might cause to disintegrate. A thick, heavy keelson had been discovered in one side of the trench. I couldn't understand that, because a keelson is placed right over the keel along its entire length, and we hadn't seen any sign of a keelson at the bottom of the trench. Despite the rough seas, I asked if I could go out and have a look.

The wind was only moderate, but we had to contend with giant swells in the sea. I went into the water with Alinat and Riquet. The keelson, which was quite heavy and made from a hard wood that was still well preserved, jutted out from the sloping side of the trench. It was clear that it hadn't been broken, because the end had been tapered and rounded off to give it an almost elegant, finished appearance. On the other side of the trench, the space between the massive garboards was filled with the crumbled remains of the keel. Above the place for the keel, the ribs got slightly thicker, forming floor plates so thin that a residue of sand had concealed their presence and made us unaware of this detail of the ship's construction.

After they had each taken several vigorous turns on the large handsaw we had purchased that morning for the purpose of cutting the keelson, Alinat and Riquet were engulfed in mud, but they weren't getting anywhere. Taking the tool myself, I put it in the half-sawn piece of wood, but the sand kept getting in the kerf and the blade wouldn't cut. Alinat and Riquet stubbornly returned to work. In the hope of breaking the keelson at the kerf, I stooped down in front of the end, anchored my legs firmly in the trench, and, sliding my hands underneath, pulled up with all my might. Since the human body is weightless under water, it's possible to exert a great deal of force that way, as long as you don't lose your grip. The wood didn't seem to be moving, but I must have loosened it because there was a fine stream of mud coming out of some small holes in the sand about a yard away. I continued my efforts for some time, paused to relax, then took it up again. This procedure caused the water to flow in around the keelson, which helped to loosen it up. We used the same method to wrench amphoras out of the soil. More and more mud streamed out of the little holes, and the sand began to run all around the buried timber; meanwhile, Alinat and Riquet kept sawing. Then there was a sudden massive shift, and the keelson emerged with sand running down its blackened sides. It had broken well beyond the saw cut. Alinat, who was short of air, went up to the surface, and Riquet looked to me for instructions. Responding to my signal, he went to get the jerrican that we used to keep the mouth of the *suceuse* out of the mud, tied it to the keelson, and filled it with air from his mouthpiece. The wood spiraled upward with Riquet and me in its broad yellow wake.

The keelson was ten inches high and fifteen inches wide. The section we had removed was five feet long. The underside, which had never been exposed to the sea, was better preserved than the rest of it and was rabbeted in a way that suggested an alternation in the hull of demiframes and frames with floor plates.

I had no idea what the purpose of this particular keelson might have been. I found it rather curious that, while all the frames I had seen at the bottom of the trench were identical, the keelson had grooves that were different. The structure of the hull must have changed under the keelson.

In 1962, when I examined the hull of the wreck at La Chrétienne, which had been laid bare by scavengers, I noticed that the mast step had a strange resemblance to the piece of timber from the *Dramont*.

The diving season was now just about over, and we had exhausted our funds. We began to tidy up the site, finish our reports, and extract the unbroken amphoras so that they would go to the museum planned for Saint-Raphaël, and not into private collections.

We had, for the most part, enjoyed favorable weather, although certain parties with more delicate stomachs didn't think so.

We stopped work for the last time on the fifteenth of October. Like the artifacts recovered at Grand Congloué, the "archaeological furniture" we removed from the *Dramont*, together with that salvaged by the Club of Saint-Raphaël, showed the importance of the wine trade in antiquity; and it added some names from the Naples area to those we already knew. My colleagues estimated that the ship had been carrying from twelve hundred to fifteen hundred amphoras, but I wouldn't hesitate to go as high as two thousand.

Sivirine wrote a report on the *Dramont* which I found very much to my liking, and if I don't agree with some of the details, that isn't his fault, or the fault of any of the other divers, for that matter. It is the fault of those who failed to allocate the funds that we needed in order to conduct this promising excavation on a more scientific basis.

It would be interesting to see, someday, the parts of the ship that are still in the sand. I personally would like to solve the mystery of the hull that we exposed with our trench.

9

The WRECK
from the BRONZE AGE

IN 1959 I RECEIVED A letter from John Huston, who wanted to know if I would be interested in joining an archaeological expedition to Turkey, on the yacht of a wealthy American. Huston was the chairman of a committee on underwater archaeology—the Americans love to form committees. After that I received another letter, this time from Peter Throckmorton, an American journalist who had explored Turkish waters with some sponge divers. The divers had shown him several wrecks, including one that was more than three thousand years old, upon which they had found copper ingots shaped like oxhides and various objects made from bronze.

I exchanged a few letters with Throckmorton to keep abreast of the latest developments concerning the expedition. The wealthy American proved to be primarily interested in collecting souvenirs for himself, and since the scientists couldn't bring themselves to work for such an unworthy cause, the project came to a standstill. It was revived the following year under more serious auspices, when the University of Pennsylvania became

interested and advanced a modest subsidy. Many scientists have
become successful divers. The biologists have managed to make
themselves useful to the military by studying the layers of protozoa that form screens which prevent submarines from being
detected by the usual means. The oceanographers have shared in
that windfall and can also offer other services to the navy and
merchant marine. The ability of geologists to locate oil under the
sea is enough to keep them in demand. The archaeologists alone
remain in the status of poor relations. They produce nothing of
commercial value and their study of warfare is rooted so far in the
past that military men living in the atomic era are not interested.

The expedition was to be directed by the university, which
would be represented by George Bass, a professional archaeologist. The delegates from England were the highly re-
spected Joan du Plat Taylor, who could give us the benefit of her
wide experience on excavations in the Middle East, and another
woman, Honor Frost, who could dive and make all the necessary
drawings of the site. I, along with another diver, Claude Duthuit,
was to represent France. According to the very ambitious plan
that had been established for the project, we were supposed to
investigate the Bronze Age wreck, which was ninety feet down
on a rocky bottom, and, in the same area, two Byzantine wrecks
loaded with amphoras and lying in sand a hundred thirty feet
below the surface.

Honor Frost, who was intelligent, cultivated, and blessed with
an excellent memory, had made some dives on the Byzantine
wrecks, so she came to brief me on the problems connected with
them. I subsequently went to London to present my point of
view, and I asked that we be provided with a core sampler so that
we could determine the limits of the wrecks in the sand before
undertaking to excavate them. A core sampler is a tube with a
cutting edge at one end, which is driven into the soil by various
means, for the purpose of getting samples of the subsoil. Miss
Taylor, who knew all about such things, procured one for us.

Archaeologists have to record the location of every object before removing it, and they register each phase of an excavation on
a series of drawings and charts, so that they can reconstitute later
on what they have destroyed in the process of extraction. In the
hope of making this work a little easier, I designed a wide, horizontal metal frame with four legs that could be anchored in the
soil. It had a vertical measuring rod that moved back and forth

along a horizontal rod which was attached in the same way to the frame itself. Three readings with this apparatus were sufficient to record the location of a given object. When work had been completed in one square area, the frame could be pivoted on one of its feet and made to cover another square.

I was going to be occupied with other duties right up until the day we were scheduled to leave for Turkey, so I left it to Duthuit, in Paris, to supervise the preparation of the parts for the frame and for a *suceuse* as well.

Spirotechnique, the manufacturers of diving equipment, were kind enough to lend me the material I needed to supplement what had been furnished by the Americans.

I left France on the first of May. In Rome I went to see the Baths of Caracalla, the vast scale of which made it easier for me to accept the size of the Roman ships that I had explored under the sea.

Peter Throckmorton, George Bass, and Duthuit had already arrived in Turkey.

In Athens I wandered about with Joan and Honor while waiting for news from Turkey, where there was a revolution going on. The two women had both had long experience with Middle East *coups d'état*, and they weren't concerned. To them it was nothing to get excited about, but just another one of those little inconveniences, like the lack of physical comfort, that you have to put up with in that difficult part of the world.

When there continued to be no word from Turkey, we decided to go and have a talk with Miss Grace, who lived like a feudal baron in a huge building in the Agora. It had a long colonnade of white marble and had been reconstructed according to an ancient model by the American School of Athens.

Miss Grace, who was tall, slender, and very sweet, had spent her entire life surrounded by amphoras. In the basement of the building where she lived she had a whole collection of amphoras that had been found on land, and which lay broken, glued together, and restored, on an extensive array of crowded shelves that reminded me of the interior of a submarine. When I compared this impressive scientific display to the sort of thing that we usually brought up from the sea, I was a bit saddened. These had quite different shapes, and the variety of types was disconcerting. Miss Grace, however, was well aware of all the subtle variations among the specimens, which is why she had never undertaken to publish the kind of classification scheme envisioned by divers, who were misled by the limited samples they found along the coasts of France. I was kindly asked to describe the work we had done at Grand Congloué. Miss Grace was of the opinion that there were two ships, one on top of the other, because we had recovered two types of amphoras that she assigned to periods seventy years apart. My objections were met with a discreet little smile. Underwater archaeology had yet to prove itself to archaeologists who worked on land. Having unearthed cities piled one upon another, they approached the analysis of sunken ships from the same perspective. It is true that certain reefs which nature seems to have deliberately created as hazards to navigation have been the scene of numerous shipwrecks. But at Grand Congloué there was only one ship.

Taking advantage of the delay caused by the revolution, I went to Iráklion, in Crete, to visit the museum, which I found teeming with what is perhaps the greatest elegance and fullest expression of the imagination that the world has ever known. I also saw the Minoan palaces, with their huge, sun-drenched terraces surrounded by an assortment of little ruins that looked like what you would find at the foot of a mountain after a landslide. Near the palace of Mallia, out in the open country parched by the sun, where the little orchards bounded by hedges were dotted with windmills, I picked up a handle from one of those enormous jars used by the Minoans for the storage of grain. The value of this precious artifact decreased with every step I took, because the ground was covered with these antique handles over an area of several miles. Something of the same sort happens on the coral reefs that lie along the shore or form islands in the warmer waters. There is such an enormous mass of colored rocks to choose from that one ultimately loses interest in collecting them at all. Near the palace the rocky, then sandy coast was lined with Minoan tombs that the peasants had broken open in order to get at the gold jewelry. The areas that had been cleared were full of potsherds, corroded bones, and perfectly preserved teeth.

It's always a delight to anticipate the warmer weather by getting onto an airplane and following the sun. Swimming around under the shallow, pleasantly clear water, I could see the remains of dilapidated buildings and rocks that had been hollowed out by human hands. Further on, the quarries belonging to the palace of Knossos extended into the sea in the form of huge rectangular excavations that were like big swimming pools. As a result of intense volcanic activity, the great, mountainous island had shifted about over the course of the ages, and the level of the sea had changed from what it was at the time when the Minoan ports were constructed, so that anyone who wanted to know anything about those ports would have been obliged to consult with geologists.

When we got back to Athens we learned that the army had seized power in Turkey and that all the airports were closed down. Joan and Honor gamely decided to take the boat. The boat was a little packet from the time of Jules Verne, but, aside from a tedious session at Turkish customs, the voyage was quite uneventful. We arrived in Izmir, the ancient Smyrna, convinced that the real tyrants in Turkey were the customs inspectors— which, of course, was as normal as the changing of the seasons.

We were met on the pier by Rasim Divanli and Mustapha Kapkin, both divers, whose charm, simplicity, and directness quickly made them our friends. They proudly showed us the equipment they had put together from odds and ends designed for other uses. Although the political situation seemed serious when viewed from abroad, all we saw were a few very orderly youth groups parading with banners and music.

At the museum I finally got to see the bust of Demeter. The Turks had not tried to restore it, which was a sign of good taste. It had simply been thoroughly cleaned, and the hard, shiny bronze gave to the expression of the model a startling air of violence that was accentuated by the damage wrought in the sea. But at least you could see it as it really was. When the statue had turned up in the sponge trawl, which is a pocket-shaped net fixed to an iron axle that runs between two wide-rimmed wheels, it was corroded, concreted, and swollen with marine life. As soon as the fishermen saw it they all broke into laughter, and they came very close to throwing it back into the sea. Instead, they left it on the afterdeck until it was faded and smelled of iodine.

Although the undersea world seems mysterious and unpredictable, it follows, at least as far as statues are concerned, a certain logic that is dictated entirely by events on the surface. After Mahdia and Antikythera, one is tempted to conclude that the

Demeter was part of a cargo of works of art on board a Roman ship engaged in the pillage of Halicarnassus.

We were joined by Peter and Bass, who informed us that our application for a permit to dig had completed its rounds of the various government agencies, and that the permit would soon be issued. In the South, if you have patience and good humor, you can eventually get things done.

Peter loaded us and our few pieces of luggage into a large jeep and got behind the wheel.

We drove off into a country that was more picturesque than Provence. There were groves of fig trees, peasants of both sexes laboring in the fields, tobacco crops, olive trees on the slopes, ochre patches of plowed land, and tiny villages that looked as if they had sprung up out of the soil. By dusk we had reached Ephesus, where we stopped for the night. The setting sun cast its oblique rays on the walls of the ruins, the marble blocks of which had lost their corners to vandals looking for sealing weights. Only the public part of the city—the main street paved with marble, the theatre, the baths, and the odeum—had been excavated. The rest of it, which extended down toward the sea on one side and climbed the hills on the other, had been left untouched. The monuments we saw, which were already covered with various kinds of vegetation, had been chosen for restoration because they were considered to be safe from the tides.

The next day we followed a road through hills whose dewy slopes hosted large clusters of blooming rose laurels. The twisting road led up toward the golden yellow mountains, and we stopped in a pass that overlooked Bodrum, the point of departure for our expedition. On a terrace that was a most unlikely place for a bar, we drank raki served on marble altars decorated with wreaths and rams' heads. Below us lay the elegantly circular harbor, bounded on the left by the Crusader castle with its ramparts, towers, and crenellated walls rising toward the dungeon in the middle, all against a background of islands that looked blue in the distance. During our stay in Bodrum I often went out to walk through the castle. The walls were covered with coats of arms belonging to all the nobles—Italian, German, French, English, and Spanish—who had, at one time or another, occupied the castle. There were even some that belong to princes of the Church. Among the graffiti that had been there since the Middle

Ages, Joan and Honor took particular pleasure in showing me one that said "Vaca Francia." Antique columns had been incorporated in the walls in order to reinforce them, and sculptured fragments from the famous Mausoleum had been put to use again to supplement the local building stone.

On the pier at Bodrum, we received a warm welcome from our friends the sponge divers. Two caïques were there waiting for us: the *Mandalinci*, which was stylish but encumbered with a deckhouse that contained the pump for the helmet divers; and the *Lufti Gelil*, which, being larger and minus the deckhouse, could better accommodate all our equipment and salvaged artifacts. The *Lufti Gelil* had in her hold, for ballast, a heavy layer of white pebbles so pure that they seemed to be from another era. I found Kemal, the stocky, muscular captain, somewhat uncommunicative, and I felt more comfortable with the first mate, Kasim. I liked the way he looked straight at you through eyes, ringed with little wrinkles, that seemed to be saying that only the two of you really understood. He probably gave the same impression to everyone, but, in any case, he was an endearing old scoundrel. Our Turkish companions, although they looked every bit like a band of Mediterranean pirates, were in truth just poor, simple men who could be very loyal once they had decided to be your friends.

I didn't, of course, understand a word they said and, as it happened, I never had the time to learn very much, but it really didn't make that much difference. Among ourselves, we divers would use our hands to describe a fish, give orders, or express our feelings.

The market for sponges was declining all the time, and every year, since the laws of diving are not something you learn by instinct, our Turkish friends would see a few of their number taken off to the cemetery. So they were only too glad to cooperate with us in what they considered our insane rush to spend large sums of American money searching for ancient junk.

The Turkish government sent an archaeologist out to supervise our activities. Akki Bey was a jolly little man who didn't quite fit our image of an archaeologist, and he seemed to live in fear of some unnamed superior. He nevertheless proved to be very helpful.

We still had a long way to go before we would get to Finike and the wreck from the Bronze Age. Some members of the team chose to make the trip aboard the two caïques, but I wanted to stay on land, so I went in the jeep. Soon we were climbing up the mountains again, trailing a cloud of dust like a diver on the bottom of the sea. I never would have believed that there were so many rivers in the area, or that they could be so beautiful.

We came within sight of the sea again at Fethiye, the ancient Telmessos, which was a large village nestled at the foot of a high, vertical cliff sculpted with tombs. Fethiye had been destroyed by an earthquake two years previously, and it had just been reconstructed according to a plan that was far too geometric. Leaving Peter and Akki Bey to deal with the garage mechanic, I went off in the direction of the cliff. There was no path leading to the tombs, so I made my way over crumbled walls and across enclosed fields populated by listless cows. Up ahead, at different heights, there were two temple façades with columns that had been built into the cliff for Lycian kings of the fourth century B.C. All around the royal tombs there were the tombs of the bourgeoisie, with house façades, and some of a more modest nature that were nothing but rectangular holes. The royal tomb that was accessible from the ground had its base blackened by recent fires, a panel missing on its massive door, and hens nesting on the three pillowed mortuary couches carved right out of the rock.

The Turks took so long to repair our sputtering jeep that we had to spend the night in a hotel where, in keeping with a Turkish custom, there was a glass panel at the top of the door and a light on in the corridor all night. It was still relatively comfortable, however.

The next morning we took the route followed by Alexander on his way to Xanthos after the occupation of Telmessos. We were constantly walking in the footprints of Alexander.

On a rocky promontory that overlooked the bend of a wide river, archaeologists had laid bare the ruins of Xanthos, which consisted of a concentration of marbles standing in place or strewn on the ground in the midst of the barren scrub. I found the sun particularly oppressive, and climbing up the tourist path left us all very thirsty. An elderly attendant came out of an obscure little cottage to welcome us, and we were seated on brightly colored divans, cushions, and rugs that were amazingly clean. Sitting on these rugs spread out on the ground, we partook of the ambiance proper to the tents of nomads, sultans' palaces, or mosques. The old man served our food and drink with great simplicity.

After eating we went to bathe in the river, right across from a tomb that had been carved in the side of a prominent rock. Only the triangular pediment was visible above the water, and we couldn't dive to see if the tomb had been opened because the current was too strong.

Back in the jeep again, we traveled through a pleasant rural area full of large trees. At the foot of another group of mountains, we came to a fork in the road. Akki Bey asked directions from some peasants, but their responses were somewhat confused and based on vague memories of relatives who had, at some time in the past, taken one of the two roads. They measured distances in hours.

The road kept climbing up higher, and the jeep, although it had four-wheel drive, labored like a diver in deep water, on the brink of exhaustion. We were continually bumping into conduits from which running water was raised through wooden gutters to where it fell on little mills. A reddish crest, riddled with rock tombs, stood out against the sky. With a certain amount of anxiety, we skirted the forest of larch trees that bordered the snowy peaks, and, as night fell, we stopped to drink some raki in the public square of a little village full of wooden houses. There we were approached by a woodcutter who showed us an antique gold coin with two heads, beautifully minted. In the face of my cupidity, Akki Bey kindly put aside his professional scruples and asked the man how much he wanted. But the price was too high for me, especially since everything else in Turkey had been so cheap.

After making our way down deserted forest roads in total darkness, we were relieved to see the lights of Elmali in the distance. Our reward for surviving the ordeal was a quiet and refreshing night in the village hotel. Peter fell asleep fully clothed.

Driving down through the forest again the next day, we passed a group of about thirty men walking along behind a stretcher in which a dead man lay wrapped up in a brightly colored shroud. Further on, four men were waiting for them with an engraving for the head of the tomb.

Before the end of the day we were in Finike, the ancient Phoenicus, a very ordinary little village by the sea. The other members of the expedition who had gone by sea were already there, red as beets from too much sun. Together we unpacked our equipment from huge shipping crates that were full of dust from the Turkish roads. As the food got worse and worse, it became good form to describe it with the word *tamam,* which the Turks applied broadly to mean good, pleasant, or beautiful.

I was captivated by the beauty and charm of Turkey, but I couldn't cope with all the little problems that came with living in such a country, and I went about totally mystified for three days, until we were finally ready, at three o'clock one morning, to get underway for the wreck from the Bronze Age.

In the southernmost part of Turkey, at the tip of Cape Gelidonia, there is a string of five little islands that were probably part of the ancient coastal roadway. The wreck was situated to the north of the third island, a white rock that was so sheer and desolate that we couldn't find any place to pitch our tents. And even though the island is called Sou Ada, which in Turkish indicates the presence of fresh water, there was none.

About an hour after we sailed off from the islands we entered a crescent-shaped bay enclosed by dark cliffs that rose at the edge of a stony beach about ten yards wide. The Turkish divers thought we ought to moor the ships right there. It looked too much like a fortress for our taste, but we did notice that there was a plentiful supply of fresh water. Behind the next cape there was another beach that gave access to the hinterland, but it was not well sheltered and had no fresh water, so we chose the narrow beach with the dark cliffs.

Peter had bought a government-surplus, dark maroon tent that was large enough to shelter the whole expedition. We put it up with its back to the cliff and decorated it with orange and white striped parachutes that reflected the light from the sun. We had to wear shoes to walk on the beach, because the pebbles burned our feet. The Turks installed the kitchen on the west side of the camp, near a little stream that trickled down the side of the cliff. They would collect the water in a can and pour it into a heavy cloth sack held off the ground by three wooden pickets.

For the sake of having something to do that would get me away from the chaos created by the Americans as they strove to organize the camp, I undertook to build a basin where we could wash the salt off our artifacts. I chose a natural pocket between two projecting rocks, in a place where the fresh water seeped into the sand. One of the Turks, whom I suspected of sharing my attitude, came over to help me. To keep the sand from running into the fault, we rolled some big rocks up to the entrance. The water began to accumulate right away. Later on, with my hands protected by a marvelous cream that insulated them from the cement, I built a wall and created a second basin under the spillway of the first.

The next day, June 15, Kemal took us to the site of the wreck. The sea was calm, the sky perfectly clear. We anchored near the island, and I went into the water with Peter. The transparency of the water afforded us a broad view of a rocky slope that ended at the crest of a small cliff. On the luminous bottom, a long, flat boulder of considerable size formed a crevice with the cliff. An oxhide-shaped ingot stood propped against a rock, and down in the crevice there was another one held fast by concretions. We were now ninety feet below the surface. Here and there we found evidence that someone had recently worked the site. About fifteen feet from the big boulder I noticed an oddly shaped platform comprised of rocks covered with algae and partially concealed by a very fine sand. Peter suddenly threw up his hands in despair. I could see that he wasn't in trouble—he was a capable, experienced diver—so I couldn't understand what he was trying to tell me. Then he started swimming hurriedly all around the site like some carnivorous beast searching for food, stopping only to throw up his hands again and again. The problem, it seems, was that he couldn't find some things he had seen there the previous year: a pile of ingots, a metal bar lodged between two rocks, and some bowls made from stone. I had been told that the bottom at the site sloped down toward deeper waters, but that proved to be an exaggeration; it just descended gradually toward the valley between the islands. I was intrigued by the rocky platform because, although it did seem to be very much a part of the terrain, there had to be some explanation for the presence of the brilliant crystal powder and fragments of pottery. Peter was wandering about in despair and I was eager to talk with him, so we went back up to the surface. When we came out of the water, he was furious. The ingots had been on the platform, but now they were all gone, stolen. Peter suspected the sponge divers, for whom the site was a veritable mine of copper.

As we steamed along the mountainous coast toward the camp, the Turks caught a small merou on a line trailed from the ship.

In a heated discussion in front of the big maroon tent, during which everyone had something to say, Kemal angrily defended his colleagues and suspicion fell upon the wealthy American. The other members of the expedition consoled themselves with the thought that, if worst came to worst, we could break camp and move on to explore the Byzantine wreck at Yassi Ada. But I was far from being convinced that all was lost, because it didn't seem to me that the site had been worked to the extent that would have been necessary in order for someone to carry off the entire cargo.

By the time we got settled back into camp again, everyone was a bit morose.

Just to create some diversion, I went out to inspect the site with Akki Bey, who had already done some snorkel diving, and George Bass, who had taken a few lessons in a swimming pool before leaving the United States. It turned out to be a good idea, because while we were there it occurred to us to make a map of the area before deciding to abandon the search.

With some frayed cables, a few rusted skeletons of anchors, and some forty-gallon barrels, we established a permanent mooring to keep the caïque over the wreck against changes in the wind and current.

Peter made a great many photographs, which Herb Grier would develop at night, in a hollow in the cliff at the rear of the tent. With a copious stream of bubbles emanating from the helmet of his diving suit, Kemal would stride about majestically on the bottom, looking immense beside our naked, horizontal bodies. When everything was in place, he would signal to us with outstretched hands. Because we wanted to make a map, Peter took his photographs from above the site; but it seemed to us that they failed to give an accurate picture of the terrain. The reliefs were indistinguishable from the flat areas, and the tufts of algae stood out more clearly than the rocks. On the beach back at the camp, I gathered up white pebbles from among the more numerous gray, and, assisted by Duthuit, spread them out on the bottom to make a dotted outline of the topography. By gluing these new photos together end to end, we obtained a good panoramic view of the site.

Some friends of the Turkish divers came to replenish their supply of fresh water and gave Peter some Byzantine amphoras, together with a block of oil lamps welded to one another by concretions. They knew Peter liked to collect the antique artifacts that came up in their trawls among the sponges.

On June 19, a Sunday, Kemal, tired of eating cucumber-and-tomato salads, went out on the *Mandalinci* to catch some fish. I was determined to get a better look at the wreck, so I took advantage of this opportunity to get underway with the *Lufti Gelil*.

Many ancient wrecks cause accumulations of sand that, added to the natural sedimentation, check the growth of concretions. When the upper part of such a ship is still visible, it will be covered with concretions that are still in the process of formation, whereas, under the soil they will all be dead and progressively thinner toward the base of the wreck. The Bronze Age wreck was a rarity, however, in that it had never been protected by sedimentation at all, which meant that concretions had been forming there continuously right from the day it had sunk.

I swam around calmly over a landscape that was radiant under the sun. A lifetime of diving had taught me, at my expense, never to underestimate the power of the sea and its ingenious methods of concealment. I had taken along a crowbar, as well as an axhammer made according to my specifications by a blacksmith in Finike. When I introduced the crowbar into a slight fault in the platform, a corner broke off and I saw a pile of copper.

The soil between the platform and the crevice looked quite natural, but in the crevice itself there were heaps of strange concretions. After making a few tours of the immediate vicinity in order to get used to the look of the natural rocks, I applied my axhammer to the suspicious rocks in the crevice and found copper and bronze embedded in the stone.

When I got back to camp with the good news, everyone crowded around to hear me.

I began with the assurance that there had been only superficial looting. The cargo, the weight of which I estimated at close to a ton, was hidden under a crust of rock and divided into two piles a few yards apart. In certain places, and particularly in the crevice, portions of it were covered with a wild, elaborate growth of spongy, brittle concretions that were easy to break with a hammer. Elsewhere, however, it was buried under a homogeneous substratum of hard, compact concretions, and the platform was nothing but a mass of objects immersed in a layer of this same substance.

At this point everyone began to talk at once, and Bass started to draft a telegram to his superiors.

I tried to temper their enthusiasm a bit by pointing out that, while it was our intention that our excavation should be methodic, systematic, scientific, and a model for others to follow, this ship was unfortunately not buried in sand like the wrecks from the classical era. It had fallen into the col of an underwater mountain range lying in the path of a strong current that swept through it like the wind in a narrow pass. During a storm the surge of the sea, which was very strong at that depth, would stir up the sand, and it would be carried off by the current. Without the protection of the sand, the wreck had become fossilized. As the bronze and copper artifacts were embedded in a rock that was as hard as cement, I felt it would be impossible, working under the water, to extract them without breakage. I therefore proposed that we cut the wreck into blocks weighing about two hundred pounds apiece, which was the maximum that our winches could raise. We would follow the lines of least resistance, in order to keep the damage to a minimum. The blocks would be reassembled on the beach according to the way they had been cut, then dissected later on. All the necessary drawings, maps, and photographs would, of course, be made under the water before the least disturbance of the artifacts, and during the course of the operation.

My proposal was adopted without discussion, and the camp came to life again as we busily prepared to start the digging.

Every morning, as part of his daily routine, Djumour, the cabin boy, would take a man-sized blowtorch down into the hold of the *Lufti Gelil* and, wreathed in flames, warm up the one-cylinder diesel engine. When the engine appeared to be ready, he would put the blowtorch, without extinguishing it, down amongst the debris in the hold and turn the enormous flywheel. But the wheel would often refuse to turn, in which case Kemal would have to go down and, in his capacity as captain of the ship, employ his considerable strength to force it into submission.

We dove from the *Lufti Gelil*, leaving the speedier *Mandalinci* free to travel back to Finike for our provisions, which were always disappointing. I was enchanted by the sun and the calmness of the sea. I had tied a rope to a rock near the wreck and put an empty drum on the other end to keep it on the surface. We would jump into the water fully equipped and head right for the drum, in order to avoid being carried off by the current. It was then a simple matter to descend along the taut rope.

After several months during which we worked every day, Sundays included, I noticed that the divers were getting tired. They came down with colds and otitis, and our production was decreasing rapidly. The decompression tables had been shown to be valid for isolated dives, but I had reservations about adhering exclusively to their schedules in our case, especially since, the recompression chamber purchased for the expedition having been held up by customs, we would be unable to give any immediate assistance to a stricken diver. I therefore adopted a work schedule that was a bit more conservative than that permitted by the tables. We would stay down for thirty minutes in the morning and twenty-five minutes in the afternoon, with five minutes of stage decompression after each period of work. I prescribed a minimum interval between dives of three hours, which was enough time for the major part of the nitrogen dissolved in the bloodstream to be eliminated. As work on the project neared completion, we extended the length of the morning dive to forty minutes, with ten minutes for decompression. For safety's sake, the divers always worked in pairs, and since the field of excavation was quite small, they would always be in sight of each other.

The water on the surface above the wreck was almost constantly swept by a strong current. Contrary to what we had been told by the Turks, this current didn't seem to have any connection with the winds, which were quite mild that summer anyway. It was, rather, a general current like that on the Riviera and was influenced by the tides. When the moon was full, the waves would come up on the beach and lap at the edge of our tent. Along the cliff near the wreck, the current would get stronger and stronger, until it ran like a river. At some point during the day, it would suddenly change its direction from southwest to northeast, and for fifteen minutes there would be large masses of water in conflict. In certain places the current rolled back on itself. The caïque would swing on its anchor as great volumes of water rose to make smooth planes on the surface and give off tiny waves. The eddies would eventually subside, to be replaced by ripples that marked the new path of the current.

The diver, meanwhile, would be caught up in the turbulence, knocked off balance, and dragged away from his work. Jets of water breaking on the cliff would raise clouds of sand that spiraled toward the surface. Once the moment of crisis had passed, the effects of the current were felt mainly on the surface.

Down below, it was seldom strong enough to disperse the mud we raised with our digging.

On the island the white rock formed a peak that towered in the sky over our heads. Every day, as I lay on the deck waiting for my turn to dive, I would see a family of eagles circling this peak and hear them singing out to each other while they glided about effortlessly on the rising columns of air. They would fly around behind the peak, then reappear higher up in the blue of the sky. A certain number would be heading straight for the coast, and others coming back. One day when they were more numerous than usual, they seemed to be having a sort of fair in the sky over the island. Although I had been warned by the Turks that the eagles were dangerous, I decided to climb the rock, along with two other members of our party. The loose stones gave way under our feet, and we clutched at rocks pitted by erosion. As we approached the summit, the eagles circled more rapidly. And when we saw how big they were, we decided to turn back—there was work to be done; our colleagues would be needing us.

Around noon, when the first series of dives had been completed, we would have our lunch on the caïque. Usually it was a salad of tomatoes and cucumbers, but sometimes we would also have powdered eggs.

Quite often when we arrived in the morning we would find that the current had caused our safety rope to become entangled with the anchor chain. On one such morning, I swam into the garden of the valley, which was full of white sand, mossy rocks, and huge, silky-black, corollaceous sponges. These sponges, the fibers of which had the consistency of coarse grass, were not used for bathing purposes. Kasim liked to use them for washing dishes; their sap must be a sort of detergent.

This morning the current had wound the slack of the cables around some rocks, pulling the floats under the water. As I swam around among the rocks struggling with the tangled cables, the Turks, whose long experience tending divers from their boats had taught them the art of giving out just the right amount of slack, showed an uncanny ability to follow my movements and anticipate my needs. With ordinary sailors, I never could have done the job alone.

In a tool chest placed on the bottom we deposited some hammers and chisels, the crowbar, and two axhammers. Everything we found on the site would be put into a large basket made from grilled angle irons which I had requested Bass to order. The basket would be hauled up to the *Lufti Gelil* on the end of its primitive, frightfully hesitant cargo boom.

I decided that we should begin by cutting out a block from the west side of the platform, where there was a jagged corner that we thought might be hiding some ingots. Looking for a place to start, I stuck my hand into a narrow hole under the platform and found a pocket of pure sand. The lower part of the ship must have disintegrated, leaving a vacuum that filled up with sand. I explored a few more of these cavities, as well as some stone pillars, and was very much encouraged. The platform was not homogeneous with the rocky soil.

For three days Duthuit and I chipped away at the stone, trying to chisel a block out of the body of the platform. Our colleagues, meanwhile, were busy taking measurements, making drawings, putting labels on the few visible objects, and marking letters on the various zones of the worksite, which was forty feet long by ten feet wide. Peter and Herb kept firing away with their cameras which, although they were built into watertight boxes, still occasionally failed due to leaks and defective electrical contacts.

When the block finally looked ready to be removed, I put the crowbar underneath and pulled up, but to no avail. Some inaccessible pillars of stone were holding the block in place.

Peter suggested that I use the jack from the jeep, but it wouldn't fit under the block, so I had to start hammering and chiseling again. There was no hurry, however, because a great many drawings and maps had to be made before anything could be done.

When at last the jack was fixed in the right position, I turned the handle and a thin white mist appeared near the head as it bit into the stone. Then there was a sharp crack and the block shook loose. After I quickly tied it with a rope, it was hauled up on board amidst the shouting of the Turks.

Peter touched the block lightly with the end of a chisel and scraped off some algae. Then, yielding to the temptation, he began chiseling delicately in order to expose one of the ingots. By the time we got back to the camp, an hour later, he had chipped away so much of the block that it was unrecognizable. I protested, as a matter of form, against the use of the chisel on any of the blocks before we had had a chance to fit several of them together on the beach. Everyone agreed.

The next time we dove, we discovered that our removing the first block with the cable had dislodged a second one, which now trailed a piece of tissue and a light, plaited rope between the ingots. These delicate filaments were out at the mercy of the current, so Bass gave me a transparent bag to put them in. Then we came across the bottom of a basket clinging to one of the ingots, and we had the *Lufti Gelil* lift the block slightly so that we could wrap it in a cloth. Protected in this way, the basket bottom, which was made of spiral-wound light rope, survived the journey to the top intact. Among the ingots there were some bronze agricultural tools that had been broken before the shipwreck.

Peter was hopelessly addicted to wielding his chisel, and since what happened to the artifacts once they were out of the water was not my affair, I no longer protested. I was anxious myself to see our finds emerge from the stone. Besides, we all more or less followed Peter's bad example.

All the vestiges of the platform, in blocks that had been thinned down or dissected, were placed on sheets near the big tent. Joan, Honor, and Bass spent hours, sometimes even whole days, trying to piece together, with the help of their sketches and underwater photos, the jumble of ingots and other little objects. Their hesitation and incertitude were reflected by the look of preoccupation on their faces, by their air of indecision, and their interminable discussions. From time to time one of them would go over to contemplate the latest arrangement of the material, then nudge one of the ingots a little or ask for help in order to move an entire pile. They would all ultimately reach more or less the same conclusions, but only after they had thoroughly exercised themselves with seemingly endless deliberations.

The oxhide-shaped ingots were two feet long, sixteen inches wide, and weighed an average of forty-four pounds, with significant variations. According to the archaeologists in our party, the fact that the ingots were shaped like oxhides was purely coincidental. What looked to us like paws were actually handles designed to make them easier to carry or to secure on the back of a donkey. All around the piles of bronze ingots we found lenticular copper ingots weighing about nine pounds, one face of which was flat and the other convex. Many of the bronze objects had markings, among which, to my great delight, there frequently appeared a Lorraine cross inscribed in a V.

The little Bauer compressor that we used to fill our air bottles was a constant source of trouble. It was always breaking down under the excessive heat on the beach. But for a Turk, anything mechanical has the same sort of fascination that draws Arabs to guns, and no sooner would the pump stop than it would be surrounded by a team of eager repairmen. They would sit in a circle around the compressor, with the torrid sun scorching the beach and all the delicate little parts of the engine lying about on the rocks wherever they had chanced to land after they had been disassembled and everyone had had the opportunity to inspect them. The Turks would invariably split into two groups with different opinions about the cause of the trouble and then stop everything in order to argue the point. Peter and Bass looked upon these episodes as something ordained by Fate and every bit as ineluctable as the wind or rain.

In the meantime, our departure for the site would be delayed, then postponed, and, finally, canceled. We would all have to find something else to keep us busy.

But we knew from past experience that, just before it was time to eat, we would hear the quick gasps of the engine as the Turks, victorious at last, celebrated by repeatedly starting the thing up, stopping it, and starting it again. The happy band of mechanics would then reluctantly go their separate ways.

Joan, who was responsible for the cleaning and conservation of the artifacts found on the wreck, set up a workshop for herself, under an orange and white parachute, right in front of the freshwater basins I had built. The proximity of the water made it seem cooler there, and sometimes a light breeze would even come along to fill the parachute with air. This area became the center of the camp, the place where anyone with nothing to do would go to chip stone from the bronze and pottery, or just pass the time of day. In the basins there would be blocks of concretions yet to be touched, objects that had been cleaned and were now slowly desalinating, and plastic bags containing the most delicate items. Nearby, the remains of the platform were spread out on badly soiled white sheets, with sandbags supporting the ingots in the positions assigned to them by the latest arrangement. The pottery, which was soft and fragile, gave Joan quite a bit of trouble. She broke a fair amount of it, but that didn't bother her because, as she said, it could all be put back together again later. To me, however, it looked like a real massacre. Among her instruments Joan had an electrically driven vibrating tool sent to her from England, which, together with her white smock, made her look like a dentist. This tool could be used only to remove a particular kind of concretion and not unless the object itself was in good condition.

The beach around our camp was divided into two parts by a gigantic wall of fallen rocks. The first time I saw it, the day we arrived, I knew what I was going to do. First I took a sledgehammer and made a path through the wall. The rocks were easy to break, and the fragments filled up the empty spaces, with the smallest pieces providing a level surface; I even found enough rock dust to finish smoothing it out. At the top of the wall I carved out a platform for myself so that I could have my own living quarters far from the big tent that was home for everyone else. I had a commanding view of the beach and slept right on the ground, on an old army mattress, with just a mosquito net hanging down from the cliff for protection. Near the camp the water trickled out drop by drop, but beyond the fallen rocks it ran fairly swiftly. I dug out under the spring and made a rampart from some large stones. The strongly calcareous water filled the pores in the sand. At night the semicircular bluff that enclosed our camp radiated the heat absorbed during the day, and I would go to lie in the basin of the spring, under the overhang of the cliff. As soon as I felt myself getting cold, I would climb back up to the platform and, exhausted, fall asleep before I could get hot again.

When the moon rose above the darkened cape, it was so bright that I had to shield my face. In the morning, however, I always woke well rested.

Joan and Honor wanted to have quarters on the fallen rocks, so I made platforms for them as well. The Turks, who used to travel up my path on their way to fetch water or to wash out their clothes on some flat rocks, were surprised that a soft-spoken individual like me could be capable of such extensive muscular activity. But I have always liked breaking up rocks, and it gave me something to do on mornings when the weather was uncertain, at the end of a day, or when the compressor was being fixed.

Honor had brought a number of bags of coffee to give as gifts, but she kept some for herself and roasted it in the cover of a tiny alcohol stove. I would grind it in the morning, using the method employed by prehistoric man, which was to spread it out on a flat stone and crush it with a round one. The hot coffee was a pleasant treat for our little Anglo-French colony.

Before dinner everyone would come up to our platforms to drink raki. Raki tastes sweeter when it's mixed with water, but I found it quite palatable by itself.

Regretfully abandoning our fortress, we would go down to have dinner, which we took while seated on crates around a table made by laying the sides of the largest crate over the tops of some others. In the distance you could hear the hum of the generator supplying current for the single bulb that we kept hanging on the cliff behind us, mainly for the purpose of attracting mosquitoes away from the dining area. We had to dress for dinner, but it was just as well, because a day in the sun leaves you sensitive to the cold.

Whenever the *Mandalinci* came back from Finike with a goat or some chicken, we had to eat it right away. The heat, which was so intense that it melted our candles, spoiled everything except tomatoes and cucumbers.

Before I left France, I had had an attack of nephritis. The fact that I was able to eat tomatoes and drink petrifactive water was a sure sign that I had been cured of it.

During the night it often happened that a few stones would tumble down the side of the cliff. A regular Turkish earthquake would have buried us all.

Near the wreck I caught a sea turtle, which I kept on the end of a line in the water directly in front of the tent. The turtle was constantly trying to swim out to sea. Although I did suggest to Peter that a turtle soup might be a refreshing change from our diet of salads, the thought of eating turtles actually brought back some very unpleasant memories. When we were filming *The Silent World* on the little coral island of Asuncion, in the middle of the Indian Ocean, sea turtles were the only source of meat, and we used to eat them all the time. We bought them from some degenerate natives who left them on their backs in the hot sun for days, on the white sand of a beach lined with coconut trees, which treatment caused the poor turtles to weep. Their flesh was tough, as if it had come from a calf that had been living in the sea, and the yolks of their eggs were so mealy that they made your mouth dry. The Turks, who considered turtles to be bad luck, frowned when I proposed that we should eat mine. I finally had to let it go.

Back when I was still in France getting ready for the expedition, it had occurred to me that directing the excavation might be easier if we had a Polaroid camera and could get the latest pictures of the wreck without having to wait for them to be developed. Bass got the camera and Davso, at the O.F.R.S., made me a large, yellow, watertight box, streamlined up front like an underwater scooter. Herb, who undertook to operate the device, made some trials with it near the camp that left us very optimistic.

The first time he took the camera down on the wreck I went with him, but I got busy breaking up concretions and didn't take much notice of what he was doing. When I got back up to the *Lufti Gelil*, Herb was already on board. He had discovered some water in his air hose and, panic-stricken, had bolted for the surface, leaving the Polaroid behind. Although I was assured that the camera would be all right, since Herb had left it near the bottom, I knew it was lost. Being perfectly balanced, it would neither sink to the safety of the bottom nor rise to the top; it would simply be carried off by the current. Peter went down to have a look, to be followed by Kasim, then Kemal, who lumbered all around the area in their diving suits with the weighted shoes. To satisfy our consciences, we sailed along in the direction of the current for quite a distance. But, just as in Musset's story about the pelican, "the ocean was empty."

Bass, having made a short visit to the nearby town of Antalya, came back thoroughly enchanted. In the course of our work we never saw anything but the sea and the beach, so the idea of walking around in a town was quite tempting, and I decided to go along on the next trip. We left on the *Lufti Gelil* one night, with Joan, Honor, Akki Bey, and me all trying to sleep under the steady spray from the spindrifts. By morning we could see Antalya in the middle of a verdant plateau bordered by a cliff from which several waterfalls ran down into the sea. In the tiny harbor, which was nestled in the rocks and protected by a huge wall, there were a few brightly colored caïques tied at anchor. The marketplace, with its caravans of camels, its craftsmen crouched in their little stalls, and its busy street life, was reminiscent of the Orient. But this exotic atmosphere was unfortunately spoiled by the presence of some modern buildings.

In the antique shops they had silver coins from various Greek cities and intaglios from the Roman era. And when we got to our hotel, then went to eat in a restaurant, it all had a kind of novelty that made us feel like children enjoying such things for the first time.

The next day we hired a taxi to take us out into the country. Arriving in Aspendus, we stopped by the entrance to the enormous, incredibly well preserved Roman theatre, which stood all alone with its back to a hill where the underbrush covered the sides of thick crumbled walls. The front of the theatre looked out on a sandy plain ringed by purple mountains. Inside there was room for twelve thousand people, and the light from the sun bouncing off the tiered rows of seats was practically blinding. The façade, where the pedestals and niches reserved for the statues of the emperors were now empty, was in the shade. On the floor of the stage, the lines showing the places for the actors were engraved right in the tiles. As my colleagues exhausted themselves climbing up the rows of seats with gigantic strides, their silhouettes grew thinner and thinner; by the time they reached the top, they were just little black dots in the sky. I went up to join them, and when I looked out over the plain there was no trace of Aspendus itself, even though it had been in its time the most important town in the area.

In the next village we drank snow from the previous winter, which had been preserved by keeping it in holes covered with branches.

After traveling on for some time along a narrow, dusty road, we came to an area full of dense brush and ruins that appeared in greater numbers the closer we got. This was Side, a city founded by the Greeks but inhabited by the Romans as well. The two public buildings that archaeologists had restored there were already overgrown with vegetation again. Among the remains of one edifice built up against a large boulder were some truncated columns and a statue of a woman that couldn't have been worth very much. A decrepit placard indicated that this particular edifice had been the library. As we walked on, the ground was strewn with broken jugs and iridescent glass that had been half melted by the last of Side's fires.

In the midst of some rather imposing ruins, by two squalid huts hidden under a fig tree, a loud chorus of flutes and drums announced the celebration of a marriage.

The ancient port consisted of two basins, one of which had been filled in by fallen earth. Honor had a special interest in such phenomena, and she went out to swim around between some still quite visible, dilapidated jetties. While waiting for her to come back, I went for a walk through the scrub brush with Akki Bey, who was all excited by the thought of the city whose presence he sensed under the wild vegetation. With the searing heat from the ground coming right up through the soles of our rope sandals, we made our way over a group of large, bluish white columns lying in pieces on the ground, then came up against the remains of ancient walls under the bushes and other ruins to negotiate. I wished that I could have lived there as a child. I would have played tag on the marbles in the scrub brush, and, having familiarized myself with the plan of the vanished city, unearthed the treasures buried in the homes of the wealthy.

On the way back we passed through Perga, where the ruins included a theatre and a stadium with a seating capacity of twenty-seven thousand. At the end of an avenue lined with columns, some of which had reliefs of tiny gods on their smooth shafts, a young girl was drawing water for her cows from a well with a marble lip.

Perga, like many of the towns in the area, was founded at the beginning of the Achaean migration, around 1000 B.C. What we saw in such places were merely the vestiges of the last inhabitants, who were in some cases Greek, but more often Roman or Byzantine. The earth had long since obliterated all the evidence of numerous conflicts with obscure seafaring peoples, the struggles with the Persians, and the occupation by Alexander.

When we got back to the camp we found that some newcomers had arrived and volunteered to help with the work. Kirk, the leader of the group, was an American soldier stationed at a base near the Soviet Union. The others were Waldemar Illing and another young German whom Kirk called Blondy.

With the addition of these new divers we started bringing up so much material that Bass couldn't record it all. He decided that we should slow down, so I went back to working alone; but I still extracted more artifacts than the whole team could draw, photograph, and locate on the map—and this in spite of the fact that everything was covered with stone! I couldn't help but wonder what would happen if we tried to apply this method of excavation to a wreck from the classical era, where thousands of amphoras would be lying about in loose sand that could be easily dispersed with a *suceuse.*

Through all the daily changes in the state of our morale, I went right on chiseling the stone in order to prepare blocks of the cargo for their journey up to the surface. I was determined that everything should be brought up before the end of the season, so that our excavation would be a success and demonstrate the value of underwater archaeology.

As the work progressed, the platform gradually disappeared. Underneath it we found Phoenician glass beads scattered among the remnants of a jar that had probably contained them. I was slowly but surely working my way toward the crevice. Kirk, who had quickly become my friend, helped me to drive stakes into the cliff at various points, and to tie nylon cords to them so that we would have some guidelines on the site. This procedure had been suggested by George Bass. Whenever the current threatened to carry them off, the divers would instinctively cling to the lines, but to no avail, because the strain would simply pull the stakes out.

The previous summer Peter had lost two ingots while trying to raise them with a rope that wasn't strong enough for the job. When work on the site was suspended again so that the maps could be brought up to date, I went to look for the ingots with Peter and Kirk. Between some large rocks there were gorges full of sand that looked like fertile ground for coral and lobsters. I scoured the bottom, poking my head into every little cavity, but saw nothing. Then I noticed Peter and Kirk off in the distance, on a rocky terrace; they had found the ingots and were busy tying them with a rope. As we were hauling them up, however, the ship started to drift, dragging the ingots along the bottom until they caught like an anchor and the rope broke. I thought something like that might happen, so I had noted the location of the ingots with respect to certain distinctive features of the landscape. That afternoon I dove again, descending rapidly in order to minimize the effect of the current. I felt pain in one of my ears, so I held my nose and blew air into it to equalize the pressure; but the pain kept getting worse. Just as I was passing over a chain of rocks, I saw the ingots. By the time I reached them, the pain in my ear had become very intense. After attaching another rope to the ingots, I went back up to look for the steel cable. The whole operation proceeded smoothly, except for my ear. When I came out of the water, I discovered that the ear had been bent forward under the hood of my diving suit in such a way that it was completely blocked and there was no pressure on the exterior surface of the eardrum. The drum had been stretched by the force of the pressure inside. There were some traces of blood in my ear, but I forced air into it and was relieved to find that the eardrum had not been ruptured.

When we resumed work on the excavation the next day, my ear was still bothering me, and I had to make my descent very slowly. Kirk, who was quite strong, helped me to break up some concretions that were holding back a block at the entrance to the crevice. On the second day the ear was still sore, and it hurt when I chewed. Joan and Honor gave me some penicillin so that I could continue to dive.

Under the block that closed off the crevice, resting on a bed of branches, there was a piece of fine metal about the size of two fists and folded back upon itself many times. As we worked away in the crevice, a big, friendly merou would come by to watch us, keeping his head just about a foot and a half from ours. The Turks wanted to cook him up, but we protected him as our friend. The merou was particularly interested in Honor's sketch board, which I used to study as well, because her maps helped me to understand the wreck. But, my job being just to supervise the divers, I didn't really have to appreciate the significance of Honor's work.

The hardships we had to endure while living "in a state of nature"—too much sun, too much salt on the skin, not enough to eat—made it more difficult for the various members of the expedition to get along with one another. The isolation of our camp eventually affected everyone's psychological reactions, and the multinational complexion of the group only made matters worse.

Some of the sand that had previously been held back by the

cargo had seeped down into the bottom of the crevice. Peter and Bass wanted to remove it with the *suceuse,* but I didn't care to waste time rigging up a hose, so I suggested that we put the sand in cans and sift through it when we got back to the camp. They wouldn't listen, however, and the *suceuse* was installed according to their own idea of how it should be done.

Under the pretext of having something to do on the site, I went down to see how they were making out. The *suceuse* was stretched out along the slope of the fallen rocks, with too little difference in height between the ends. Bass was cautiously probing the crevice with the mouth of the hose, which discharged at the other end into a metal basket. Then the *suceuse* suddenly reared back, flinging Bass up toward the surface. I burst into laughter, and my mask filled up with water.

The next day, July 17, Bass asked me to work with him. I declined, saying that I didn't like the way the *suceuse* had been installed, and I predicted that it would get stopped up the next time they tried to use it. Bass went down without me, but before long he came back up again to report that the *suceuse* wasn't working. When Peter investigated, he found that it was full of sand.

Although Peter and Bass, armed with a smaller *suceuse* and the knowledge gained from experience, made a few more attempts to remove the sand by suction, this approach was finally, to my great satisfaction, totally abandoned.

As time went on and our compressor began to fail with alarming frequency, it occurred to Peter and Bass that, by hitching up the sponge divers' pump to the motor on the *Mandalinci,* we could replace our aqualungs with "narghiles" consisting of flexible hoses that would carry the air from the pump to low-pressure escape valves strapped on our backs.

Peter extolled the virtues of the narghile to the sponge divers, in the hope that they would adopt it in place of their helmeted diving suit. He was convinced that the new device, which was cheaper to assemble, would also enable them to increase their production. Kemal seemed to be sold on the idea, but the others wisely preferred to wait and see.

Both the caïques were now moored over the wreck and, there being hardly any breeze that summer, we were continuously engulfed in blue smoke from their engines. The air drawn from the little cabin on the *Mandalinci* smelled of tar, exhaust fumes, and even Kasim's old, worn-out shoes.

The current took its revenge on us by seizing our hoses, shaking them violently, and causing us to drift constantly off toward the west like members of some nomadic tribe, or Americans caught up in the California gold rush. You had to use one hand just to keep your balance while you tried to work with the other. Everyone would instinctively grab onto our guide ropes to anchor himself, but the ropes, which had already been damaged by that sort of thing, naturally gave way under the strain. Worst of all, the hoses would get tangled up, cutting off our air.

One day, absorbed in my work, I didn't notice that my air hose had caught on the lifeline. For a minute or so I found it hard to breathe, then I suddenly had no air at all. I started up, got carried off by the current, and found myself suspended near the surface, still with no air. In my fear I struggled with all my might to reach the top. I finally made it, shocked and thoroughly exhausted. I could, of course, have simply detached the hose, but when you're desperately in need of air you don't have much presence of mind.

Early in August a swell that came in from the high sea sent waves crashing up under the tent, sowing panic in our midst. Everyone dragged his own belongings up to higher ground, then returned to help transport the salvaged artifacts onto a narrower, steeper slope near the basins. The advent of such an extensive flood at a time when the sea was relatively calm made us realize that a storm could cause waves that would wash everything away. There was talk of moving the entire camp up into the area where I had built my platforms, at which point I decided that it might be prudent to stop teasing everyone all the time. But the swell quickly subsided, and, the crisis having passed, nothing was done.

The part of the cargo situated in the crevice formed an extension of the line from the platform. Although there were a few small objects that had landed at some distance from the wreck, the shape of the mass of ingots corresponded to the outlines of the ship. The disposition of the ingots in the crevice proved to be not so regular as it had been on the platform. My explanation for this disparity was that the end of the ship located in the crevice must have come down on the rocks there and been kept slightly elevated until the hull collapsed. When the ingots hit the irregular bottom of the crevice they fell into disarray.

I guessed that the ship was approximately thirty-three feet long and not more than six feet wide, which was quite a bit smaller than the average commercial vessel used by the Romans. The few extant pieces of the hull seemed to indicate that the ship was of light construction. Those who sailed with Ulysses could have pulled it up on the beach at night.

As the area under excavation grew larger, I was pleased to see that my first impression of the site had been correct: the cargo was indeed divided into two piles several yards apart. The space in the middle might have been where the crew lived, but it was hard to tell, because the Turks had known about this source of copper for some time. Another possibility was that the central portion of the hold contained a cargo that was perishable.

Three oxhide-shaped ingots in the crevice had taken on so many concretions that they now formed a solid slab at the foot of the cliff. I chipped away at the periphery of this slab for days, until Bass finally sent the Turks down to help me in their helmeted diving suits. Working like children happy to be at last among the adults, they gave a practical demonstration of their famous strength by freeing the slab on their first dive.

With the problem of raising such delicate objects in mind, I had brought from France several large balloons similar to montgolfiers, which, when they were inflated, could lift more than two hundred pounds. We attached one of these balloons to the slab and put in some air from our mouthpieces. With a little practice you could replace the mouthpiece without swallowing any water. Soon the slab became weightless, and we were able to lift it by hand. The underside of it was hard and clean, so we finished inflating the balloon. As a precaution, however, I tied on an extra rope so that I could regulate the speed of the ascent from below.

Under the slab of ingots there was sand that had filtered in when the substratum of organic matter shriveled up. Beneath this sprinkling of pure sand we found some lightly concreted bronze objects embedded in a sand that was hardened but still crumbly. Under that layer, a black sand mixed with organic debris covered the branches that protected the hull. The hull itself had been flattened out on the bottom, and all that remained of it were a few rotted planks. Some of them were rather narrow and fixed in the interior of the ship, across the axis. They were resting on longitudinals that were probably jointed and must have constituted the planking. A piece of timber eight inches wide and three inches thick was lying nearby. There was an abundance of slimy white matter, soft pulp that the water carried away, some bent pieces of thin metal, bronze tools, and weights made from black stone.

Although I couldn't deny that it was necessary for everything to be sketched and marked on the map before being taken out of the water, I did think that following this procedure forced us to leave fragile objects and even more fragile organic matter exposed to the action of the sea for too long a time. Having been protected for several thousand years by a matrix of stone, these delicate items had remained in a state of arrested decay. Once the stone was removed, a new phase of corrosion began. But the damage wrought by movements of the water, by curious fish, and by the carelessness of draftsmen or photographers was especially catastrophic. By the time all the paper work was done, there wasn't much left of the fragile matter.

At the bottom of the crevice we found three scarabs of the Egyptian type with hieroglyphics. After that we jumped every time we saw a periwinkle shell, because they had the same size and shape. The white periwinkle shell has been in copious supply around almost every Mediterranean excavation.

One morning, diving after Honor and Bass, I saw from a distance a black mist rising from the crevice. I couldn't imagine where it was coming from, because the mud raised by the previous divers would have already disappeared. As I drew nearer I surprised two mullets rummaging around amid the newly exposed delicate matter. I chased them off with my hand, but that made them angry, and they quickly returned. Only when I threatened to harpoon them with a graduated stake did they decide to forage a bit further off—but not too far. Bass subsequently made it a practice to cover the bottom of the crevice every night with a plastic sheet weighted down with pebbles.

In amongst the remains of the cargo we came across a collection of rocks, some of which were the size of an egg and others as big as your head. We called them "ballast stones," but I had serious doubts about their origin. In the faults around the wreck there were rocks that hadn't come from the ship. And on the

1. Merou in his cave.

2. M. Dumas's first amphora, Port Cros, 1939.

OFF MAHDIA:
(photographs three through eight)

3. The grinding stone found off Mahdia.

4. The *Elie Monnier*.

5. Pillar and anchor stock.

6. Commanding Officer Alinet has a cornice placed on the bridge.

7. A pillar on the bridge; in the background is Father Poidebar.

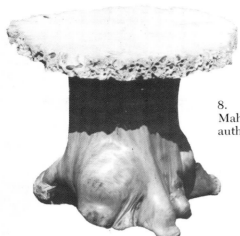

8. Section of a Greek column found off Mahdia and made into a table by the author.

9. Mr. Benoit looking at an amphora at Grand Congloué.

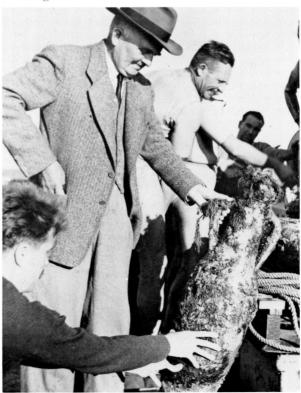

10. Marble statuary taken from the wreck near the island of Antikythera in 1901.

11. A porthole from the wreck of the *Panama*.

THE BRONZE AGE WRECK: (photographs twelve through twenty)

12.   The two boats at anchor in front of the expedition's camp.

13.   The two boats anchored over the wreck.

14.   A view of the expedition's camp.

15.   The rinsing basin of fresh water and a view of the worksite.

16. A block of the wreck's cargo lying on the bridge.

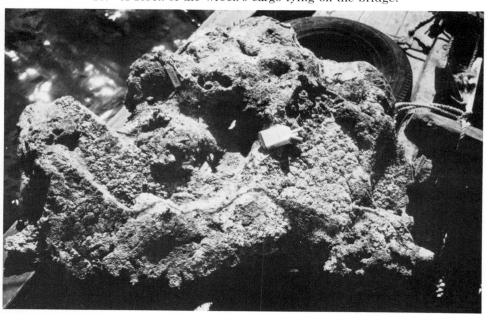

17. Bronze objects from the wreck.

18. Herb Grier sketching objects from the cargo of the wreck.

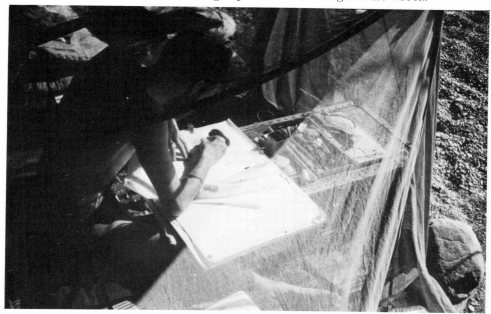

19. The last block raised from the wreck.

20.   A view of the ruins of Xanthos.

21. Ingot in the shape of an oxhide.

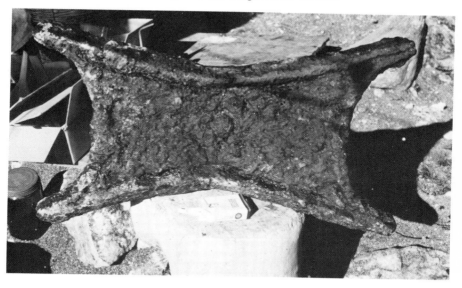

22. Bodrum seen from the château of the Crusaders.

23. A block detached from the wreckage is hoisted on board the boat.

24. Some bronze instruments removed from the wreckage.

25.   Lycian tombs carved from the cliffs of Féthiyé.

26. The Roman theater at Aspendos.

27. An amphora from the Chrétienne A wreck.

28. A cavity in the wreck's mast step to hold the mast.

29. The extremity of the mast step.

30. View of the bottom of the boat seen in relief on the sand.

31. Roman bath being lifted from the water.

32. Roman bath with child in it.

33. Different kinds of bowls from "the wreck of the bowls."

34. Lead ingot found below the tower of Magnons.

35. Inscription on another ingot.

36. Roman amphora resting on its side on the floor of a coral reef at Shab Rumi.

37.   The amphora after recovery.

38.   View of the wreckage of the bilge pump with pipes.

39. Driftwood eaten by shipworms.

40. Wreckage of a ship loaded with Roman amphoras, which
foundered against the rocks.

41. Concrete block containing 127 silver pieces of the Doges of Genoa.

42. Piece of a block from a jetty eaten by date mussels.

island that overlooked the site the seams of pudding stone that ran between the boulders represented a virtually illimitable source of "ballast stones."

Waldemar Illing, who, because he was still considered to be a visitor, had the right to dive wherever he wanted, opened up a new area of excavation by going to explore the little faults in the rocky soil beyond the big boulder that bordered the crevice. There he would find various small objects that had been displaced by the movements of the sea and caught in the faults. These isolated bronzes were well preserved, whereas those that had been thrown into contact with the mass of other metals had been affected by electrochemical processes, and many of them were ready to crumble under their still smooth surfaces. Herb hurried to finish taking his photographs so that he could go and dig in one of Wlady's faults. They came back with some more black-stone weights. It now appeared that these weights were of two types, one of which was cylindrical and shaped somewhat like a barrel, while the other was conical. We didn't pay much attention to these gleanings until one day when Wlady showed us a little stone roller engraved with the images of three persons in different styles of dress. The first two were facing the third, who was wearing a large hat with horns. The archaeologists in our group judged this seal to be older than the ship itself and suggested that it might have been handed down in the captain's family.

The beauty and importance of this piece led Bass to exaggerate the probability that the cargo had been dispersed over the area, and he gave official status to Wlady's efforts. Some lines were put down on the side of the wreck opposite the cliff, dividing the site into several sections. Each diver was assigned to a section, within which he was authorized to break up concretions and obliged to dig out the contents of the smallest fault. This scheme yielded very few objects, however, as the artifacts turned out to be pretty much concentrated in one location.

It made Bass a little nervous to see the delicate part of the wreck exposed in the crevice. The current would carry off his numbered labels and the photographers sometimes tore them loose as they maneuvered about or braced themselves to keep from being swept away.

Lying face down at the bottom of the crevice, I chiseled away at the soft rock that lay under the magma and supported it. The block lifted out properly, but some of the remains had unfortunately disappeared since the layer of hardened sand had been removed. What was left was a conglomeration of tools, branches with bark and twigs still attached, twisted metal, and remnants of planks from the hull.

We still had our doubts about the concretions at the base of the cliff, but we decided to leave them to the Turks in their helmeted diving suits. They had a good old time for themselves with their sledgehammers, raised a cloud of diluted dust, and found nothing.

Back at the camp, Joan packed the bronzes in cases, put on labels, and numbered and classified all the artifacts. Those of us whose previous experience had been limited to the excavation of amphora ships, on which you rarely found any crew's instruments or personal belongings, were amazed at the variety of items we had recovered.

In our collection of oxhide-shaped ingots, about forty were complete and another dozen or so only half their original size. The majority of them had been stamped with the manufacturer's trademark before the metal hardened. We came across quite a few fragments of these ingots that had escaped from the ship before it sank. There were, in addition, about twenty of the lenticular ingots. We thought the two piles of whitish material might be tin oxide, which was mixed with copper to make bronze. Small bronze artifacts turned up just about everywhere on the wreck, and in some places they were still grouped together, probably as the result of having been kept in some kind of basket. Among the objects we collected were: tools—double-bladed axes, axes with just a single blade, adzes, a bronze block with varied holes and channels for making nails, and a mirror; arms— spearheads and halberds; and cooking utensils—skewers, tripods, and bowls. There was a predominance of agricultural implements—picks, hoes, ploughshares, and shovels. Almost all these objects had, even before the shipwreck, been either broken or worn down to such an extent that they were entirely useless. The sailors apparently bought scrap metal, like our own country junkmen, and stored it on the ship beside the broken ingots until they had time to melt it down. The presence of the copper ingots and the tin led us to believe that some bronze articles were made right on the ship, but we didn't find a single mold. The glass beads and two transparent crystals must have served as a medium of exchange. It was most likely that the few pieces of pottery—jugs with handles and some storage jars—as well as the two mortars were used by the sailors themselves. We even found some traces of their food in the form of fishbones and olive pits. It was obvious from the number and variety of whetstones on the ship that a tool made from bronze needed to be sharpened rather frequently. Having examined the ingots and other artifacts, the archaeologists concluded that most of the cargo had been taken on in Cyprus, and that the ship had sunk sometime around the year 1200 B.C. As far as its nationality is concerned, the foreign articles in the cargo suggested that it had come from Syria.

Bass, who was only a novice diver when we arrived at the site, had come to appreciate the great promise of underwater archaeology. I sometimes had to curb my sailor's impatience with his hesitations, yet they were justified. I sensed that he was uneasy, but he knew what he wanted to do. Under his direction we brought up from the sea, with maps of every phase of the operation, the most important collection of Bronze Age artifacts found to this day. My first estimate of the weight of the cargo proved to be within two hundred pounds of the actual weight, which was about a thousand pounds. I was lucky, of course, because I could easily have been wrong by as much as a hundred percent. Having an estimate made by intuition turn out to be correct is more gratifying than the success of an hypothesis based on actual calculations.

There had been a precedent, however. A large number of Bronze Age artifacts had been recovered in 1923 during the dredging of a channel in the Spanish port of Huelva.

With the expiration of my unpaid leave drawing near, I got ready to return to France. Two days before I was scheduled to leave, I took a walk along the shore on the relatively accessible part that we skirted every day before arriving at the beach. The Turks had enticed me there with stories about a fault in the cliff where those who lived in the mountains were able to gather wild honey.

We scaled some enormous boulders by the edge of the sea, and crossed a steep, overgrown slope that had once been under cultivation. After making our way slowly toward the red cliff, we came to the foot of the fault where the honey was supposed to be. The Turks were very disappointed to see that there weren't any bees buzzing around. All along the fault, which was quite high, there were heavy vines caught in the rock, and anyone who cared to take the risk could have climbed them. But when you haven't had a chance to take a walk for a long time you really enjoy it, so we decided to continue on our way.

As we were coming back down, the Turks showed me a little pond around the edge of which you could see the freshly laid tracks of a pack of wild boars. This was the source of the freshwater stream that ran down to the beach. Some of the vines had grown wild and climbed high up into the trees, like lianas. A little further down there were some ruins reminiscent of the dilapidated sheep pens you see on the hills of the backcountry in France. The village looked as if it had been abandoned for several decades.

I was surprised to find the interior walls of the houses covered with a mixture of mortar and crushed brick. I had seen walls like that before. Then I examined some fragments of tile and pottery scattered on the ground, and I realized that the houses had been built by the Romans.

10

The Tiles

AS SOON AS I GOT BACK from Turkey, my friend Beuchat took me to Marseilles to dive on the wreck of a ship that had been carrying a cargo of roof tiles—not all the vessels on the bottom of the sea are amphora ships.

We dropped anchor about forty yards from the northwest coast of the Ile Pomègues, where a poet-fisherman came by to sell us some sea urchins. The water was cool, clear, and about sixty feet deep. Just beyond the furthest rocks, the cargo of tiles formed a slight but easily discernible relief on a gentle slope of sandy ground covered with posidonia.

Having become accustomed to the disorder of the average load of amphoras, I was surprised to find the large, flat, double-lipped tiles standing on edge in neat rows, like books in a library. Some of the rows ran in different directions. There were also a few half-round gutter tiles like the ones we use on our own roofs, but I couldn't quite see the way they were arranged. On the periphery of the wreck the tiles had fallen into dissarray when the sides of the ship collapsed.

The visible part of the ship occupied an area about twenty-three feet long and sixteen feet wide. At one extremity, barely protruding from the sand, were three clearly recognizable white-pine hull planks, about an inch and a half thick and decreasing in width toward their ends. The stem—or the stern—had to be close by. I had the impression that this ship was much smaller than the big cargo ships used in the wine trade.

In ancient times all the houses in the Mediterranean region were covered over with the wide, flat tiles, which were called *tegulae* and laid down so that there was a slight overlapping in the direction of the slope. The interlocking lips were capped by a row of the half-round tiles, called *imbrices*.

It's easy to imagine how such heavy, cumbersome, and fragile materials, for which there was considerable demand, might come to be transported by sea. That they were is plain to tell from the large number of wrecked ships having these tiles as their only cargo. Just a few hundred yards from the wreck I was exploring was another ship with tiles; and at Porquerolles, on the northern spur of the Cap de Mèdes, there was one that had been knocked about by the rocks and extensively pillaged. The Club de la Mer discovered one lying intact in a bed of posidonia off Juan-les-Pins. In Turkey, the Diving Club of Izmir knew of several such wrecks, and some English archaeologists reported seeing one near the island of Chios. All the tile wrecks found on the coast of France up to the present appear to have been ships of medium size.

Since roof tiles were not the sort of thing that could be sold on the black market in antiques from the sea, we thought we could save the wreck at Pomègues for excavation at a later date. We did it, though, at some risk. Despite their lack of commercial value, the tiles still attracted divers, the urge to pilfer being so strong that a goodly number of tiles were hauled off to be used as tabletops and as bricks for a garden wall or patio.

11

The
SLAVA ROSSII

A NUMBER OF LITTLE CAPES on the coast of France are called
Pointe de la Galère (Galley Point), and I've always thought that it
was more often the shape of the point, rather than the presence of
a sunken galley that was responsible for the name. But the Pointe
du Roucas Roux, on the Ile du Levant, is also known as the *Pointe
du Russe* (Russian Point) because of a wrecked ship.

When some divers saw cannons near this point, Captain Davin,
a retired naval officer who knew a great deal about the history of
Toulon, did a little research in the archives of the port administration, the results of which he was kind enough to communicate to
me.

In 1780, Louis XVI, busy with the American Revolution,
agreed that European seas should be neutral. At the time, a
squadron of ships belonging to Catherine the Great was tied up
at Livorno.

On November 3 the squadron came into the vicinity of Toulon,
and, during the night, one of the ships, the *Slava Rossii* or *Glory
of Russia,* lost contact with the others. With the white sails,

blown by the raging wind, flapping about in the dark, the Russians didn't see the Ile du Levant until it was too late to avoid it.

Launched in 1774 at Archangel, the *Slava Rossii* was commanded by Lieutenant Captain Jean Baskakov, whose rank was equivalent to that of a lieutenant commander in today's navy.

Six or seven crewmen were drowned. The rest of the ship's company, four hundred forty-six officers and men, were able to reach safety on the island, for the bow of the ship had caught on some rocks and remained above water.

Monsieur de Saint-Aignan, lieutenant general of the navy and commanding officer of naval forces at Toulon, sent "the King's tartan armed for war," under an officer named Rabaud, speeding to the rescue.

Twenty-four of the seventy-four cannons were saved. Lieutenant Captain Baskakov was invited to stay in Toulon, but he chose instead to go to Hyères to wait for a frigate he had requested from Livorno. It arrived December 10.

On February 5, 1782, another frigate came to Toulon for the twenty-four salvaged cannons.

In March 1961 we went out in the *Elie Monnier* to have a look at the remains of the Russian ship. At the place indicated on our map, we saw three almost identical rocky points, and I went into the water without knowing which of them was the one we wanted. At a hundred thirty feet, in the sand at the base of the cliff, there was a colony of lobsters. I couldn't resist the temptation to gather them up, for I had mastered the technique. At first I used to extend my hand rather stealthily, but the lobster, feeling about with its long antennae, would become nervous and retreat into its hole. Then I changed my tactics for a while and tried just making a quick stab at my quarry. The water agitated by my gesture must have reached the lobster before my hand, because I missed quite a few. I next attempted to attract the victim by gently wiggling my fingers in front of him. Responding to the stimulus, the lobster would advance timidly and touch my hand with the ends of its antennae. I would then seize the antennae and pull the lobster right out of its hole, so that I could grab it with the other hand. The antennae are firmly rooted, but you have to act quickly, before the lobster's defensive reflexes cause the arrested members to come apart at the base. Those who dove after the first team would always see numerous abandoned antennae lying around on the bottom.

One day when I wasn't even thinking about gathering lobsters, I put out my hand from force of habit and caught one anyway. From that time on, I used to pick them up as casually as if I were shopping in the marketplace.

I had been so busy catching lobsters that I had forgotten all about the *Slava Rossii,* which, in any case, was nowhere in sight. At a hundred thirty feet we could stay down for only fifteen minutes, so I took my seven lobsters and headed up to the surface. The other divers found the wreck a short distance away.

We returned to this wreck twice that year, since we were beginning to lose interest in the wrecks we had been exploring and were looking for new ones.

Near the rocks where the bow of the ship had come to rest, at a depth of about thirty feet, I came across their sounding lead. It was long and heavy, and I could use it as an end weight whenever I had to descend to the bottom along a lifeline— especially if I happened to be working with divers who didn't subscribe to that practice. I could also let the lead trail along the bottom on the end of a light rope and, holding the other end of the rope in my hand, feel the lead grate against the sand, glide over the posidonia, jump on the rocks, or strike the hull of a wrecked ship.

As I moved away from the rock, the sand was covered with concretions that were typical of those you would find on a wreck. I followed the slope of the bottom and passed over a mixed pile of heavy bricks and small beams that must have been the remains of the oven. A little further down, there were a few sand-filled cannons and, in a grayish jumble of debris, the shining ends of some bottles—of vodka, no doubt. Much of what I saw consisted of vague forms fused together in such a way that I couldn't distinguish any familiar object and had to content myself with categorizing them according to their geometric form—rods, spheres, and slabs. Around a hundred thirty feet this array of unrecognizable refuse came to an end on the edge of a plain full of barren sand. Turning back again, I found a soggy leather saber case, from which the blade had disappeared, leaving only the stone-encrusted handle and hilt. When, back on the deck of the *Elie Monnier,* I broke through the matrix of stone, I saw that the hilt was made in the shape of a heart and that the bronze of the twisted handle had apparently been gilded. The Russians must have had small hands. As I passed by one of the cannons I

scratched it with my knife, and it got shiny. I scratched another
one with the same result. They were bronze!

Some of the other divers were skeptical, however, and they
went down to see for themselves. It turned out that I had
scratched a lead plate located at the point where the cannon
rested on its base. The cannons were actually made of iron.

A midshipman brought up a shapeless block of concretions and
proceeded to break it up while the other men looked on with
unconcealed amusement. But they all turned pale with envy
when, from the black, slimy block, there emerged a handsome
little bronze mortar complete with ornamental moldings. It was
probably a showpiece used only to fire salutes. Another diver
came up with the remains of a musket, on the bronze bedplate of
which were engraved some large letters interlaced beneath a
crown. We also recovered a blown-glass bottle. The amazing
quantities of bottles we've seen on sunken ships make it tempting to conclude that the vessels foundered because the crews
were drunk. The bottles of antiquity were the amphoras.

When Bargiarelli brought up a block of concretions fused to a
piece of board, the other divers, remembering their experience
with the mortar, refrained from comment, and everyone crowded
around to watch him open up his little surprise package. It
proved to contain a cannon charge made from a wooden rod fixed
to the center of a circular base. Around the rod were thirty cast-
iron balls two inches in diameter, arranged in five layers of six
balls apiece, for a total diameter of six inches. The balls, which
were still covered with grease, were contained by a cloth sleeve
tied to the base and to the end of the wooden rod.

I got to keep one of these balls for myself; it now weighs only
one-fourth of what it did at first, although the greased surface
remains intact. I have repeatedly put it to soak in fresh water,
frequently changed, but the same thing happens every time: as
the ball dries, it secretes little beads of rusty moisture.

We tried using a *suceuse* on the Russian ship and struck wood
about a foot down in the sand. I thought it was probably the hull,
but I couldn't say for sure. I was more familiar with the wood on
ancient ships.

In the course of our raids on the *Slava Rossii*, we hauled up a
cannon with which we hoped to decorate the terrace of our headquarters at the Undersea Research Group. Under the crust of
stone, the surface, engraved with an inscription, was perfectly

preserved, but it was easy to penetrate with a knife. Every time it rained, the cannon gave off a stream of rust, and the terrace became an eyesore. So one day we just took the cannon back to the wreck.

Of the seventy-four cannons that had been aboard the ship, twenty-four were recovered shortly after the accident. One bronze and nine cast-iron cannons were recently salvaged by a navy team under the direction of Philippe Tailliez. There should therefore be forty cannons still on the bottom, but only very few remain visible.

About this time we also made some dives on the wreck of an Italian ship that had been part of the fleet of Andrea Doria and had left Genoa to attack Nice. This wreck, like the *Panama* and the *Slava Rossii*, had the settled look common to sunken ships from the classical era.

The hull had been crushed by some neighboring rocks; there were thick growths of posidonia on every side and sand in all the hollows. The riches within were camouflaged by blocks of concretions that were very much like the concreted rocks on the periphery of the site. Under this new, four-hundred-year-old seabed lay a hidden chamber that was as inaccessible as the garret of a Renaissance château; I nevertheless enjoyed swimming all around it. Cannons were strewn about the area like the amphoras on an ancient wreck. But the cannons weren't quite so tall as the ordinary pile of amphoras, and they would get buried before they had been in the sea as long as the jars of Greece and Rome.

12

LA CHRÉTIENNE A

ALTHOUGH I HADN'T SEEN the wreck at La Chrétienne since 1950, I had heard news of it from other divers, so I did have some idea of what had happened to it in the meantime. I knew that the letter A had been added to its name and that it had lost all its amphoras.

In 1953, Barnier found there a leaden anchor stock with part of the shaft still in place—something that is very rare. Later on he worked the site with the members of the Undersea Mountain-climbing Club of Cannes and picked up, near the same spot, two rather curious blocks of concretions. When he saw that they were hollow and contained a liquid black residue, Barnier decided to cut them open with a saw. He filled the cavities with plaster and obtained perfectly molded replicas of a carpenter's ax and adze. After that, archaeologists began to treat these amorphous blocks of concretions with greater respect.

I became friendly with Jack and Jane Issaverdens, who had a house near the sea that faced out toward La Chrétienne. In the summertime they used to explore the vast underwater garden with its stretches of white sand, prairies of posidonia, huge steep rocks, and exotic concretions the like of which you wouldn't find anywhere else on earth. Often, when the mistral was raging in Toulon, I would go up to visit with them and enjoy the better weather. They would take me out to view their discoveries, which I was only too glad to do, because it gave me the opportunity to dive for pleasure and forget about whatever I happened to be working on for the navy.

Before the construction of the lighthouse at La Chrétienne, many a ship had run afoul of the rocks there. We saw several wrecks on our very first dives in the area.

What made the reef even more dangerous was that it was the meeting place for two winds coming from opposite directions. Several times a year this otherwise peaceful spot became the scene of a clash between violent winds from both east and west. First one, then the other would be the stronger, and the narrow, irregular line of battle would shift constantly back and forth. Any sailing ship caught in this turbulence would be hopelessly trapped.

On May 28, 1961, I went out to have a look at the wreck I had come to know so well many years before. I've rarely seen a site changed so much. After being picked over by divers, it had been further transformed by the sea, until it was no longer just an abandoned excavation but an entirely new archaeological field.

I've always liked to observe the actions of the sea. When I was small, I would run down to the beach as soon as the first late-summer storm began to appear on the horizon. Each wave would come up a little further on the sand that had been trodden underfoot by bathers for a period of two whole months; and, sometimes, to my great delight, I would find a few lost coins. Everything on the beach—pieces of wood, bits of paraffin, old sandals, worn-out bathing caps, broken toys, and countless other signs of the summer's activity—would be swept out to sea. But when the storm was over the tide would bring it all back, sorted as if by hand. I knew in advance where the last waves would deposit each category of objects.

In the deeper water the shifting tides aren't nearly so dexterous as they are in at the shore, but they can still stir up the sand and change the shape of the bottom. So much white sand had accumulated on the Roman ship at La Chrétienne that everything below the tip of the mountain of amphoras was completely obscured. For fifteen years various divers had worked the site, and every year the sea had patiently leveled the sand, removing the surplus and thereby facilitating the task of the next wave of vandals.

What had once been a considerable mound was now just a vast, sandy basin at the bottom of which there lay exposed a heavy piece of blackened wood. I thought this was probably a keelson, but I wouldn't commit myself, because I was anxious to get to work on another exciting project, and I didn't have time to investigate.

I returned to Anthéor in September with the intention of showing the keelson to Honor Frost.

But the sea and the divers had disturbed the sand to such an extent that we couldn't find the keelson at all. On the other hand, there was a well-preserved portion of the ship's hull protruding from the soil among the oddly shaped potsherds. Under the interior floor of white pine the oak ribs were still quite solid, and the joints between the hull planks scarcely discernible. We made some drawings, took measurements, and photographed the site. I removed a section from one of the ribs so that I could study it on land and was surprised to see the outline of the rib traced on the hull with a blunt instrument. Here was another reason to believe that, contrary to the way it is done today, the hull of an ancient ship was assembled before it received the ribs.

Honor made a drawing of the rib section and asked me for a sample that she could analyze. When I tried to cut it, however, the saw passed through a soft layer of soggy wood and then came up against a hard inner core that was difficult to penetrate. I finally left the half-cut wood under a hedge in my backyard. When I went to trim the hedge the following year, it was still there. The soft outer layer had shriveled up and peeled off like the bark of a tree, exposing a smooth, slightly fissured surface beneath it. I cut off a piece and, to remove the salt, put it to soak in some fresh water, which soon became permeated with a dark red liquid. I let the wood dry in the shade, then sanded and waxed it until it took on a beautiful polish. I subsequently used it as a paperweight. Little by little, the sun brought back the natural color, the grain of the oak began to appear, and the wood shrank slightly, narrowing its fissures. The paperweight kept absorbing more and more wax, until it finally looked newer than the wood of my furniture. It amazed me just to look at it.

June 17, 1962, was a very lucky day for me. At noon that day the sea around Anthéor was as smooth as glass, and the perfect calm was enough to put you in an acute state of euphoria. Jack was afraid some Sunday divers might find our hidden treasures, so we went out to La Chrétienne to see what the situation might be. Everybody knew that the wreck was desolate.

When we arrived at the site, the keelson was once again protruding from the soil, a black patch on the white mantle of sand. I exposed one of the ends by fanning the water with my hand, which is a technique used by every diver and called *la vente*. With a vigorous stroke of your hand you force water down onto the soil, sending the sand, potsherds, and concretions floating upward in a murky cloud. In order to maintain good visibility, you have to determine the path of the current and push in that direction. I always begin by raising a small cloud and watching the way it drifts. If it doesn't move at all, there's no current, so I have to create one by making periodic broad sweeps of the hand as I dig. With my left hand I remove any debris that is too heavy to dislodge with jets of water. I'm always amazed when I come up after using this technique and find the muddy water lying on the surface as far as the eye can see.

The end of the keelson was chamfered, which meant that it had not been broken but started right there in the center of the ship. The end was seated in a special floor frame recessed to house it. The adjacent frames fitted into grooves on the underside of the keelson. As I continued to dig, the sand got thicker and the width of the keelson increased with carefully measured regularity. This made it obvious that the piece of wood before me had been designed to serve as something more than just a keelson.

Removing still more sand, I uncovered a rectangular hole in the keelson. It was the mast step, the heart of the ship and something that had never been seen on an ancient wreck!

With mounting excitement, I expelled all the sand from the hole, at the bottom of which I discovered a bronze coin fused to the wood by oxidation. I vaguely recalled seeing something like that before; it seemed to me that the coin had been put there for a reason. Having decided that it might be worthwhile to reflect on the meaning of this token that had lain under the sand for two thousand years, I went back up to the surface.

Suddenly I remembered that a friend of mine had once put a gold coin under the mast of his yacht, and I realized that the bronze coin must have been a votive offering.

Then I began to have second thoughts, which is only natural.

People would say that the coin had fallen out of someone's hand, or through a hole in somebody's pocket; and that it had slid down between the amphoras before coming to rest at the bottom of the mast step.

I was dying to scratch the oxide from the surface of the coin, and only its symbolic character kept me from doing so. I entrusted my find to Professor Mollat, who kindly arranged for it to be cleaned at the Cabinet des Médailles of the Bibliothèque Nationale. It was in excellent condition and engraved with the image of an arrogant woman wearing an Egyptian headdress. On the other side was a laurel wreath that framed an illegible inscription.

Monsieur Yvon, the curator of the Cabinet des Médailles, identified the coin as having been struck at Cossyra, on the island of Pentelleria, between 217 and the first half of the first century B.C. The inscription was in Phoenician, despite the fact that the island had by that time been occupied by the Romans. This identification tallied with the opinion given by Benoit, who estimated that the ship had been on the bottom of the sea since 75 B.C.

I subsequently learned that the custom of placing a luck coin under the mast is still practiced in Spain, in England, and in France as well. In my book *Epaves antiques,* I devoted a long chapter to La Chrétienne, but I was afraid to mention the luck coin because I thought the archaeologists would laugh at me.

In September 1962 the remains of a Roman ship were discovered in the bed of the Thames by workmen engaged in making repairs on Blackfriars Bridge. The following year, Peter Marsden, a young student, found in a hollowed-out section of the ship's hull a bronze coin that bore the image of the Emperor Domitian and had been struck in Rome in 88 or 89 A.D. The piece of wood in which he found the coin was comparatively small and, what is unusual for a mast step, lay across the axis of the ship. Peter Marsden made some inquiries in England concerning the custom of the luck coin. It was practiced there until about thirty years ago. One shipbuilder said that until 1914 his father used to put a gold sovereign under the mast, but that after the war he reduced it to a half crown. On small boats with removable masts, the builders would, as a precaution, put the coin in the mortise of the stem- or sternpost. The manager of one of the shipyards Peter visited told him that, because of the luck coin, a carpenter called upon to repair a mast would always be closely watched. The custom apparently died out as iron construction came into general use.

When my friend Chevalier excavated a Roman ship at Port-Vendres in November 1963, he uncovered the mast step and found a bronze coin bearing a likeness of the Emperor Constantine lying inside. It had been struck in London at the beginning of the fourth century B.C. Since my publisher was a bit behind schedule, I had time to insert a note in my book making the luck coin an official part of my description of the wreck at La Chrétienne.

Although the luck coin is associated with a joyous event, i.e., the launching of a new ship, it is still somewhat like the obolus put in the mouths of the dead to pay Charon for their passage across the river Styx on the way to Hades. The obolus helps to fix the dates of tombs, while the luck coin will, in certain cases, settle controversies arising from the pottery found on sunken ships.

Scholars should now trace the origins of this custom, follow it through the upheavals of the Middle Ages, and look for evidence of it among the various nations of every historical period.

Was the coin simply a good luck charm, or did it correspond to a specific myth that became a tradition? Did it represent a vestigial form of the sacrifice made to the gods when a ship was launched? What important person had the privilege of depositing the coin? Was it placed with the face up or down? What was put under the mast before the invention of money?

There had been ships on the sea for quite some time when the first coins appeared in the seventh century B.C. But the luck coin was a later form of an even more ancient custom, that of the "foundation deposit," the placement of precious objects in the basement or foundation wall of a building so that the gods would favor the project. Like the rite of the luck coin, the foundation deposit has survived the passage of time and it's not unusual today to see a cabinet member lay the cornerstone of a public building.

On today's ships the mast is just set in a hole from which it never moves. On the ship at La Chrétienne, however, the mast step was rectangular and divided into an upper and lower part, the upper being just a shallow recess cut out on the surface of the wood along the four sides of the lower, which was wide and deep. The coin had been placed at the bottom of the lower part, where the heel of the mast would rest. The upper recess looked to me as if it had been put there to receive a chock. Chevalier, in fact, found such a chock on the mast step of the wreck at Port-Vendres. And, although the ship at Port-Vendres was four hundred years younger than that at La Chrétienne, the steps were almost exactly alike.

The complexity of the ancient mast step leads one to believe that it may have been designed to allow a certain degree of movement, so that, for example, the mast could be lowered.

Strangely enough, we have yet to see the heel of a mast in place on an ancient ship. A mast that could be folded down might very easily, once the ropes broke, have toppled over in one piece and wound up at the mercy of the sea. It might also have floated up to the surface. But the best explanation may be that the mast was simply made from a species of wood that can't withstand the rigors of life under the sea.

The axis of the ship at La Chrétienne ran the length of a basin that measured forty by twenty feet. The wreck was slightly inclined in the direction of a rocky barrier. Near this barrier, at exactly twelve feet from the mast step, the ends of six ribs protruded from the sand, an indication that a considerable part of the hull had been preserved. There was, in general, very little sand covering the wood and, at sixty-five feet, it would be easy to remove it. I was tempted to take advantage of the favorable conditions and conduct a small, one-man excavation, by hand, as a demonstration for the hesitant archaeologists. My friends had generously given me a place to stay, and I could use their inflatable dinghy to transport myself across the half mile of water that separated us from the wreck. It was only June, so I had the whole summer ahead of me.

My work for the navy left me free to go out to La Chrétienne on weekends and also to take a few days' leave from time to time. I never dreamed that my project would require as much work as it did.

In order not to lose a minute once I was in the water, I used to think about the wreck as I was driving up to Anthéor. I would try to anticipate what might develop on the site and to prepare myself for any eventuality. It's only seventy-three miles from Toulon to Anthéor, but you had to pass through crowded villages on a road so narrow that traffic backed up for miles whenever two trailer trucks met along the way. As the road wound in and out, I would come up against a line of traffic comprised of a wheezing old truck followed by several two-horsepower Citroëns that would be constantly darting to the left, hoping in vain for an opportunity to pass. Lush green vines ruled the plains and clambered up the hills. During the grape harvest, you had to contend with hordes of odd little carts drawn by horses who looked as if they might expire at any moment.

I dove in the morning and late afternoon, coming up when my bottles were empty, which in this instance was after forty-five minutes. Sometimes, if the work was particularly strenuous, I would consume more air and be forced to surface early.

Since I had planned to limit myself to a cursory examination of the site, I started out just digging here and there to satisfy my curiosity. As I went along, however, my curiosity grew stronger and stronger. In one place the hull would be in excellent condition, but a little further on it would, without any apparent reason, be decrepit and eaten by worms. I could tell the difference between the damage wrought by the sea and that which had been caused by divers.

I didn't remove the sand, but merely displaced it. Every time I dug a new hole the old ones got covered over, and I would invariably find something at the bottom of the new one that would lead me to enlarge it or go back to the old ones again for the sake of comparison. At the end of each stay in Anthéor I would fill in the holes and conceal the visible parts of the hull under some blocks of concretions, for I was not the only one poking around the site. Divers from Germany, Switzerland, and Belgium used to come over from the international camp near Cape Dramont, and I would sometimes even see local divers there. They were both intrigued and disquieted by my continued attention to a wreck that had already been extensively pillaged. After I left they would rummage around and frequently steal pieces of the hull.

Although the wreck had been plundered for fifteen years, I still occasionally unearthed a broken amphora. I would deliberately leave it out in the open, to disappear overnight.

My fellow divers eventually discovered another mine of amphoras behind the rocky barrier. Their preoccupation with this new lode distracted them from the destructive raids on the basin. As I arrived on the site that day, all I saw was a big cloud of mud and some footfins moving about. They were working blindly, with small picks, feeling around with their hands for the amphoras. After they left and the mud drifted away from where they had been digging, I went over and gathered up some magnificent stoppers that were identical to those in the basin. I knew then that part of the cargo was separated from the main body, but I didn't know why.

Before starting in to work I had bought a sixty-foot nylon-plastic tape measure and a stainless steel folding yardstick. I made notes and drawings on a sheet of plastic which I had sanded so that the pencil marks wouldn't rub off. In order to keep the pencil from falling apart, I had to wrap it with adhesive tape or force it into a plastic tube. I measured angles with two flat, plastic rulers riveted together at one end. Friction between the rulers kept the measured angle constant until I could record it on my drawing board. I didn't use a protractor because I was afraid that I would misread it in the muddy water. To provide for the measurement of horizontal angles, I attached a small air-bubble level to one of the two rulers. I carried everything in a transparent bag, which made it easy to pick out the instrument I wanted.

Sketching the various parts of the ship became so tedious that I began to envy the other divers around the site, who were there just for pleasure.

After each dive I would, in spite of the burning summer heat, labor at making fair copies of my drawings, a practice that directed my attention to problems which I had overlooked under the water and which would determine the plan of the following dive.

Although an underwater excavation is usually a complicated affair involving ships, personnel, a budget, and adjustments to other people, at La Chrétienne I enjoyed, reveled in, total autonomy, my only obstacles being the sea and the sand.

As the weeks went by, however, I began to realize that I was not autonomous at all. I was subject to the site itself, which imposed its own method of procedure, thereby relieving me of what had actually become a rather burdensome responsibility. I was now no longer conducting the excavation—it was conducting me.

The best time to take photographs of the wreck was early in the day, because the water was very clear and I had an unobstructed view of the bottom sixty feet below me. In the afternoon the water would get turbid, as it does, according to our experience, in all the seas of the world. The light from the sun must cause the microorganisms, or plankton, to multiply and rise toward the surface.

In the morning the mud I raised would be carried off by a small current, but in the afternoon it would accumulate to form an immobile cloud. Sometimes I would just give up, swim out into the clear, and have a look around. On one such excursion I found a bronze bracelet with two finely carved fish heads at the end, and an earthenware oil lamp on which there were still some traces of black varnish. Having fallen into a hollow in the rocky barrier about five feet above the level of the soil in the basin, the lamp had escaped the attention of the vandals, probably because they never thought to look up so high, in such an obvious place.

The current that usually sweeps across the Riviera from east to west was, unfortunately for me, especially weak that year. Most divers are familiar with this current, which, when it strikes an underwater shelf or enters a narrow pass, gains momentum and interferes with their work. It varies in strength from day to day, occasionally reversing itself or failing to appear at all.

Some days I would find the cold, clear layer right at the bottom. The Mediterranean is never, as a body, entirely warm; when summer bathers splash about in water that is pleasantly tepid, the diver encounters the colder layer quite close to the surface. Toward the end of the summer it drops down to about a hundred thirty feet. The coastal current affects only the warm layer, and I often prefer to brave the cold rather than to fight against the current. When there's a mistral, the cold layer rises and reaches the surface within a few days, then rapidly descends again once the wind subsides. The separation between the warm and cold layers is sharp and abrupt; from a point in the warm layer you can touch the cold water with your hand.

At La Chrétienne the cold layer stayed close to the bottom, and the effect on my photographs was disastrous. Since the index of refraction was different for each layer, the water appeared to vibrate like the air near the surface of a road heated up by the summer sun.

The efficiency of a diver is influenced to a considerable extent by the weight of his own body, which is regulated with pieces of lead tied to a belt around his waist. If he is too heavy, he will have trouble moving around and will get tired rather quickly; if he is too light, he will be forced to swim with his head lower than his feet and will be unable to work on the bottom without being carried off by the current. I used to go into the water with eight two-pound lead weights, which were enough to send me floating effortlessly to the bottom. When I wanted to take photographs, I would remove the weights, so that I would be suspended in the water and not raising clouds of mud with my movements. In order to make measurements, however, I would add weights until I felt more stable but not so burdened that I couldn't move. For digging I liked to be quite heavy, so I would attach all eight of the weights. I even had another ten pounds that I could put on if it was necessary. Each time I felt the weight return to my body I experienced a bit of anxiety, but there was really no reason to worry, because the belt could easily be discarded.

I made a few halfhearted attempts to dig trenches with a coal shovel and to cover them over with a little rake, but with tools like that you can't make the water circulate the way you can with your hand, and I was very soon engulfed in a cloud of mud. To me it's essential that I be able to see; moreover, I believe that fanning the water by hand is a much more efficient way to dig.

I had to have a certain amount of patience, but not nearly so much as Jack and Jane, who spent many idle hours up on the surface waiting for me to complete my work below. Jack couldn't resist the challenge of pursuing our investigation right to the end. Jane, however, wanted nothing to do with the Roman ship; as far as she was concerned, I should have been busy clearing up the mysteries that surrounded some of the items she had discovered herself.

The looters eventually resumed their activity in the little valley that extended off to the northeast side of the wreck. In one of the newly dug holes there was a length of square-cut white pine with a tenon at the end. It wasn't part of the hull, and I wondered if it could have come from the rigging. Although I was reluctant to extend the area of my investigation, I was intrigued and began to dig. The original length of wood turned into a huge, thick, ever-widening beam with a groove in one side. After it attained a foot in diameter, it became square again. I had never seen anything like it on a Roman ship. A little further away I uncovered a second, similar piece of wood with a leaden cap at one end, which led me to think that both pieces might have been mooring bitts. The sand was full of various fragments of wood, amphora shards, tiles, and fine pottery. I sensed the presence of a structure that had collapsed, but it would have taken a systematic excavation with charts of each phase in order to determine what had happened, and I didn't have time for that. Afraid to dig any deeper or further, I covered everything up.

Two months later I was emerging from a mud cloud at the end of a dive when I noticed the piece of wood with the groove in its side lying on some posidonia. Some divers had wrenched it free, carried it away and abandoned it, no doubt temporarily. I was out of air, so I asked Jack to go down and put a rope on it. It was enormous; on the round end there were traces of a leaden cap, and a piece of the white pine in which it had been housed was still clinging to its side. The mooring bitt was put to soak in a protective bath for three years, under the watchful eye of Bouis, and then slowly dried out before a decision could be made concerning its state of preservation.

Whenever I exposed the interior floor of the ship, called the *vaigrage*, I would find a bed of slender branches that reminded me of the thicker branches under the cargo of metal on the wreck from the Bronze Age. They were apparently intended to protect the hull.

The inclination of the wreck, measured along the mast step, was twenty-five degrees toward the east. A large portion of one side was in perfect condition and had kept its shape. But near the axis there was a slight separation between the hull and the frames caused by the excessive weight of the amphoras on the side that lay on the bottom. The west side, which was not so well protected by the cargo, had broken up and disappeared.

The number of amphoras and the size of the mooring bitts gave me the impression that the ship was quite large. The only way to be certain of its dimensions, however, was to uncover whole sections near the mast. With my hand I dug a trench a foot and a half deep to completely expose one of the ribs. The effort left me exhausted. Fearing that I had buried all my instruments, I felt around in the sand for them. When the water cleared up again, I stretched a string from the mast step to a stake placed at the end of the rib, a distance of about twelve feet. I then went on to record the vertical distance between the string and the rib at intervals of eight inches, which required a total of nineteen measurements. Busy to the point of forgetting the water, I was slow and quite maladroit. I made the same measurements on a second rib five feet away, with slightly different results, which was evidence that the ship had been elegantly shaped. The wreck was inclined in the direction of the rocky barrier and, since the oil lamp, together with other scattered fragments, had landed there, the height of the deck must have been at least equal to that of the barrier's crest. I therefore made the crest part of my sketch of the hull section nearest to the mast and extended the lines of the section to meet the crest. This projection gave the ship a width of about twenty-six feet.

The length of a Roman ship was usually three or four times its width, so this one must have been eighty to a hundred feet long, and could not have been completely contained in the basin.

The pillagers, in fact, found amphoras on the other side of the rocky barrier, which meant that I had to enlarge my map of the site. But a rock twenty feet high sat astride the axis of the ship. I placed a buoy on either side of the rock with the floats set quite high. In the absence of any current, the buoys remained almost perfectly vertical, and Jack helped me to measure the distance between the floats.

I had to conclude my study of the Roman ship without having seen any portion of the hull except the one nearest to the mast. At that point the structure consisted of an alternation between half frames and full frames with floor plates. The ends of the half frames met to form a bevel above the keel, leaving room for the bilge water to run through. The floor plates south of the mast had, on the underside, a channel cut out for the same purpose and called the "timber hole." In the center of each triangular plate, moreover, there was a hole an inch and a half or two inches large, of the kind that had already been noted at Grand Congloué, and the function of which was still a mystery. The floor plates north of the mast had no channel and no hole in the center. The reason for this discrepancy was far from clear, but, while I was unable to offer any explanation, being content merely to present the facts, I felt that it was a significant detail.

I wore myself out trying to find the bow of the ship so that I could get a better understanding of the asymmetrical mast step. The presence of the anchor and mooring bitts to the north suggested north as the forward end, but they could also have been located at the stern. And the pieces of tile near the bitts came, according to the iconography, from a deck shelter that was situated toward the stern. Too much of the evidence I needed in order to resolve the issue was lacking, and probably nothing short of a complete excavation could have provided it.

Before leaving the site I wanted to protect the mast step. With the aid of a balloon I raised a heavy block of stone that I had found at the foot of the light tower, about a hundred sixty feet away. It always fascinates me to see the air, imprisoned by water, transformed into a powerful, disciplined worker. Jack towed away, but while I was deflating the balloon the current caused us to drift, and the block fell at a distance from the wreck. When we recovered the balloon it was all wrinkled up; nevertheless, we managed to reinflate it just enough to get the block over the wreck again. I eased it onto the mast step, then covered the rest of the wood with all the heavy concretions scattered in the basin. The wreck would thus be protected from the sea, but not, of course, from vandals.

I don't mean to give my readers the impression that my study of the wreck at La Chrétienne was an authentic piece of archaeological research. Amateur archaeologists like me lack competence and discipline, and we have to limit ourselves to the sort of exploration that will simply turn up enough material for a summary description of the site. I never intended to go any further than that; if I did, it was only because of my desire to understand the ancient wreck and my fear of seeing its vestiges rapidly destroyed.

What I saw as I dug in the sand was, for the most part, just what I was looking for. I was there to observe, but also to interpret, and preconceived ideas are harmful to observation, which should be considered as an end in itself. I failed to record certain important details which my notes, being incomplete, could not elucidate. A little detail that hardly seems worthy of notice can sometimes turn out to be the key to a significant problem.

The archaeologist in charge of an excavation doesn't necessarily interpret the documents he compiles on the site; if he does, it will be only much later. He is trained to observe everything, recording the smallest details. It has often been written that an excavation destroys a site, leaving behind only the documents collected there. I will go a bit further and say that an archaeologist considers extremely dangerous the all-too-human tendency to interpret at the risk of giving a particular orientation to an investigation that should go off in every direction.

13

The BATHS

NEAR ALMOST EVERY lighthouse built on a reef there is a wrecked ship from the Roman era.

In March 1957 the *Elie Monnier* was sent to La Ciotat on official business, and we took advantage of the opportunity to visit the wreck that had been discovered at the foot of the lighthouse between the Ile Verte and the Bec de l'Aigle. There I came across two iron anchors from a Roman ship welded to a rocky slope by concretions that had reduced them to pipes of stone. Further on I found a leaden anchor stock, then descended into a fault where amphora shards mingled with posidonia and the soil had been recently disturbed. As we were bringing up a few amphoras we saw, at one end of the site, a large, thick, oddly shaped piece of pottery sticking up out of the ground. Once the *suceuse* had been installed, I straddled the nozzle, which I held between my knees, and proceeded to remove stones, concretions, and amphora shards along with the sand. As the mysterious object, which was the color of lead, began to emerge from the soil, I perceived that it was a piece of earthenware shaped something like a slipper bath* turned upside down. The water had become turbid, and I was numb with cold; I was also afraid that I would be unable to finish digging the thing out before the end of my dive. I planted my feet in the sand like an octopus and got a firm grip on the piece of pottery. The sand quivered encouragingly. I continued my efforts until the object finally came out of its hole in the midst of a yellow cloud. To my great dismay, it appeared to be an air vent! In my disappointment I ran my hand along the tapered end, which I thought was designed to pass through the deck, and was relieved to find it sealed up. When the mud cloud drifted off, it became evident that the object was indeed a slipper bath, big enough to be the shoe of a giant.

Although Benoit already had some amphoras taken from this particular wreck, all of which bore markings connecting them to families well known in Campania, our latest discovery would be a unique item for his museum.

"This type of bath," he said, "was used in Greece from the fifteenth century B.C. right up through the Hellenistic period. This one doesn't have the bench that the Greek baths had."

Antique bathtubs couldn't be that rare in the sea, because I found another one five years later. I was then working feverishly at La Chrétienne, and, pressed for time, had prolonged my weekend by taking a day of leave. There was a great deal to be done there. Jack and Jane, meanwhile, continued their leisurely exploration of the area. For two days they had been very excited over a dolium, the neck of which they had seen poking up out of the sand on the other side of the rock that served as a base for the lighthouse. A dolium was a huge spherical vessel kept on every Roman ship to contain the supply of fresh water. The site that Jack and Jane had been working, extensively pillaged and quite disorderly, didn't interest me at all. The sand concealed pieces of wood and amphora fragments from several ships that had foundered on the reef and come to rest there. I call that type of site a "complex."

Jack and Jane were so insistent about showing me their dolium that I knew I would, sooner or later, have to give in and lose some of my precious time.

In the afternoon, as I was preparing to dive on La Chrétienne A, Jane looked so forlorn that I relented and followed her off

---

* A partially covered bath shaped somewhat like a slipper, used in Europe.

toward the dolium. From a point high up in the water, I saw a lip in the midst of a cluster of posidonia, at the foot of a small, isolated rock. The lip was quite handsome and decorated a rectangular form, the side of which curved inward instead of flaring out. Even before I reached the bottom I recognized the object as a bathtub.

Crouching to get a good hold on the lip, I gave it a few pulls. I thought I felt it move, but I knew I would never be able to extract something that big from the roots of the posidonia. I took a *main de fer*, which is a small, three-pronged gardener's tool, and clawed at the roots until I had exposed the lip that was intact—the other one was partially broken. With the whole perimeter of the tub projecting from the soil, I gave a few more pulls, but the effort made me dizzy and I had to return to the surface.

It being vacationtime in all the countries of Europe, there were looters everywhere. I had to leave Anthéor that night, and we thought it would be foolish to leave such a choice morsel out where it could be seen. So, despite the lateness of the hour, we went to fetch a balloon, a device that had often been used, with considerable success, to pilfer amphoras.

Jack sent down a two-bottle air supply in which there remained just enough air to inflate the balloon. I took the rope attached to the lower end of the balloon and tied it around the tub. The compressed air rushed into the balloon with the sound that always surprises me, but the big yellow balloon just lay motionless on the bottom, and I began to get worried. Then I gave the tub a vigorous pull. The earth around it trembled, and the tub rose majestically out of the sand. It took off slowly, like an airship, then steadily gained altitude, clouding up the sky like a forest fire.

The bathtub bobbed about on the surface, full of posidonia roots coated with sand. While we were towing it toward Anthéor we drifted quite a bit. Once there, we had to get into the water and remove all the roots before putting the tub away in a safe place. It was a magnificent specimen shaped in the normal way, with markings on the lip.

Benoit, who was delighted to have this new example of a different type of bath, deciphered the name of the manufacturer, C. SABIN(us) COMM(unis) AUCTYS FEC(it), and concluded that it had been made during the first century.

There doesn't seem to have been any such thing among the

Ancients as a passenger ship, but only cargo ships that carried passengers and must have been rather uncomfortable.

We thought that it might have been the custom to bring a bathtub along when there was a distinguished passenger on board.

Several times we went back to the site to look for the piece that had been missing. As we poked around we came across many an item from the same period, and we were thrilled to see amphoras only half-covered by the sand. Jane claimed that the missing piece was probably already in Switzerland or Belgium.

14

The BOWLS

ON DECEMBER 6, 1960, I saw a story in the *République*, a newspaper published in the Var, about the discovery of an old wreck that had been carrying a cargo of bowls.

In July 1962 we went to Corsica on the *Elie Monnier* to recover, for a board of inquiry, the remains of an airplane that had crashed in two hundred forty feet of water off Calvi. The sea was very clear, and I took photographs by the light of the sun. I had never taken pictures at such a depth.

Back on the pier I had the good fortune to meet the man who had seen the wreck with the cargo of bowls—Raibaldi, a young diver happy to contribute to our knowledge of sunken ships. He was the founder of a local diving club. He graciously offered to take me out on his boat with a few discreet tourists.

We followed the rocky, irregular coast until we passed one last cape, when Raibaldi dropped the anchor. The wreck wasn't there, but he thought it better to let his clients dive before we got to it.

When they had finished, we moved to a spot about a hundred

feet from the cliff, and I went into the water with Raibaldi. At sixty feet we came upon some rocks that had tumbled down a gentle slope toward a sandy plain marked with a few meager posidonia. In the spaces between the rocks, where the algae grew like moss, there was an incredible farrago of old bowls lying in heaps. Some of them were still stacked one inside of the other, and quite a few had tumbled down the slope or come to rest on one of the flat rocks. This strange display extended along the coast for about a hundred feet and down the slope for perhaps thirty. If I had to give a figure for the number of bowls, I would say ten thousand.

In the middle of this field of crockery there were some prominent rocks where the bowls were not so numerous. The ship must have foundered there on the crest.

Many of the bowls had already been shifted about by curious divers, and those that were broken or chipped had naturally been left behind. They were all enameled, having for decoration, in the center, a sort of inlaid chrysanthemum of a darker color, or a strange cross.

A group of fish came out from between the boulders, then disappeared among some rocks a little further away. As I watched these fish it occurred to me to explore the crevices between the rocks, which yielded a number of unbroken specimens. The area where the rocks had tumbled down had remained hollow, and the water circulated there at a considerable depth. I swam off in every direction without seeing the slightest trace of the ship itself. With only the bare rocks for support, the hull of the ship had not been preserved by the residue from the disintegration of its upper parts, because this residue had simply filtered down between the rocks instead of forming the usual protective bed. Exposed to the effects of the sea, the hull had crumbled away and dumped its cargo on the rocks. With the passage of time, the bowls had acquired a thick coat of concretions. I brought all my specimens up to the surface in a net bag. Concretions that are still wet can be easily removed with a knife, but if you let them dry they adhere like cement. I've tried putting concreted objects in the water again, but once they've dried it's just too late. The layer of concretions remains hard and fast.

The bowls were enameled in maroon, yellow, buff, cream, green, and white. Most of them were decorated with a chrysanthemum, but there were also crosses and geometric designs which varied from piece to piece. The sizes and shapes varied as well. Some of the bowls had a large horizontal lip that made them look like deckled plates.

I had found fragments of this kind of pottery once before, on a ship of war that was probably Italian and, in the opinion of archaeologists who had examined some silver coins discovered on board, built during the first half of the sixteenth century.

15

The INGOTS

IN 1962, ON THE FERRY between Bandol and Bendor, a nearby island that is the home of the Centre de Plongée, I heard someone mention that the instructors at the diving school had found a number of marked ingots. I questioned a friend of mine at the Centre de Plongée about the ingots and was told that they had been discovered all by themselves at the foot of the lighthouse at Les Magnons. I asked my friend to take the ingots to Benoit at the Borély Museum, but we live in the South and they didn't arrive until the following year.

Benoit was enthusiastic, however, so I decided to inspect the site myself.

On the twenty-fourth of August we made the trip out to Les Magnons in an inflatable rowboat that pitched and tossed so violently I could hardly believe it. We crossed the bay in almost no time at all. At the base of the sloping rock that supports the lighthouse, at a depth of fifty feet, we poked around in the clusters of posidonia that grew all over this landscape I knew so well. Then we went to dig in the gravel around some small rocks and found a few ingots of lead. I pricked my fingers on some sea urchins.

Among other more or less naïve questions, a diver is often asked: "What is the most dangerous animal in the sea?" I always reply, without hesitation, "The sea urchin." The first time I said that, at the beginning of my career, I was just trying to be funny, but now, as the result of long experience with sea urchins, I am convinced that the statement is true. The common sea urchin lives among the rocks and algae, concealing itself as much as possible with a camouflage of dead algae, shells, and gravel, which it holds fast by a multitude of tiny tentacles. Sea urchins like to hide under rocks, and when I think of it I remove them before starting in to work, or even turning over a rock. Their spines cause the formation of small, barely perceptible abscesses on the tips of my fingers, which bother me for months. If I remove the spines from my flesh, which is hard to do, they don't cause abscesses but leave my fingers sore and sensitive for the next few days. As bad as it is, however, the common sea urchin is not quite so treacherous as the kind that lives in the sand. This species, asymmetrically oval and as long as a human finger, has a coat of spines so thin and sharp that I never try to pick one up unless I'm under the water, where the creature is weightless. I often encounter this type of sea urchin in the sand on ancient wrecks.

Around the lighthouse at Les Magnons, however, there is no sand.

Encouraged by the discovery of a few ingots, I removed the stones that bordered the rock. There I found another lead ingot and, under about eight inches of gravel, some small, very thin bars of copper that were from eight to twenty inches long and only slightly oxidized. There wasn't a single piece of pottery that we could use to date the artifacts.

At that point I asked if we might return to Bandol, which we did, this time without all the pitching and tossing. I scratched one of the little bars of copper; the metal underneath the crust proved to be yellow and shiny—an alloy. The bars were easily twisted and didn't look like bronze, which wasn't transported in the form of ingots anyway. One of the instructors thought that they were gold.

The little bars had apparently been poured into a gutter-shaped mold, because one face was flat and the other convex. The ingots of lead, which were crude and poorly formed, seemed to have been made from a hole dug right in the ground. The letters that made up the inscriptions had the kind of angular contours imparted by a chisel. There were short inscriptions in large letters, or signs, and longer ones in small characters that included triangles, circles, and crosses. One sign that resembled a crank handle occurred rather frequently. Some of the characters appeared to be Roman and others Greek, while a few didn't seem to be either. But epigraphy is not my field. Still, I couldn't help feeling that these ingots were more important than any of the amphora ships we had explored.

An archaeologist with a new inscription is like a child with a new toy. Benoit, although not surprised by it, seemed to be very much interested in the connection between the small yellow ingots and those made from lead. Despite the fact that the inscriptions were quite legible, Benoit was unable to identify them. The best he could do was to give me a list of languages in which they were not written. This mystery led me to believe that the ingots were part of a cargo that predated the Roman occupation, and I decided to bring them all up. I thought that an accumulation of inscriptions might give us some clues.

On October 22, I returned to the lighthouse at Les Magnons with my friends from Bendor. Since I was used to operating in the forbidding gloom of the deeper water, I welcomed the chance to work close to the surface, where the bright light from the sun had yet to be dimmed by the sea. The ship carrying the ingots must have struck against the rocks that loomed just below the surface, far away from any warning light. From my house in Portissol I could, during the equinoctial storms, look out and see the big waves crash against the base of the lighthouse. The ingots, buffeted by the shifting masses of water, must have tumbled down the slope, fallen between the rocks, and been buried by the gravel. I dug a small trench from the foot of the slope up to a cavity that began where the rock became vertical. There I gathered up a few ingots of lead and of the yellow metal as well. Had we exhausted the site? In shallow water all the remains of a ship get carried off by the current, and the pottery, of which there is a certain quantity on every vessel, is dispersed throughout the area. At Les Magnons, where there is such a jumble of debris from ancient wrecks, it would have been impossible to find any of the pottery that went with the ingots, especially since we didn't know what era they came from.

For the sake of my conscience I went back again and dug down a bit deeper, but I found fewer ingots.

At the Borély Museum my nineteen lead ingots with inscriptions looked rather sad next to the handsome Roman specimens from other sunken ships. The inscriptions are still a mystery. The ingots weighed from fifteen to sixty pounds, making the total about five hundred fifty pounds of lead, which isn't much for the cargo of a ship. If the ship at Les Magnons was loaded with just metal, it could have spilled some of the ingots at the moment of impact with the rock, then been carried off by the sea to sink elsewhere.

I asked a friend who is a chemist to analyze the yellow metal. It was seventy-nine percent copper and twenty-one percent zinc. There was no lead, nickel, or tin. This mixture was within one percent of the composition given by the Grand Larousse for the ancient species of brass obtained by heating an amalgam of copper granules and zinc oxide, at a time when pure zinc was still unknown. Some people think that the mysterious orichalc was nothing more than bronze made in such a way.

I always bring up the subject of the ingots whenever I meet anyone who might conceivably be able to help me solve the enigma of their origin. Everyone pretends to be interested, but I know they're just being polite. Is the language of the inscriptions one of the pre-Hellenic tongues spoken by the seafaring peoples who, highly skilled in navigation, invaded Asia Minor during the last years of the Hittite empire? Or is it corrupted Greek from the early Byzantine era? Was the ship sailing along the coast toward another destination, or was it heading for a port in France?

16

SHAB RUMI

SHAB RUMI, WHICH IS THE name of a small island in the Red Sea, means "reef of the Christian," a fact that links the island in a rather curious analogy with La Chrétienne, where I learned so much about ancient ships.

It was on this murderously hot coral reef that, in July 1963, we set out to film *Le Monde sans soleil*.

To the men of the *Calypso*, the Red Sea was an old friend. We loved the blue, transparent water, cloudless sky, and complete serenity of this narrow sea on whose coasts the white sand rises toward the buff-colored slopes of purpled mountains. In the winter, the climate is ideal and the warmth of the water good for the skin. There are so many fish that each meal is like a banquet. Even the presence of roving bands of sharks was not enough to dampen our enthusiasm.

The sort of delays that are inevitable on a project of such magnitude had put us behind schedule, and it was already summer when we arrived on location in the heart of the Red Sea, about twenty-five miles from Port Sudan and twelve from the coast. The heat was oppressive. On the long, low atoll, a single beacon was the only thing that rose more than a few feet above the smooth surface of the water. The exterior walls of the reef descended almost vertically to a depth of one thousand feet. In the lagoon it was a hundred feet to the bottom. *Calypso* was anchored outside the reef, and you had to go down more than two hundred feet below the ship to get relief from the heat. To make matters worse, we had to dive in winter gear, because that was what the scenario called for. The heat was just as bad at night, so we filmed from one end of the day to the other, in a state of semiconsciousness brought on by overwork, fatigue, and exposure to the sun.

Simone Cousteau, who was sunburned and suffering from a heat rash as well, was never so gracious. With tireless good humor, she expended an incredible amount of energy helping us out and making things more comfortable.

The Italian freighter *Rosaldo,* which had transported the houses for the village under the sea, was moored in the lagoon, where it had entered by some miracle through a narrow pass. On the afterdeck, across from the *Calypso*, the Italian sailors sat under a tent sipping iced drinks, playing cards, or just enjoying the gentle breeze. Sometimes, just for distraction, they would collect shells and pieces of coral, which they would cement together to fashion little sculptures that were in dubious taste but a delight to their creators. Whenever we had a minute to spare, we would go over to the *Rosaldo* to say hello and to take comfort from the sight of their wanton idleness.

One day, as they went about gathering up the materials for their pastime, they found some amphoras.

The next morning, at about six o'clock, Bébert and I, who had been in the water since two o'clock, had a cup of coffee and went off across the lagoon with the Italians to see what they had found on the other side of the reef. As we approached our destination we had to walk on the coral and pull the dinghy from the *Rosaldo* behind us. We continued slowly making our way until we came upon an amphora lying on its side atop a pillar of coral, like the rocks that cap the chimneys of fairies. The Italians had pried up one just like that the day before. I put on my mask and got down flat on my stomach to have a look around. There were some shards and a handle embedded in the dead coral, which was as hard as cement. I wondered what else might be hidden in the reef. Although I knew that Roman ships had sailed in the Red Sea, I was still surprised and somewhat excited.

The amphora was right at the surface, but the ship it came from couldn't have gone that far. It must have broken up somewhere out to sea, leaving its debris to drift on to the coral table and be welded there by the marine life. It could also have smashed against the sheer outer wall of the reef and sent a few amphoras off toward the shallow water before sinking down so far that only our "diving saucer" could have found it. If the ship had gone down in the lagoon, it would have been covered over with the white sand that was in constant production on the reef. Perhaps there hadn't been any shipwreck at all, and the amphoras had been thrown empty from a passing ship at a moment when the wind was blowing toward the reef.

I wasn't really tempted to look for the wreck because of the sand. On a coral reef, more than on any Mediterranean coast, you learn to appreciate the importance for underwater archaeology of the formation of sand and its behavior in the sea.

The erosion of dead coral by the sea was one source of sand. And schools of enormous fish would butt the clusters of coral with their heads to shake them loose, then grind them up with their teeth for nourishment, spilling out floods of sand at the other end like dump trucks. Parrot fish did likewise. This continual production of sand was a bane to certain animals who had to live in it. There was a sort of pale little lobster that spent all its time going back and forth in its burrow in order to expel the sand, pushing it along with its opened claws like a bulldozer. The frail fish that shared the lobster's hole would follow its movements with interest. Some small, colorless fish would also go in and out of their holes, giving off a stream of sand with each exit. Other animals, however, lived in harmony with the sand of the reef. Pairs of mating *balistes*—fish about the size of a large dorado, with big eyes that they roll like a comedian making a funny face—came to dig their funnel-shaped nests in the sand on the fringes of the reef. One of the spouses would blow water on the gel of newly laid eggs while the other darted about in every direction to ward off predators with designs on the eggs and any divers who happened to be around.

From time to time, excess sand from the reef would cascade into the vertical faults in the exterior walls and form narrow beaches on the deepwater shelves.

To prepare the site for the village under the sea, we constructed a series of terraces twenty-five or thirty feet below the surface, using a sort of plow-shovel rigged up by Bébert and manipulated by means of a cable from the winch on board *Calypso*.

The pure white sand shifted around by our tool formed a slope that ran down toward the point where the reef dropped off and descended almost vertically to the lower depths. As I swam about in the deliciously tepid water, I would, just to see the effect, disturb the equilibrium of the sand by digging a furrow with my hand at the foot of the incline. The entire surface of the sandbank above the furrow would then, by degrees, start to move, and the sand would run for a few seconds to regain its equilibrium.

When we got back to France, Benoit said that our amphora was of the type made on the island of Cos during the Roman era.

This discovery isn't particularly important from the archaeological point of view, but the fact that the amphoras were embedded for two thousand years in a reef formed by marine organisms should be of interest to scientists who study coral and its process of growth.

17

MEDEON

IN AUGUST 1965 COUSTEAU asked me to go to Greece for a week to supervise the installation of a pipe that would convey liquid bauxite wastes from an aluminum factory into the sea.

Calypso had assisted on a project like that once before. The men followed the pipe in their aqualungs down to a hundred sixty feet, then took to the diving saucer. The pipe in Greece was all ready to be sunk.

My two little girls, Juliette and Hélène, were spending the summer with me. I was reluctant to leave them and also worried about getting back, because projects like the laying of a pipe were often subject to unforeseen delays.

Whenever anyone mentions bauxite, I always think of the time that a group of very kind but incompetent people who had formed a committee to oppose the dumping of chemical wastes in the sea met at Sanary to protest against the installation of an underwater pipe that would have spilled bauxite wastes into the bay at Cassis. Having heard about radioactive materials being dumped into the sea, the residents of the area were worried and suspicious. Were they being told the truth?

Bauxite, a red clay that is the source of aluminum, is discharged from the processing plant in the form of an unusable sludge that is annoying but harmless. If it were discharged in Provence, it could destroy the landscape, but it is easily absorbed by the sea.

Along the rugged coast between Marseilles and Cassis there is no road, so I had to go to the site by boat. The massif of white, barren, windswept and sunbaked rock, full of creases and peaks, dropped off sharply toward the sea. Above the waterline there were grottoes that begged to be explored, but were unfortunately out of reach. The few clusters of pines that had survived the periodic, devastating fires in the area stood in nooks where the shape of the rock prevented the mistral from spreading the flames. The cliff plunged straight down into the deep blue water to a depth of a hundred thirty feet, where it gave way to a garden of red coral, gorgonians, and sponges growing in the sand.

At the foot of the cliff a flood of raw sewage from Marseilles emptied into the sea. For miles around the water was thick, gray, oily, and strewn with filthy debris; it gave off an insipid, disgusting odor. A swarm of sea gulls flew rapidly back and forth around the arch at the mouth of the sewer.

I'd like to get all the antibauxite committees, all the defenders of the purity of the sea, on a boat and take them out for a picnic in the waters fed by that sewer.

After a while it ceased to be fashionable to worry about bauxite wastes. Then, with the entire Riviera bottled up by summer traffic, the government announced plans to build a superhighway. Here was a new challenge for the local committees. They would oppose the superhighway—by demanding that it be rerouted through one of the neighboring towns!

I flew to Athens with two of Cousteau's divers. Péchiney had made all the necessary arrangements, and we had a car to take us over the narrow, twisting roads that ran through the mountains overlooking the Gulf of Corinth. As we came down out of the shadow of Mount Parnassos, there wasn't a cloud in the sky, and the sea was a picture-postcard blue.

On the edge of the beach, the village constructed to house the small population of the factory stood waiting to be weathered by time. All that remained of Aspra Spitia was a fisherman's dwelling that had escaped from the bulldozer because of its quaint appearance and typically local color.

The engineers from Péchiney greeted us very cordially. The factory would be ready to function once the pipe was in place. In the meantime the pipe, which was more than seven miles long and still supported by floats, stretched out in the gulf like the line on a sea chart that indicates the best route to take.

I wasn't quite sure about the purpose of our trip, and I had the uneasy feeling that we had come to Greece for nothing. But as I talked with the engineers I began to see that the situation was rather complicated, and I felt better about it. The big steel pipe had incurred some damage which got worse as the pipe was made longer. It was far from certain that the pipe could be laid during the next few days.

We spent our days in the sea, swimming along the length of the interminable, monotonous pipe. Every once in a while we would be startled by a small but intense prick of the skin. It was the season for jellyfish. The burning sensation from their sting lasted for half an hour after each dive, and when the dose was too strong I felt feverish. On land the heat was unbelievable for Europe.

The factory was located in a valley that ran down from the mountains, with some of the buildings right at the edge of the sea, and all of it bathed in a harsh light reflected from the freshly wrought sheets of aluminum. The olive trees around the site and the ruins of a Byzantine chapel had been saved from the bulldozer.

The road we took every day from Aspra Spitia to the factory at Saint-Nicolas passed by the foot of an enormous rock that jutted out over the sea. Every time we went by I would sneak a look at the crumbled walls with their huge stone blocks, which had once supported the Greek city of Medeon. On the way back, if it wasn't too late, we would poke around inside the walls, which were all that remained of the city except for some cisterns carved out of the rock and shaped inside like gigantic jars. Facing the sea on the vertical cliff was a wall, now partially collapsed, that had afforded the cramped village a bit of extra space and made it impossible for anyone to climb to the top. Even in 1965 it was still tempting to throw stones down from the cliff, and it didn't take much effort to imagine victorious enemies heaving the statues of kings and gods into the void just to see what kind of splash they would make when they hit the water. On the terraces and slopes, there were as many potsherds as pebbles.

Just beyond the road, on the side of the mountain, there was a cemetery with a great variety of tombs—sarcophagi in stone and terra-cotta, holes bordered with tiles and stones, and holes without any border at all.

One morning when we arrived at Saint-Nicolas, we found everyone in a state of consternation. During the night the last two miles of the pipe had sunk into the sea, and more of it was expected to follow. The end of our stay in Greece was drawing near; it would have taken another week to describe the condition of the pipe and the damage that was likely to occur in the future.

Mr. Lugagne, the manager of the factory, had invited us to dinner. Lugagne was not the industrial vandal that you might have imagined from the way his factory blighted the admirable landscape of the gulf, but a learned and sensitive man who was very much interested in the city of Medeon. On the day we were to dine with him, we came back from inspecting the pipe a bit early, and we had a good half hour on our hands. I suggested that we might, just for recreation, make a short dive in the waters near the ancient city, about a hundred yards away. My colleagues told me that Bébert had already explored the area and found nothing. The water was turbid, and the cliff continued to descend almost vertically, with only very small steps. About fifty feet down, the rock disappeared into a mound of bare white mud, but the water, while colder, remained clouded. The big blocks that had fallen from the rampart were probably in that mud somewhere. I followed the slope down to ninety feet, but the bottom there was hopelessly barren. When I got back I watched Canoé and Kiki very carefully, out of a sort of childish fear that they might find the statue of the local goddess before I did. The fact that the sand and mud had been accumulating at the foot of the cliff for two thousand years led me to think that it would take heavy equipment to penetrate very far under the surface of the monotonous slope. The other divers did a little digging with their hands, but they just stirred up a lot of mud, without making any inroads into the sediment at all. I thought it better to return to the cliff, where nothing could be concealed.

I zigzagged up and down along the length of the rock, which was full of little holes made by date mussels, and, in a vertical fault, picked up a pewter chalice of the kind you see in churches or antique shops. On a narrow shelf covered with muddy sand, I spied what appeared to be the neck of a small bottle. I came up with a long, pot-bellied copper vase reminiscent of the long-

necked bottles that they use in the Middle East to make narghiles. I shook it in the water in order to wash off its belly, which,
although only slightly crumpled, had a hole in it that looked as if
it could have been made with a spear. It was time to return to the
surface. The other divers came up empty-handed.

The old Greek sailor with the brillant eyes and his young cabin
boy hid my treasures in the launch.

As I walked across the pier, holding the chalice and vase, I was
pursued by an army of excited customs agents all talking at once.
They insisted that I surrender the artifacts to them, but I refused,
saying that they would have to discuss the matter with Lugagne,
whose name carried quite a bit of weight.

At dinner I told Lugagne that I hadn't wanted to arrive with
empty hands, and I offered him my souvenirs of the last religious
cult to flourish in his beloved Medeon. The chalice and vase
looked as if they might have been from the Byzantine era.

Lugagne promised to let me know what became of the artifacts,
and he kept his word.

At Christmastime the news wasn't good:

"The local agent of the archaeological service got wind of your
discoveries, and I had to turn them over to the museum in Thebes
for a determination of their archaeological value. I haven't heard
anything from them yet, but I hope to get the artifacts back,
because I consider them worth having, both as objets d'art and as
souvenirs."

On June 5, 1966, Lugagne wrote again, this time to inform me
that, after many dealings with authorities, he had managed to
recover his souvenirs:

"These objects have a definite value, which is why I had such a
hard time getting them back. According to our experts, the artifacts date from the fourteenth century, and their quality suggests
that they must have been given to the monastery of Osios Loukas
by a great Byzantine lord, perhaps even by the emperor of
Byzantium. How did they come to be at the bottom of the sea?
Nobody knows."

Like a balloon that is inflated under the water to raise a heavy
load, my pride swelled at the idea that, with a slight reversal of
roles, I had performed the same act of generosity as a Byzantine
emperor. And the more I thought about it, the more the comparison with the Basileus seemed to favor me, because when I made
gifts of the chalice and vase they had become antiques as well.

18

The BILGE PUMP

IN OCTOBER 1964, Robert Delattre, who was the director of the diving program at the Yacht Club of Hyères, came to see me at the shipyard in Toulon. He asked me to go out and see something that his team had discovered in ninety feet of water. It was a wreck with a square hole in the center, from which there protruded a pair of lead pipes. They had seen only three or four amphoras.

I doubted that a hatchway like that would have been found on a Roman ship. The sea holds a great many surprises, but, even so, one shouldn't let oneself get carried away.

With the advent of winter, the club's launch was taken out of the water, and I regretted not having gone to Hyères right away.

In the spring I alerted my friend Chevalier. From the earliest days of the government's involvement in underwater archaeology, Chevalier had served against the winds and tides with devotion and self-sacrifice.

On the twelfth of July a group of divers were waiting for us at the entrance to the complex of buildings that had recently sprung up around the new port of Hyères, and they gave us a warm welcome. The launch from the Sauveteurs Bretons took us out to join Delattre and the members of his diving school.

We descended through a surface layer of warm and turbid water, then penetrated another layer that was cold and clear. Below us the landscape was full of thick vegetation, with clusters of posidonia scattered about like bushes, and coarse sand formed from shells and calcified debris. On the plain, there was a long, narrow, slightly elevated mass of rock. In the soil at the end of this rock you could see the square hole. It had a flat growth of concretions around its edges and was full of sand, with two amphora bottoms showing just above the surface. The two lead pipes, after they left the square hole, curved harmoniously and extended out to the edge of the strange wreck. The big rock, regular in shape near the hole but contorted in spots further on, looked to me like a block of concretions formed on an imposing mass of materials, including iron bars, which I recognized from the distinctive appearance of their matrix of stone. All around the long, elevated rock, down at the level of the soil itself, there was a bed of concretions in the oval shape of a ship's deck. My investigations on the site all led me back to the central hatchway, which fascinated me. When Chevalier, beating about in the water with his footfins, forced the sand and dust out of the hole, a rectangular block of lead appeared between the pipes.

The divers from the club, pleased by my unconcealed enthusiasm for their wreck, had tactfully left the site undisturbed. Such an attitude is rare, and I let them know how much I appreciated it.

After dinner at the Yacht Club, during which the young divers filled the air with noisy chatter, they showed us some earthenware jugs decorated with a colored monogram of Christ, Italian ceramics made sometime between 1450 and 1550. They had also found, in the same place, some tin pitchers, a bronze powder case, and a marble ball. All these latter objects were familiar to me, because I was slowly sorting out a whole collection of them on the wreck of a great ship of war. They had been buried among cannons of every caliber, which, in the navies of the sixteenth century, were still loaded at the breech with marble balls and powder cases that, like miniature cannons, were rammed into the breech at the moment of firing. The flames shot out in every direction, reducing the efficiency of the cannon. The mobility of the powder case caused it to wear down rather rapidly. This method of loading a cannon, which even then had been abandoned on land, ceased to be used at sea during the seventeenth century, and it was not until modern times that breech-loaded cannons appeared on the scene again.

The wreck at Hyères left me somewhat perplexed. The pipes no doubt led down to the bilge pump. On the wrecks at Lake Nemi, the Italians had found pumps with two barrels. Before the destruction of the wreck of the *Dramont,* there had been some large lead pipes above the amphoras. In order to perform their function, these pipes had to discharge above the waterline. This seemed to be the case on the wreck at Hyères as well, but I couldn't believe that all of the ship was still there, even when I admitted the possibility that the rapid growth of the posidonia might have protected it. Something wasn't right.

I asked the divers from the club to keep an eye on the wreck, even though there wasn't a single souvenir out where it could be stolen. The few pieces of pottery that were visible being embedded in the stone, it would have taken an act of vandalism to damage the site.

On February 2, 1966, I saw Cousteau at a meeting of the board of directors of the O.F.R.S. When I told him, during a break in the meeting, what I had found at Hyères, he became very enthusiastic. He was quick to grasp the unusual character of the wreck and, to please me, offered his assistance. With Cousteau's help our project was guaranteed to be a success.

I was reluctant to talk about an official excavation until I knew what was there.

Jacques put the *Espadon* at my disposal. On February 14 an icy mistral whitened the sea off Toulon, and at the pier inside the harbor, which was sheltered by a closed roadstead, the *Espadon* bobbed about in the water. For the previous ten days, I had been suffering from a bad case of the flu, with fever and fits of coughing. We agreed among us that we would try again the next day. The *Espadon* would come by before dawn, in order to take advantage of the fact that the mistral is usually in abeyance at night.

Chevalier picked me up at my house in a station wagon belonging to the Ministry of Cultural Affairs. The ministerial seal painted on the car conferred on the occupants a certain air of importance that wasn't always in harmony with the way I was dressed.

We arrived at the harbor in Hyères at the same time as the *Espadon*. In the calm early morning air, the smoke from the ship's stacks rose straight up, and I could hardly believe it. We're always touched to see the weather show signs of benevolence.

The divers, under the direction of Albert Falco, arrived by land with a large amount of equipment. Since our days at Grand Congloué, Bébert, our best diver, had become a valuable technician. He had already made more than three hundred dives at the controls of the "saucer," the ingenious, highly perfected little submarine that was one of the best of the many new tools conceived by Cousteau and his team. In 1960 Bébert had taken me aboard the saucer for a slow descent of the sheer, rocky cliff at Nice. Face down on a mattress, with my eyes glued to the porthole, in darkness so black that the searchlights could hardly penetrate it, my body powerless in this world that was, nevertheless, my own, I was afraid.

The team was made up of Canoé, still just as strong, Raymond Coll, whose reticence was all the more regrettable since he was a keen observer under the water, Bonnici, and Omer. The last three had been among the six "oceanauts" who had participated in Conshelf Three a few months before. Such a deployment of forces seemed to me to be more than I, as an amateur archaeologist, deserved, and I was flattered. But in practice, given the difficulty of performing even the slightest task underwater, there wasn't a man too many, and their wide experience made things easier for me.

The previous night I had gone to spread the word to Delattre and Salvatori. During our visit to the wreck in 1964 I had taken some bearings, but, since we were not tied to a fixed mooring, they were not exact. In the course of our conversations that night I kept asking for details of the landscape that, put together, would help to situate the wreck.

As I guided the *Espadon* the next day, I was secretly rather worried. But the mistral had cleared the air, improving the visibility, and, just as I was beginning to think of the ridicule I would have to endure for having lost the wreck, I recognized one of the landmarks described to me by Delattre and Salvatori.

We dropped anchor, and Canoé and Chevalier went down along the buoy rope. In the turbid water brought in by the storm, the visibility was poor. An error on my part of as little as sixty feet could have caused them to miss the wreck entirely.

To my great relief, however, their air bubbles came straight up, which meant that they were not swimming and must have been right on the wreck.

The buoy had fallen a few yards from the hole. The manometers indicated ninety to ninety-five feet. Although our modern instruments appear to be very precise, it's still not that easy to get an exact measurement of depth. The old, rather impractical sounding lead, which we're just too lazy to use, continues to be the best tool for the job.

Tempted by the unusually warm winter sun and the stillness of the air, I decided to suit up in spite of my illness. I knew that, as I descended the ladder, the cold of the water on my feverish skin would make me feel guilty and apprehensive, but I also knew that I would forget about all that as soon as I had gone down a few yards.

I dove with Bébert. With his extraordinary knowledge of the undersea world, Bébert didn't need me to evaluate the site, and if I chose to go along it was only because I would then, once we got back, be better able to discuss it with him.

The water was quite murky until we neared the bottom, where it became somewhat clearer but only dimly lighted by the rays of the sun filtering down through the turbid mass above. I found the site a bit cleaner than it had been in July. In the south of France, where the trees are always green, the change of seasons, as far as vegetation is concerned, is perhaps more evident under the sea than on land. The hole was carpeted with the dark red ribbons of dead posidonia that had been collected there by the current like dried-up leaves caught in a whirlwind. A pair of lobsters dallied about in their nest, but I decided that there were too many of us on board to make a meal out of just two, so I passed them up. I had brought down my probe, a stainless-steel rod six feet long and five-sixteenths of an inch in diameter, the permanent finish of which reduced friction with the soil to a minimum. The probe, which had become like one of my organs of touch, slid quickly through the mud, but I could feel it grating in the sand, and I had to bear down on it. Here, as is the case in every field of posidonia, the sand mixed in with the slender roots remained loose, and the probe penetrated the soil around the periphery of the wreck without meeting much resistance. I would call Bébert from time to time in order to show him the probe buried up to the hilt just beyond the last concretions. This was possible because the wreck had a definite shape that was unlike anything I had found on other sites, which were just piles of amphoras. At one end of the elevated block the wreck stopped abruptly. Beyond the square hole I ran into a flat, slightly sunken matrix of concretions that also ended all at once. The entire mass of stone in the soil measured roughly sixty by twenty feet, for a ratio of length to width of about three, which, once you take into consideration the probable disappearance of a narrow section at either end, is normal for a Roman ship.

On the flat part of the wreck beyond the square hole, a semicircular, heavily concreted object sticking up from below looked as if it might be metal. Delattre, who had scratched it, said it was bronze. A little further on there was a bare, freshly broken, concave fragment of an amphora embedded in the stone.

In the raised block I noticed, aside from a few local, altogether legitimate disorders, some horizontal cavities that surprised me. They seemed to be due, not to any movement of the cargo, but rather to the disappearance of pieces of wood after the iron had been concreted. The sea, however, isn't the ideal place to think.

Empty-headed and suffering from the cold, I signaled to Bébert that I was going up. Viewed from above, the lead pipes looked as if they weren't quite where they should have been.

The official mission of the *Espadon* that morning was to test a special sounding device designed by Edgerton to graph the different layers of the seabed and any obstacles it might be hiding. The part of the sounder that sent out the electronic impulses was kept submerged alongside the ship at the end of a rigid shaft rigged up for the purpose. The addition of this shaft forced us to maneuver rather slowly. A small gust of wind, or a slight current, would throw us off the course toward the wreck. We passed by the buoy twice before we realized that it had drifted away from its original position. Nylon rope, being elastic and slippery, sometimes escapes from a knot, like a snake, and plays tricks on you. After several passes along the best line of position, we still had found nothing, probably because the graph, designed for the representation of geological phenomena, had been printed on a scale that made it impossible to detect the presence of the wreck.

My stint in the water hadn't exactly improved my health, and I spent the whole night coughing. In the morning, with a strong wind blowing in from the east, there were low clouds and waves crashing over the top of the jetty, so we decided to stay in port. I had learned from experience not to get upset about bad weather.

Taking advantage of the respite, I went to the headquarters of the G.E.R.S., of which I was no longer a member, to see Dr. Barthélémi, who always came to the rescue when I got sick. He said the fever had spread to my lungs and, threatening me with the direst consequences if I were to dive, he filled me up with antibiotics.

I'm always amazed at the way the weather changes in the South. The next day, the wind had subsided and, while the sea was still rather rough, the sky had cleared.

It seemed to us that the square hole was the key to the enigma of the wreck, and we were all agreed that it should be dug out. Bébert directed the work. Bonnici tied one end of the *suceuse* to the wreck and the other to a large metal ball. When we put compressed air into the float to make it lighter, it kept the *suceuse* hanging over the wreck, independent of the changes in the ship's position that are inevitable with a temporary mooring. The *suceuse* was fed by a Junker compressor from which the muffler had been removed so that it sounded like a machine gun, and the afterdeck area was filled with so much noise that our voices were completely drowned out. I took refuge on the mess deck, where Bébert and Bonnici informed me of the latest developments as they changed into their clothes again. The lead block was at an angle in the hole—it must have fallen there with the two amphoras—and it appeared to be larger than we had supposed. The next diver would no doubt get a look at the bilge pump.

But, in fact, he found that the pipes ended at the block of lead, which left us thoroughly confused.

Coll brought up some huge, open lead rings. Lead ages very little in the sea, and the rings could have been part of the sunken ship, although I had seen the same sort of thing on trawlers, of which there were a great many in that area.

The compressor broke down from time to time, giving our ears a rest. During these periods of delightful calm, I would come out of my lair to talk with the divers. They were having trouble manipulating the *suceuse* in the limited space left to them in the hole by the lead block, the pipes, and the parts of amphoras embedded in the walls. With another team I would have been worried.

Bébert extracted from the hole one amphora without a neck and another one that had lost everything but its bottom. Back on board, he put a water gun into the first amphora and flushed out muddy sand full of shells that had been blackened by contact with the iron. I had seen snail shells like that before, and I knew that no octopus was capable of breaking them; the amphora must have been inhabited by a lobster. On the wall of the hole, Bébert had seen some fragments of wood that were the remains of a coffer around which the cargo was stored.

I asked Omer to make a diagram showing the position of the lead block and the pipes, an idea that appealed to him. I advised him to sketch what he saw, then take measurements for the actual dimensions.

When he came back up, his sketch was totally unintelligible, but he had filled the entire drawing board with writing. He had so much trouble making sense out of what he had recorded that he decided, without any prodding from me, that he ought to go down again in the afternoon. His second diagram was perfect. The block of lead was two feet long, two feet wide, and one foot tall. The pipe on the south side of the wreck was set in the lateral face of the block, right near the top, and the pipe on the north had become detached from the opposite face. As he was measuring the block, Omer discovered, to his surprise, that he could put his hand into the part that was resting on the bottom of the hole. What we were dealing with wasn't a block at all, but a bucket turned upside down. The walls of the bucket were about five-sixteenths of an inch thick. There was no pump in sight, but we hadn't reached the bottom of the hole yet.

The site was beginning to make sense to me now. Peter Throckmorton had recently sent me a sketch of a V-shaped bucket with two pipes attached that the Spanish had found on the ancient wreck at Palamòs, in the Formigas Islands. The whole thing took up about fifteen feet. The bucket we had dug up must have been designed to hold the overflow from the bilge pump. It would have been situated on the deck, above the well, with the slightly flared ends of the pipes set into the base of the bulwark. When the ship fell apart, the bucket and pipes had tumbled down into the well, where the bucket had come to rest upside down. The north pipe had slid and moved further from its original position than the pipe on the south. Although I felt, illogically, a bit disappointed, I was now convinced that the top of the wreck didn't correspond to the level of the deck, and that the closely packed cargo of metals occupied only the lower part of the hold. The bucket and the pipes must have fallen from above.

A few rather strong gusts of wind blew across the water, but we weren't concerned, because we were protected by the island of Porquerolles, which was close by. After several unsuccessful attempts to detach an amphora neck that was held fast at the bottom of the hole and would have been extremely valuable for dating the wreck, we got underway.

As we sat around down in the mess talking among ourselves, we were all somewhat preoccupied. Since our days at Grand Congloué, where we had found some rather mysterious pieces of lead, we had encountered a host of other enigmas and had learned to accept the fact that, because we were dealing with antiquities, certain things would have to remain unexplained. But the bucket was such a simple, uncomplicated device that we felt we should be able to explain it. My theory of an overflow for the bilge pump wasn't entirely satisfying, because the same thing could have been accomplished with just a pipe from the pump to the exterior of the ship. Someone suggested that the bucket might have been used for bathing or for washing dishes, but those operations have never been a problem for sailors. Then Bébert remarked that the ship could have been equipped with a noria. That was the answer! Only a noria would have necessitated such a large well right in the middle of the cargo area, or a vessel that could, like the bucket, take in a great volume of water and, oscillating with the movements of the ship, discharge it through the pipes to the port or starboard side, according to the list of the ship as it proceeded under sail. The noria, a simple device that applied the principles of mechanics to the task of drawing water, must have been the first pump. In his excellent book on the excavations at Lake Nemi, Ucelli mentions that vestiges of a noria were found on each of the two ships. He calls the device a *sentinaculum*, i.e., a bilge pump. The lowermost part of a ship is called the *sentina*.

When a sunken amphora ship falls apart, the cargo tumbles out and gets scattered, while the bucket and the pipes, pulled in different directions and broken into pieces, come to rest among the amphoras that fill the central well from which the noria draws its water. We had often found fragments of the pipes; and we had also come across the central well, but, in the muddy water of a salvage project, we had dismissed it as just another accumulation of debris.

Only a systematic excavation in which the position of each amphora is recorded would make it possible to analyze the movements of the amphoras during the compression of the cargo. From such an analysis one could draw some conclusions about the structure of the ship and the position of the well for the noria. But right now, at a time when sunken ships are freely pillaged and the sporadic official excavations are in the nature of salvage operations on sites that have been profoundly modified by looters, it is impossible to form an opinion on the frequency of this particular type of bilge pump.

The wreck that we had been exploring was unusual in that the cargo had formed a solid block before the collapse of the hull. One could also suppose that the cargo, being closely packed and neatly stowed in the bottom of the hold, had remained in place when the wood collapsed and had become welded together afterward. The hull had not benefited from the shelter of a scattered cargo, and its walls must have disappeared before the natural rise of the soil had been sufficient to protect them, but the lower part would have survived.

I wished that I could have seen the junction of the well and the hull, so that I would be able to recognize it on wrecks that were poorly preserved.

Up to that time, all the antique iron objects brought up from the bottom of the sea had been found by themselves or among other, different, materials. I wondered what happened inside a mass of iron weighing two or three tons. What form would the metal be in? I didn't dare dig into the wreck to see.

I estimated the total length of the ship to be a minimum of seventy-three feet, because the extremities went at least six feet beyond the cargo.

The next morning the weather was fine, and Delattre and Salvatori got underway with us. I was eager to have them participate in our study of their wreck.

Our divers did such good work and understood my problems so well that my task was greatly simplified, and I began to think that I wouldn't go into the water myself—unless it was necessary. But I didn't like that idea, because I really need to have contact in order to get some sense of the way a wreck is formed and of how far it extends under the soil. A knowledge of the landscape helps to define problems, and, since no one can really describe the appearance of the concretions, you have to have broken a great many before you can learn anything from them.

The antibiotics were keeping my fever under control, so I decided to take a tour of the site and think about the conclusions I had drawn. I might have gone beyond my evidence.

As I went down through the turbid water the light faded quickly, and when I got to the bottom it was all yellow like a large city at dawn; but once my eyes adjusted to the conditions I could pick out the smallest details. After having seen so many chaotic heaps of amphoras, I was delighted with the hole, which was clean, neat, and had reached a depth of two and a half feet. A good piece of work! The vertical walls were studded with a quite regular array of nodules about the size of a fist, which must have formed on the ends of the iron bars. It would have been difficult, in the black, hardened sand, to dig any deeper. Although I had already made numerous photographs of the site, I wanted to get some of the well after it had been dug out.

I always use Tri-X film, because its high sensitivity is ideal for shooting under water, and using the same film simplifies the choice of camera adjustments. I usually set the shutter speed at 1/125 of a second, but, even then, the huge shutter release on the "Calypsophot" sometimes causes the pictures to come out blurred. I wasn't very far below the surface and the water near the bottom was clear, so I thought I would have enough light. Just to be sure, however, I set the shutter speed at 1/60 of a second and the aperture at f/35, the maximum. My photographs turned out so badly underexposed that they were useless.

I went looking for pottery that could be used to date the ship and saw a few pieces embedded in the stone. They proved to be rather untypical ship's crockery. Archaeologists know everything there is to know about fancy china, but simple, everyday crockery has yet to be studied. The crockery was concentrated at the beginning of the raised block, in the vicinity of the hole, which suggests that the galley was right up above. Near a little niche inhabited by a lobster, I noticed the rim of a plate sticking up out of the stone. When I cut in around the plate with my axhammer, it gave off a black liquid, which indicated the presence of corroded iron. The concretions were so hard that I got discouraged; the lobster, meanwhile, hadn't moved an inch. Everywhere I struck with the hammer I got the same little black cloud.

The other divers had uncovered a pair of lead ingots which were now quite visible and likely to attract the attention of looters; but I didn't have time to extract them to see if they were marked. I also saw some recently broken slabs of iron with a square, empty space inside.

When I put my probe, at an angle, into the soil under the edge of the wreck, it encountered a hard wall for about a foot, then penetrated under the cargo, which did indeed have the shape of a hull. By this time I was so cold that I couldn't concentrate on anything, and I began to lose interest in the wreck. It was time to go back up to the surface.

We subsequently changed the location of the *suceuse* so that we could dig in the soil against the side of the wreck. With the constant din from the Junker compressor assaulting our ears, my colleagues devoted six dives to this work, but it was hopeless. In the mixture of sand and roots, the *suceuse* was practically useless; the nozzle penetrated, but made a hole that was too narrow for our purposes. It was true, as I had concluded after testing the soil with my probe, that the vegetation had existed before the sinking of the ship.

The wreck from the Bronze Age had shown that it is impossible for divers to dissect a sunken ship so thoroughly concreted as the one we were confronted with. The recovery of a ship like that is the sort of job that can only be done by a salvage contractor. He would have to dig a trench around the perimeter of the wreck with a powerful dredge, then refloat the ship, either all at once or in parts, and turn it over to the experts.

As Dalattre and Salvatori were suiting up, I told them to bring back some lobsters so that they wouldn't have to go home empty-handed. When they surfaced, with the lobsters, they were ecstatic. "You were right," they said, "it really is the wreck of a ship." They had found it freer of vegetation, but that wasn't any doing of ours, because winter is the off season for algae.

Preoccupied with dating the wreck, I asked that the amphora neck at the bottom of the well be extracted before the *suceuse* was removed. But all the divers brought back were vague potsherds. Delattre was sorry to see our labors coming to an end, and he asked permission for Salvatori to bring up the bronze ring. As it happened the ring broke in his hands, but even someone as strong as Salvatori would have had a hard time extracting a bronze ring of that size from such tenacious concretions.

The following day, a Saturday, the east wind was raging once again. The *Espadon* had a schedule to meet, and the men liked the idea of spending Sunday on land, so the ship returned to Marseilles.

On Monday I went to the Borély Museum. Bouis, to his surprise, had found nothing but sulfur in the blackened contents of the concretions.

I couldn't help thinking about the cargo on the wreck at Hyères, because it was so unusual; no one had ever seen such a quantity of iron from the Roman era. Suddenly, my thoughts turned to warfare. All the square bars, I said to myself, were probably destined to be forged into ballista shafts, lances, and javelins by the Roman soldiers, who were blacksmiths as well as farmers. I even went so far as to attribute the curious cavities in the central block to the disappearance of the wooden parts of weapons that had been dismantled for shipment.

I found Benoit engrossed in the writing of a new book. To pedestrians hurrying by outside, the light in his window stood out conspicuously against the darkness that enveloped the rest of the huge building. Benoit said that the amphora belly was most likely from the first century B.C.—the century of the Gallic Wars. I told him how I was tempted to invoke the needs of Caesar's army as the explanation for such a large shipment of iron.

As time went by, I realized that I had concentrated too much on the bilge pump, to the detriment of the cargo. A nagging doubt made me wonder if the compacted mass in the soil was really composed of iron bars. My instincts could have betrayed me.

On June 11, Cousteau lent me the *Espadon* once again. The distant coast was obscured by a fair-weather fog, but I had, fortunately, also taken some bearings on the island of Porquerolles, which was still visible through the haze.

On the bottom the light was stronger and threw the details of the landscape into relief; the thermal cycle that ordains the seasons under the water was a bit behind itself, with the result that the usual clusters of algae had yet to invade the wreck. Some dead posidonia had accumulated in the well, but the wreck hadn't been touched. On the raised block, toward the end opposite the well, I noticed some fragments of tile that were probably traces of the covered shelter located, according to ancient iconography, at the stern. I wanted to remove a large sample of the ship's flank, some iron bars that had fallen from the raised block, and one of the ingots. I started in to work with a hammer and chisel. I had also brought a jumper bar, but that was a crude tool and, as far as I was concerned, only a last resort. Coll, who cared very little for the subtleties of archaeology, found the bar quite efficacious. It didn't take us very long to get our samples. Underneath the crust of the main body of the cargo, which was very hard but not too thick, there was a black, spongy substance that had once been iron. I was pleased to see clear indications that the iron had been in bars, because I had been worried that it might turn out to be just ore. The sides of these bars measured about two inches, while the sides of the bars in the raised block measured a little more than an inch. The ingot, which was shaped like a flattened ellipse, was nine inches wide and twenty-two inches long, with, on the surface, concretions and corroded iron that could have been hiding some markings. Coll brought up a welter of bars that had fallen from the raised block. In among the bars there was an amphora shard, as well as a vaguely cylindrical piece of wood and a lead cap about four inches in diameter.

After dinner I went down again to take some photographs and to have a last look around. In a hole situated toward the end of the raised block where I had seen the fragments of tile, I found the remains of an earthenware pot. When I stuck my hand into the muddy soil at the bottom of this circular hole, I came up with sand and a few shells. I thought this cavity might have been left by a mast that went down through the cargo area. My arm was too short to reach down any further, but I put in the jumper bar and, at two and a half feet, encountered hard sand like that at the bottom of the noria well. The circular hole appeared to be too close to the end of the wreck to have contained the foot of the mainmast. Ancient ships did have a small mast up forward, the ancestor of our bowsprit, but the presence of the tiles seemed to indicate that I was back aft.

The other divers had installed a hauling line and were busy plugging up the noria well with sacks which, on the previous day, they had filled with sand from the beach. I hoped in this way to protect the bucket from the onslaughts of the summer. The shadowy forms of the divers were engulfed in a yellow cloud like those stirred up by sandstorms in the desert.

With the jumper bar lying right next to the second ingot, I

couldn't resist the temptation, so I pried the ingot loose, tied it to the hauling line, and sent it up to the surface. It was cleaner than the first one and had an inscription on its flat face. One of the faces had, apparently by design, been given the shape of a dish. We thought these pieces of lead might have served as counterweights for some sort of weapon, but they showed no evidence of having been attached to anything.

Two days later I went to the museum with Chevalier. Bouis was not in his little attic laboratory, so we made use of it ourselves. Chevalier put one of the ingots into the sink and filled it with hydrochloric acid, while I worked at removing the concretions from the lead cap, on which there were still some remains of a corroded iron bar. After a while a piece of copper band appeared under the stone, which I thought was rather strange. As I continued my cleaning, I realized that what I had was the butt end of a cast-iron navy shell casing, perfectly preserved right down to the scratches made on the band by the rifling in the cannon bore. The area around the wreck had been used for many years as a firing range, and the bottom there was strewn with shells. There was a great big one in plain view right on the wreck itself.

As Chevalier brushed and rinsed the ingot in the sink, which was filled with frothy suds, two letters of an inscription appeared on the flat face. Viewed from one direction they looked every bit like Roman characters. Even so, when we turned the ingot around they read MN, which could have been an abbreviation for "Marine Nationale." A little further on some more letters, CVM, emerged from the dirty suds. All we could think of for that was "Cercle de voile militaire" ("Military Sailing Club"). We looked at each other in bewilderment. our minds full of doubt. We thought that the ingots might in reality be the two halves of the bulb keel of a small sailing vessel. We began to have doubts about the wreck itself, and I had to come up with some solid arguments to assure myself of its authenticity. When struck with the hammer the metal rang true, so it wasn't lead; yet it was quite heavy, and its surface was shiny, with iridescent, leaflike patches similar to those that appear on freshly galvanized tin. The other ingot had the same inscription; their weights were sixty and seventy pounds.

We had found the ingots touching each other, buried under a Roman bar, the iron from which had formed a crust on the ingots that had been practically stabilized for many centuries.

We consulted a work on Latin inscriptions, and under MN was written "metalla nova." I liked that as a name for the strange metal of the ingots.

When I entrusted a small sample of the metal to my friend the chemist, he found it to be pure tin. Tin, which is mixed with copper to make bronze, had been used in the form of oxide since the early ancient period and was common as a metal during the Roman era, so much so, in fact, that I wondered if MN really did stand for "metalla nova."

19

IN the
MALDIVE ISLANDS

IN MARCH 1967 WE EXPLORED the Maldive Islands with the
Calypso. On the fringes of the reefs the coral was thick and, in
places, superabundant. The tropical fish, of which there were a
great variety, seldom strayed from the channels swept by the
tidal currents. A few of the species were new to us.

The archipelago begins about three hundred thirty miles from
India and, like a wide ribbon, extends from north to south for
almost six hundred miles, right down to the equator. Its eight
thousand little islands, tiny clusters of coconut palms and exotic
vegetation on a base of white sand projecting from the sea, are
grouped in huge atolls ringed by barriers of coral that descend
almost vertically to the lower depths. The largest of these
islands—or, rather, the least small—are inhabited by natives who
emigrated from Ceylon at the beginning of the Christian era and
now number about a hundred thousand. These friendly, timid,
selfless people, whose skin is black or dark brown, have been
protected by the ocean from the effects of tourism and from
foreign influences. They live rather poorly on fish and coconuts;

often, the natives on one island will invite those from a neighboring island to dine with them and be entertained by music played on drums with heads made from ray skins.

Their only building stones are blocks of coral removed from the shallow water and used for walls, houses, jetties, sculptured funeral columns, and anchors.

Their sailing ships, which are long, thin, and low in the water, are manned by a crew of about ten. They look quite a bit like those used by the Vikings and by the Mediterranean peoples of the pre-Hellenic era, except for the fact that their sails are triangular instead of square.

The prows of the ships, which are high and curve back toward the stern, grow wider at the end like the crest of a helmet. They're impressive to see when the ship is under sail, but they must be impractical in the congested little harbor at Male, the capital, because they are then removed and hung up with some of the other implements.

Calypso had dropped anchor off the island of Alifuri. On the beach, under the first coconut trees, there was a row of shelters built from palms. Inside the shelters, a number of carpenters were at work on ships in various stages of construction.

When I saw that the interior of one of the hulls was smooth and bare, it startled me, but I wasn't quite sure why.

The garboard strakes were attached by long wooden dowels that still protruded from the underside of the keel. The planks of the hull were joined to one another by dowels driven into their edges. Then it hit me—that was the way ancient ships were built! The only difference was that these modern carpenters used round dowels instead of the flat tongues which, although they involved considerable labor, were preferred by the ancients.

I tried to get my colleagues from the *Calypso* to share my excitement, but I had to admit that, if the moment was intense for me, it was because I had been prepared for it over a long period of time.

The construction of a ship today begins with its skeleton—the keel, the stem- and sternposts, and ribs—and only when that is completed are the hull planks attached. We are so accustomed to this way of proceeding that we are inclined to think it derives from the laws of nature. At La Chrétienne, however, I had seen a line on the hull marking the place for a rib, which seemed to me to indicate that, in ancient times, the hull was assembled before receiving the ribs, according to the method called "shell first" by the English.

I returned to the island whenever I could.

The keel, the stem, and the stern are all made from mangrove, which is the hardest wood to be found on the islands. The hull planks are cut from the trunks of coconut trees. To make the joints fit as closely as possible, they rub the edge of the plank that is in place with charcoal, then put the following one on top of it to show the points of contact, which are then planed down until the two planks come together perfectly.

The caulking is made from thin slivers cut out of the fibrous husk of the coconut, which is rarely seen in Europe. They put the caulking in place before tightening up the joints, but they claim that the joints are so well made that the ship would be watertight without any caulking at all.

Each succeeding plank is first pierced with holes and then hammered onto dowels that protrude from the previous plank. The holes for the dowels are made with a drill operated by two men pulling by turns on opposite ends of a rope. In the Persian Gulf the same kind of drill is manipulated by a single man using a bow. The planks themselves are cut out with hatchets and adzes.

When the bare hull is finished, they place frames, which are stiffened by three or four horizontal rails cross-braced vertically in quincunxes, between two blocks attached to the inside of the planking. These "perforated frames" reach up to where we would put a deck, and the ship's company can walk on them. The slender ribs are subsequently placed between the frames. They are cut to fit, then adjusted and attached with dowels. On Roman ships, a copper nail was also driven into each dowel.

Each of the frames has a thick part at the base, with a semicircular recess above the keel to allow for the passage of bilge water. This recess was triangular on Roman ships.

The mast, which is cut from the wood of the coconut tree and can be folded down in the direction of the stern, sits in a step carved out of a frame that is stronger than the others. In this arrangement the base of the mast step lies across the axis of the ship, but the ship is relatively small and the mast doesn't create any considerable stress.

A strong guardrail, consisting of a massive hardwood gunwale over a heavy coconut-wood stringer rounded off in the interior of the ship, strengthens the cohesion of the hull. This feature of the ship's construction reminded me of the only large piece of wood that had been seen in Turkey on the wreck from the Bronze Age. Judging from its location on the site, it must have been situated on the upper part of the hull. According to some representations, Roman ships were also reinforced with a guardrail.

In the Maldives, a ship under construction is supported by logs fixed vertically in the ground. Six men work on it all day long for a month. They don't use any gauges or other tools of measurement, relying entirely on the eye of the carpenter to achieve the symmetry and perfect elegance that they give to the hull. The wood is coated with shark or turtle oil.

The anchor, which is made from coral, just as primitive anchors were made from stone, consists of a head cut from a heavy species in the shape of a skullcap and hafted to a branch that grows thicker or has a small fork at one end.

I have been told that these ships are quite different from the barks constructed by the natives of Ceylon, and that the hulls of those built in the Laccadives, which lie between India and the Maldives, are sewn like the hulls of some primitive ships.

Since the earliest civilizations sprang up along the Persian Gulf and the Indian Ocean, it is quite possible that the first genuine sailing ships plied their waters. Unfortunately, we have yet to find the remains of any ancient ship from that area, so we have nothing to compare their modern vessels to except ancient ships from the Mediterranean region.

20

ANCIENT SHIPS

IT SEEMS ILLOGICAL THAT scholars today should know so much about classical antiquity and so little about the ships that were the instruments of its opulence.

Before the recent advances in the technology of diving, the study of ancient ships was restricted to the interpretation of texts and of iconography.

The galley used in combat, or long ship, has often inspired writers and artists by the grandeur of its destiny and the elegance of its lines. Nevertheless, the best available source of information is still the portion of the archives from the Athens shipyard that was engraved on marble plaques and found in a Roman or Byzantine sewer in Piraeus. The commercial, or round ship, which was a modest, hardworking vessel, and a prime factor in the establishment and development of economic and cultural relations, has remained in the dark, so that we have very little information about it.

Many ancient writings have come down to us through scholiasts and lexicographers who knew nothing about naval sci-

172

ence. Numerous errors and interpolations have found their way into the texts.

Artists have always been attracted by the elegance and decorative value of ships, which they have reproduced on coins, medals, seals, vases, frescoes, mosaics, bas-reliefs, and columns.

Prehistoric man, who was even then haunted by moral anxieties of a religious nature, has left us, from one period of great productivity, some surprisingly realistic mystical portraits of living beings. After that his painting evolved toward a sort of symbolic writing in which men and animals were nothing but conventional signs. The Egyptians, with a certain kind of statuary, the Greeks, and other peoples have portrayed living beings with realism while, at the same time, exalting their beauty. The representation of objects, on the other hand, has long been of a decorative nature, marked by symbolism or by a concern with lines, to the detriment of veracity. And, finally, the reproduction of a ship on a coin or vase necessarily involves some sacrifice of proportion and detail.

A conventional image of ships became established and, having been modified in accordance with contemporary tastes, was perpetuated from one generation to another; it is often difficult to separate the evolution of artistic style from that of ships.

The sea is a very special domain, and sailors have reason to think that landsmen don't really know too much about ships. Archaeologists, without the instincts of the sailor to guide them, have approached ships as if they were buried edifices. Seafaring men interested in ancient ships have lacked the special training that enables archaeologists to weigh the value of sources, or to interpret them as the work of serious creative artists. Such men have often fallen victim to a theory and been led to simply search for any sort of argument that might confirm their personal opinion. Others have been content to repeat the opinions of their predecessors, or to make a partial effort to contradict them.

The irritating problem of the number and disposition of the oars on a galley has given rise to many a half-baked theory. People with fertile imaginations have drawn arguments from such sources as the chapter in Homer in which Ulysses constructs a ship to take him off the island of Calypso, the famous account of Saint Paul's shipwreck written by his companion Luke, and Athenaeus's writings about an age that he was far from having known. The laborious dissections performed on these texts and the tortures inflicted upon each word are sadly reminiscent of the interrogations that have been a feature of certain political trials.

The archaeologist excavates abandoned cities that were already dead before being covered over by the soil. He digs into necropolises and tries to reconstruct the lives of the deceased from his examination of their tombs; but when it comes to describing the life of the Romans, he is content to base himself on the miraculously preserved ruins of Pompeii, which, aside from Herculaneum, is the only city to have been buried while still inhabited. The miracle of Pompeii, although highly extraordinary on land, was repeated every time a ship sank.

A single ancient ship carried a sampling of objects from its era that it would take more than a lifetime of patience to find, as debris, in the soil of abandoned cities. In the course of its journey from port to port, a ship would take on products from a number of different countries. To retrace, on land, a commercial route with such an abundance of details would be a prodigious task.

A ship that has sunk has deposited a slice of life on the bottom of the sea, without the sort of confusions about time and space that occur on the sites of cities, which are always being rebuilt. A sunken ship is not a puzzle.

Enormous piles of the amphoras used in the Roman wine trade are still lying on the bottom of the sea, making it possible for us to locate the wrecks of the ships that carried them. The astonishing publicity given to the amphoras has caused them to be associated in the mind of the public with ancient wrecks.

The ships that transported wine no doubt came back loaded with other produce, but such putrescible cargoes have simply disintegrated. I imagine that some of the ships that bore perishable cargoes are still extant, but difficult to detect.

We have uncovered many different kinds of cargoes on the bottom of the sea. The two famous Roman ships discovered and excavated at the beginning of this century, at Antikythera and Mahdia, had been transporting works of art. Numerous wrecks loaded with tiles have been discovered in the Mediterranean. There have also been cargoes of sarcophagi, blocks of marble, millstones, architectural elements, dishes, mineral ore, copper ingots, lead ingots, and alloys. Wrecks from the Middle Ages or from the Renaissance, which are distinguished by their enormous anchors or by their cannons, are still little known to the public.

In addition to the cargo, a wreck is usually full of articles from the daily life of the sailors, who quite often had no other place to live and kept the things they were attached to—souvenirs from various ports of call or family heirlooms—on board the ship. Like a house, a ship was equipped with tableware, tools, other implements, and everything that was necessary to sustain life on board for long periods of time.

Some partial excavations have shown us that sunken ships can yield surprising information and that the lower part of a hull is usually well preserved. This latter fact has encouraged us to think that we might someday find ships that have come to rest on one side or, although it is rather unlikely, upside down. If we did, we would have the opportunity to see how the upper parts of an ancient ship were made. We might even find whole ships buried intact in loose mud; or see, lying in the soil under yards of sediment, the rigging of a ship that has come to rest on its side. Once we have seen a galley of the type that was used in combat, we will know what its remains look like and will be able to find others.

Underwater archaeology has yet to give us an understanding of the ancient ship as a whole, but it has uncovered important details of construction and raised questions that will be answered by future excavations.

The planking, which is comprised of heavy boards joined together and attached to the ribs, is the watertight skin of the ship. Today's shipbuilders simply put the boards together and, using a special chisel, caulk the interstices with oakum. The swelling of the wood creates a watertight joint.

We have examined wrecks varying in date from the third century B.C. up to the beginning of the fourth century A.D. The planking on these ships was always put together with mortise-and-tenon joints. A multitude of tongues made from a supple and resilient wood were set into the edges of the planks and locked in place with wooden dowels. Once the planks were attached to one another in this way, they couldn't separate or become disjointed by warpage. They formed a turtlelike shell that gave a ship great solidity and allowed a sampling of wood that seems to us to be a bit meager. The joints were fitted with such precision that they are still, after two thousand years in the sea, hardly visible. The carpentry required by this method of construction is unthinkable for us because of the high cost of labor. The staggering amount of manual labor that the ancients devoted to the various things they made is, for me, the most amazing thing about them. The tenon-and-mortise technique seems to go back to very early times, and we still don't know when it was abandoned. When George Bass, in Turkey, excavated a Byzantine wreck judged from gold coins to belong to the first half of the seventh century A.D., he found that the upper part of the hull had been put together by modern methods, whereas the rest had been constructed in the classical way, with tenons and mortises. The nails were made of iron and driven directly into the wood; those on older ships were copper and were driven into dowels, which took more work. The Byzantine ship was probably built during a period of transition.

The technique of holding the planking together with tongues makes it hard to imagine how the hull could be repaired in the same fashion. In the report on the ship from the Roman era discovered in London in 1910 there is a sketch of a section that appears to me to be a repair on the hull. The edges of the old planks have been stepped to fit together with the edges of the new ones, which are also stepped, and the joints have been reinforced in the interior by an additional plank.

We have found evidence of the coexistence, at various times in history, of ships that were plated with lead to protect them from shipworms and ships that had no such plating. The reason for this is unclear; it could have been a question of economy, of local customs, or of some technical consideration that has so far escaped us.

Only a few specialists concern themselves with the details of the construction of ancient ships, and we haven't as yet brought up enough information from the sea to satisfy them. Moreover, any general speculation in this area could be made premature and at once outdated if someone were to discover and carefully examine an entire, well-preserved hull. I believe that such an eventuality is both possible and imminent.

Benoit has had the courage to approach the problem posed by the fact that some ships had pointed hulls with half frames, floor timbers, and no keelson, while others had flat hulls, frames that were all alike, and a keelson. This difference is rather perplexing and needs to be explained. I have seen some hulls that were pointed and others that were flat. Strictly speaking, I should say that I have only glimpsed them, because I've never actually seen more than a small part of any particular hull. It may be that several types of naval construction coexisted or succeeded one another in the various geographical areas encompassed by the Roman Empire. On the other hand, the structure of a ship is complex and the shape of the hull varies from one point on its axis to another. According to pictorial representations, ancient ships grew narrow at the ends, and it's not surprising that a ship should have a hull that is flat in the center and pointed at either end. But we have, so far, never been able to say about any of the pieces of hull we have uncovered that it definitely came from one or another part of a ship.

In the trench we dug across the axis of the *Dramont,* the bottom of the ship was flat, with identical frames and no keelson. From the sand in the side of this trench I extracted what I believe to be a piece of the mast step. On the underside there were some small notches and also some full-sized recesses, indicating an alternation of half frames and frames with triangular floor timbers. Were there two different techniques corresponding to the flat and pointed parts of the same hull? All our previous excavations had been conducted rather hurriedly, so it was hard to tell, but the wreck of the *Dramont* made me wonder.

In the same trench, the hull on one side of the ship rose slightly at a certain distance from the keel and had been flattened on the other side. A hull is made to be supported at every point by the uniform density of the water. When a ship comes to rest on soil that it can't sink into, some parts of the hull are unsupported and are liable to be deformed under the weight of the cargo. The hull can break right off near the keel, as was the case at Mahdia, or just become slightly detached from the frames, which is what happened at La Chrétienne. If the hull is almost flat, it can get even flatter as the wood grows soft. Only a minute examination of an entire hull, like those recovered from Lake Nemi, would enable us to sort out the various deformations and to know exactly what the shape of the hull was before the sinking of the ship.

Despite these considerations, I believe that there were in ancient times, just as there are today, some ships that were flatter than others.

The two ships exposed by the draining of Lake Nemi in 1928 were, respectively, two hundred forty feet long by eighty feet wide and two hundred thirty-four feet long by sixty-six feet wide. They have been attributed, without conclusive proof, to the emperor Caligula, who reigned from 37 to 41 A.D, and are supposed to have been floating casinos that had nothing in common with ships built to sail the high seas. But why, then, were their hulls sheathed in lead, which would have been unnecessary in a lake devoid of shipworms? The lead plates were fastened beginning at the stern, so that the overlapping would be in the right direction with respect to the ship's course through the water. This practice, it should be noted, provides a valuable method of distinguishing the bow from the stern on wrecks plated with lead.

The wrecks discovered since then by divers have had the same kind of structure as the ships at Lake Nemi. We think we might someday find ships in the sea as big as those at Lake Nemi. And that wouldn't be surprising, since the Romans were capable of conceiving public buildings on the colossal scale of the Baths of Caracalla.

Athenaeus speaks from hearsay of a gigantic ship constructed by Hiero II of Syracuse and used at Alexandria during the reign of Ptolemy II. More credible is Lucian's description of the merchant ship *Isis*, which was a hundred seventy-five feet long and brought wheat back from Egypt during the second century A.D.

The members of the Club d'Etudes Sous-marines of Tunisia calculate that the ship at Mahdia was a hundred feet long. I think that the ship at Grand Congloué was longer than a hundred feet, and that the one at Albenga was even larger. We know of many Roman ships that were smaller, but a length of a hundred feet was quite common.

Not until the advent of ships made from iron were there any that exceeded the size of those found in Lake Nemi.

It has been estimated that the *Santa Maria*, with which Columbus discovered America in 1492, had a total length of eighty feet, for a keel of fifty-six feet and a width of twenty-six feet. The *Vasa* of King Gustavus Adolphus II of Sweden, which sank in 1628 and was brilliantly refloated by the Swedish in 1961, had a total length of a hundred eighty-eight feet and a maximum width of thirty-nine feet. The *Victory*, commanded by Nelson at the Battle of Trafalgar in 1805, carried a hundred two cannons and eight hundred fifty men. It had a total length of two hundred twenty-eight feet, for a keel of a hundred fifty-two feet and a maximum width of fifty-two feet. The English clipper *Cutty Sark*, which was launched in 1869 and is now on display in a drydock at Greenwich, is two hundred fifteen feet long and thirty-six feet wide.

21

AMPHORAS

AN AMPHORA IS AN EARTHENWARE vessel with a neck made rather narrow so that it could be stoppered. It had a vertical handle on either side and a pointed bottom that sometimes had a knob at the end. Although amphoras seem to us to be cumbersome and hard to manage, they were widely used. To pour out the contents, a person would put one hand on the handle and the other on the pointed end. The ancients had to decide whether to employ a vessel with a flat bottom, which would stand up by itself, or the amphora, whose pointed end could serve as a grip. For more than a thousand years the civilized world preferred the latter solution.

In private homes and in the shops of merchants, there were wooden or earthenware stands built to hold amphoras. In warehouses they were stuck in the sand or leaned against the wall, then against one another. In the holds of ships they were stored vertically and kept in place by the sides of the hull. The pointed ends of the second layer were wedged between the necks of the first, and so on. We have often seen three layers of them. At Grand

Congloué there were more, but a deck or between decks separated the layers into two groups.

Earthenware, unless it is varnished, is porous. Amphoras, to make them watertight, were coated on the inside with a pitch made from the resin of certain trees—terebinth, lentiscus, cypress —and noted for the pleasant taste it imparted to the wine. The remains of this pitch are well preserved in the amphoras found in the sea. Even now the Greeks continue to put resin in their wine to give it the flavor they prefer, and which always surprises us at first.

The ancients used amphoras to hold all sorts of liquid, pasty, or solid foodstuffs, including water, wine, garum, pitch, olives, grains, and pickled fish.

Filled amphoras were brought to the home by foreign tradesmen, and they accumulated there in the same way that bottles accumulate in homes today. People used them again for putting up preserves or just to store provisions that they planned to consume right away. Amphoras also served as urns for the ashes of the dead and could be cut in half to make coffins for children. Sometimes the pointed ends were broken off so that the jars could be strung together to form a conduit. A long, thin variety of amphora was even utilized to support the roof on houses built during the Later Roman Empire.

Fragments of these jars accumulated in dumps, as do our broken bottles and the new plastic containers.

Archaeologists on land rarely find the stoppers that bore the mark of the wine merchant, because they had to be destroyed before the wine could be poured; on sunken ships, however, they are always in good supply.

Many of the amphoras that we find have been marked before firing with the seal of the potter, on the handle or neck, and these marks have greatly facilitated the study of such pottery. Virginia Grace, the prominent American specialist, says in her little book *Amphoras and the Ancient Wine Trade* that forty thousand marked handles have been found in Athens, and that the count has already reached more than ninety thousand at Alexandria.

22

The
FORMATION
of a WRECK

THROUGHOUT THE COURSE OF my career as a diver, I have been
fascinated by sunken ships, whether ancient, medieval, or modern. When a ship is resting on the bottom, you view it in a different light and, observing the changes it has undergone, gain a
better understanding of the sea.

In the beginning I thought of sunken ships, which are all as-
similated by the sea, as just a particular aspect of the new world I
was discovering. Little by little, however, they became familiar
to me, and I tried, in a gradual way, to understand them.

At a time when underwater archaeology didn't exist, or was just
taking its first tentative steps, I participated in disorderly salvage
operations that can hardly be characterized as excavations, and
visited wrecks from various eras without having any means of
investigating them. It wasn't easy to learn about sunken ships
from their external appearance alone. The analysis of amphoras
taught me a great deal.

Many objects that wind up in the sea disintegrate or take on a
natural form and aspect that conceal them from a diver. But the
sea has been unable to hide all its amphoras.

Not every ship, of course, had a cargo of amphoras, but they all had a certain number on board for the storage of provisions to be consumed en route.

For several centuries around the beginning of the Christian era, the Mediterranean was the center of an extensive commerce in wines produced, for the most part, in Greece and Italy. The hold of a wine ship was completely filled with a cargo of amphoras, which, as an aggregate, assumed the shape of the hull. After a shipwreck, the amphoras would spread out in a more or less organized disorder, in accordance with the topography of the bottom and the manner in which the hull fell apart.

An amphora can be broken by a moderate impact, and each one serves as a strength gauge, indicating by the size and disposition of its fragments the nature and intensity of the stresses or shocks endured by the different parts of the cargo. The analysis of this data could give us a certain amount of knowledge about a ship.

Every time we have worked on an ancient wreck, I have heard visitors inquire about the cause of the ship's demise. That, as far as they were concerned, was the important question, and they believed that we were trying to find an answer to it. We would, of course, have liked to know whether it was poor seamanship, damage to the hull, or a storm that caused the ship to sink, so that we could determine the responsibility of the captain. The accumulation of such information would shed some light on the methods of navigation employed by ancient sailors, and on the nautical qualities of their ships. Unfortunately, it is generally impossible—except in the case of fire, which sometimes leaves traces—to discover the cause of a shipwreck from the examination of extant remains. We know that a particular ship has crashed against a certain shore or reef, but we can formulate any number of hypotheses about the circumstances of the accident.

A storm can drive a ship toward the shore with such force that a collision is inevitable. The only recourse against this menace is to drop the anchors, if the water isn't too deep, and hope that they will hold; which is rather unlikely if the storm is violent. It's interesting to inspect the anchors in the vicinity of a wreck, but there are so many antique anchors along the coasts of the Mediterranean, and such anchors have been so little studied, that it is difficult to assign an anchor to a given wreck simply because it has been found nearby. A shipwreck can be caused by a navigational error committed in the dark of night, or by a reef that has been improperly charted. If the wind is strong enough, a ship at anchor can break its mooring lines, or drag its anchors and get smashed against the shore. For every ship which seems as if it might have come to grief in one or the other of these two ways, we can also suppose that, there being a fire on board, or a leak in the hull, or a pirate in pursuit, the captain deliberately ran the vessel aground in order to save the crew. Finally, a sailing ship out at sea can sink as the result of a fire, be disabled and fill with water, or be capsized by a storm.

I like to think that ancient sailors served an apprenticeship during which they learned to detect the slightest eddies around a hidden rock and the aroma peculiar to each part of the coast. Floating algae, to them, were not just debris, but an indication of something. They could distinguish the subtle shades of blue in the water, and knew the extent to which it darkened near the mouth of each river. In view of all this, I have to wonder, like our visitors, why ancient ships, despite the luck coin placed under their masts, sank so frequently. The only reason I have been able to think of is that, in some cases, a greedy shipowner might have loaded the vessel with so much cargo that it became unsafe.

Often, when a ship sinks, one of the ends will precede the other and the whole thing will go down at a sharp tilt. Both the cargo and the ship's equipment, as they hit the water, lose some of their weight. Anything that is lighter than water will float or, if it has been dragged under, return to the surface. Light objects that are attached to the ship will be forced upward. The inclination of the ship will cause heavy objects to shift about, or even fall into the water. These movements are accentuated by the relative current and by the turbulence created by the sinking ship. We find amphoras dispersed all around a wreck. Some of them have been dragged away from the ship by trawlers, while others, having tumbled from the hull as it sank, simply fell on the periphery of the site. A few apparently reached the bottom before the ship itself, because we have found them under the hull. There have also been ships that have clung to rocks before eventually coming to rest on top of their lost amphoras.

The disorder produced during the sinking of a ship should not be exaggerated, however, because the cargoes were solidly packed.

When a ship strikes the bottom the impact causes a sudden change in the inclination, and perhaps even more disorder, especially if the ship rebounds onto the steps of a cliff or falls across the tops of some rocks.

Many ships have come to rest intact on a bottom that is flat. Later on, the hull, weakened by the water and the marine life, has collapsed under the weight of the cargo, producing the greatest possible disarray and leaving each object in the permanent position in which we eventually find it. When the sides of a ship that is resting upright on a flat seabed give way, the mass of amphoras, left unsupported, fans out, and some of them slide or tumble down to fill the empty spaces. On the smooth, sloping bottom at the foot of a Mediterranean cliff or reef, a ship is more or less inclined, and the amphoras spill out in the direction of the slope.

To understand the disorder surrounding a wreck, you have to explore the periphery and estimate the role of the slope in terms of the axis of the ship, which is indicated by the length of the mound of amphoras.

I have inspected the wrecks of wooden ships that were of recent construction, or old without being antique, and I know that they deteriorate quite rapidly in the sea. The huge frigate *Panama*, which lies in a hundred eighty feet of water, is now, after sixty years, nothing but a plateau of mud with vague projections that are difficult to recognize. The *Slava Rossii*, which sank a hundred eighty years ago, has rotted away and disappeared under the sand; anything that escaped from burial has been covered with stone by the concretions. The ship has long since taken on the appearance of an ancient wreck.

The disintegration of Roman ships didn't take place by a regular process stretched out over the course of two thousand years. If that were the case, it would be impossible to explain the fact that objects extracted from their debris are virtually intact and their lower hulls amazingly well preserved. They took on their definitive form within a few years.

A wooden ship that sinks to the bottom of the sea represents an enormous, unexpected source of nutrition for teredos, worms, microorganisms, and a whole parade of other fauna. Each animal attracts another one, by which it is eaten. The wreck becomes the site of a huge feast, a monstrous carousal. The table is set for all comers and is bathed by the currents, which are vital to life in the sea, just as air is to that on land. The superstructure of the ship collapses, and the weakened hull, which has been partially devoured, yields under the weight of the cargo. Sometimes one of the sides will wind up under the cargo and be preserved, but not so well as the bottom of the hull, because it has had more exposure to the action of the sea. Shipworms eventually reduce the wood to something like a sponge, and soon even that disappears, leaving the white, tubular shells of these molluscs as the only trace of its presence in the sand.

The upper part of the ship will have formed, in disintegrating, a sediment that filters down through the cargo and protects the lower part.

In a few years the exposed timbers will have been thoroughly devoured and the banquet will be over; there will no longer be any edible remains accessible to the organisms in the sea. The wreck will have come to resemble just a low platform, which is the way it will look when we discover it.

Organisms that live in the sea are fond of the reliefs on the bottom, where they find the water more favorable for their growth. Once the animals and protozoa that move about in search of organic matter have left a site, they are succeeded by fixed, sedentary forms of life nourished by the water. Algae spring up everywhere, and animals that look more like plants settle in, secreting skeletons or calcareous shells whose debris will filter down into the mound to add to the protection provided by the mud from the decomposition of the ship. Lobsters and crayfish come to grind up the living matter and accumulate its wastes. Fish circle around and then station themselves in the interstices. Octopuses set up house in the amphoras, where they leave the remains of the shellfish they subsist on. Concretions form a crust of stone over the wreck, turning it into a regular fossil. They fuse the amphoras together and preserve the outlines of iron objects that gradually disintegrate under the crust, leaving behind, after two thousand years, nothing but a black liquid. They can also make a statue look perfectly hideous. Concretions are still forming today on the visible remains of sunken ships. When such concretions are extracted from the soil during the course of an excavation, they are white and bare, and they diminish in number as the digging proceeds, which is an indication of the way the ship got buried with the passage of time. This is true because, after the relatively short initial phase of its formation, a wreck enters into the realm of the mineral, which changes as slowly as the geological structure of the earth.

Whenever it rains, soil from the land is washed into the ocean and into rivers that convey the products of erosion toward the sea. These materials are sorted and distributed by the waves and currents. The coarse products remain near the coasts, and only the fine particles are borne out to sea. The plain of mud begins gradually when the coastal sand diminishes.

Where the marine life is intense, it adds its debris to this sediment and contributes to the rise of the sea bottom.

A wreck located at the foot of a cliff gets covered with debris that falls down from the wall above—shells, sea urchins, and calcareous fragments from the area lapped by the waves, where the concretions form a sort of curb. Rocks and stones from above the water, loosened by erosion, also accumulate on the site.

The rise of the bottom is generally much more pronounced along the coast or on coastal reefs than out at sea, but it varies considerably everywhere, depending upon the nature of the coastal terrain, the presence of rivers, the shape of the coast, and many other factors.

The composition and texture of the soil on the bottom are especially significant for the preservation of a sunken ship. The softer the bottom, the more the ship will sink in at first and the better it will be preserved, once the electrochemical phenomena that might modify the materials have been taken into account.

In the Mediterranean, a ship that has sunk at the foot of a rocky coast is generally covered with a loose sand which is sometimes free of mud and can be easily removed by hand. Those further from shore are often embedded in a compact mud that is in the process of hardening and has the consistency of clay. You can penetrate this mud with your hand, but it takes a certain amount of effort and the hole doesn't close up again the way it does in the sand. The nature of the bottom determines the conduct of an excavation.

At depths where the shifting tides still stir up the sand so that it gets carried off by the currents, some wrecks, as new obstacles to the movements of the sea, have retained the sand, which, having run down under the hull, has formed a sort of cradle to keep the ship from losing its shape. There are also some wrecks on which the sand has crept in to fill the spaces between the hull and the interior floor and prevented the floorboards from breaking between the ribs, as they have done in so many other cases. Other wrecks have caused turbulent currents which have buried them in the same way that winds create dunes in the desert and drifts in the snow.

We have discovered diving and become interested in ancient wrecks at a time when many of them are on the verge of becoming impossible to detect with the naked eye. Some have already been covered over, especially those with perishable cargoes or, like the galleys used in combat, no cargo at all. We will continue to find wrecks at locations far removed from the land or in coastal areas where the sedimentation is rather limited.

When a diver encounters broken pottery, he can't always tell whether he has come upon a wreck or just an anchorage where a ship might have been stationed to wait for a change in the wind, to get shelter from bad weather, or to engage in trade. Locations that served as anchorages for many centuries are now forgotten, because methods of navigation have changed and ports are more numerous. Such places are full of anchors that caught on something and broke their ropes, various objects that fell into the water by accident, and pottery thrown over the side after getting broken on board ship.

What distinguishes an anchorage from a wreck is that the disposition of the anchors, pottery, and other objects in the soil is quite different from that assumed by the remains of a ship. The potsherds on an anchorage will be found in layers that correspond to historical eras, but a diver is seldom in a position to give dates to such fragments.

Besides, the stratigraphy isn't always perfectly regular. People who are strangers to the sea have a tendency to think that the elements alone determine conditions on the bottom. They forget about the intervention of men and animals. In an area that has, over the years, served as an anchorage for numerous ships, pieces of pottery have sometimes been dislodged by anchors. Nets placed on the bottom and hauled in again have stirred up the potsherds and kept some of them out of the soil. This sort of human intervention has left parts of amphoras visible on wrecks that were completely buried and has caused pottery on the surface of other wrecks to be dispersed.

Burrowing animals also falsify the historical data. Octopuses make their homes in the soil, using pebbles, shells, bits of glass, and potsherds to erect little walls and pavements similar to those built by children and which, by stabilizing the sand, prevent the movements of the sea from filling in their holes. I even suspect them of making off with materials from the surrounding area, without respecting the needs of archaeologists. Whenever we find an object in a jar or amphora that an archaeologist says is not from the same era as the pottery, we blame the octopuses.

We are amazed at the ingenuity with which beavers and certain birds build their homes, but the octopus is just as clever. One time, on a bare, smooth bottom, there were some flat rocks half-covered with sand. The octopuses had raised some of these rocks just a bit and had propped them up with pebbles; they had then proceeded to construct a little suburban garden in front of each of the buildings. On another occasion, when I was working at a depth of a hundred sixty feet, I wouldn't have noticed an isolated, almost completely buried Massalian amphora if an octopus hadn't dug away the sand around the neck and made a hole inside. The entrance to this venerable dwelling had been paved with pebbles.

Amateurs who dive for pleasure rarely venture out to sea to swim over the flat, monotonous bottoms where you don't see anything, and where access is often difficult because of the depth. They prefer to explore the rocky bottoms frequented by fish, where they will find sponges, decorative gorgonians, coral, or lobsters. These divers discover ships that have sunk on such coastal rocks and thereby, without realizing it, practice a sort of selection that puts this kind of wreck in the forefront to the detriment of wrecks buried on sandy coasts or out at sea.

Our chances of finding a particular wreck are determined by its appearance, which varies according to the nature of the coast.

Some sandy coasts in the vicinity of the deeper water are struck by the full force of the waves and swells. Ships that sink on such coasts are often destroyed, and their cargo is dispersed before sinking into the sand. Other sandy coasts drop off slowly, and the water is shallow over such a long distance that the waves have lost their force by the time they reach the shore. Lateral currents periodically displace large masses of sand and bury a wreck before the cargo gets dispersed. Some years the sand is swept away so that a wreck becomes visible again. And at certain points along the coasts of the Atlantic there are forests of laminaria that inhibit the violent movements of the ocean. Wrecks that have sunk into these forests have been preserved by their shelter.

On rocky, gently sloping coasts that are exposed to the effects of storms, many wrecks have been dislocated by the sea, but traces of the ship and its cargo have remained on the rocks, where they can be found welded down and partially concealed by algae and concretions.

The sheer rocks common along the coasts of the Mediterranean are the best sort of terrain for the preservation of wrecks. The cliff continues under the water with the same steep, often vertical slope and, toward a hundred or a hundred sixty feet, there is a bank of fallen rocks on the edge of a sandy, then muddy, plain that slopes gently toward the high seas. A ship pushed by the wind or current toward such a coast, will, unless it is saved at the last minute, dash against the rocks for a certain length of time, then suffer a break in the hull and sink, without further damage, down to the foot of the cliff, where it will be immediately protected from the violent movements of the sea. Quite often it will miss the bank of fallen rocks and come to rest in the sand, which will keep it intact for archaeologists of the future.

Conditions are also very favorable where there are reefs with a steep underwater slope. Such reefs, situated on coastal shipping lanes, have, over the ages, been the ruin of many a vessel. These stricken vessels, depending upon the length of time it took them to sink, have come to rest at various distances from the reef, some of them as much as a quarter of a mile away. It is always moving to discover, on a bare, white bottom and in the blue, shadowless light of the deep water, the dark mass of a wreck with several thousand amphoras. It always begins abruptly. The first amphoras just barely protrude from the sand to form the base of a rising mound of jars lumped together in a solid mass that, at the peak, is often several yards high. All the jars are covered with elaborate concretions and a coat of slimy vegetation; there are also patches of black in the form of solid or corollaceous sponges. Fish colored like the water circulate above the mound while others, less eerie, play around in the cavities, bringing some life to this organized disorder that was once a cargo of clean, shiny vases carefully arranged in the hold of a ship. Perfectly defined on the sterile plain, the vestiges of the ship retain its oval shape, and the amphoras, still upright, poke their heads out of the soil, under which their mass grows increasingly larger.

On certain reefs there are several gutted ships from different eras lying one on top of another. If the water is shallow, their remains will have been spread out and mixed together in such disorder that it is difficult to determine the number and identity

of the ships. These "complexes" can yield some interesting artifacts, as well as information about regional trade and navigational routes. But they make it very difficult to examine a wreck
in its entirety.

There are some rocky areas, like underwater cols, that are
swept by a current which carries off the sediment and locally
produced sand. A ship that comes to rest in such an area is not
protected by the soil, and it gets covered with concretions, sometimes to such an extent that the entire wreck is hidden under a
layer of stone.

Something similar happens when a ship lands on a bank of
fallen rocks that consists of boulders with spaces between them
through which the water can circulate. The organic matter from
the decomposition of the ship filters down between the rocks to
mix with the locally produced sand and other forms of sediment.
There is no bed to protect the hull. Only those parts of the ship
that are impervious to rot will remain on the rocks, where they
will be more or less concreted.

Along the coasts of the Mediterranean, between the shore and
the point where the water reaches a hundred thirty feet in depth,
vast expanses of the bottom are carpeted with heavy growths of
posidonia. These growths, called mattes, aren't strictly
homogeneous. They are interspersed with sandy-bottomed depressions called intermattes, which vary in depth and width from
twenty inches to two or three yards. These depressions form basins and sinuous or rectilinear trenches that can be as long as a
thousand feet. The sides of the depression are vertical, with a
recess at the base.

A ship that lands in these posidonia is often very hard to detect;
its tumulus is almost indistinguishable from the natural hillocks,
and the plants disguise its surface. It could probably be located
with a sounding device equipped to give a profile of the different
layers of soil on the bottom.

A few of the many ancient wrecks in the posidonia are still
visible, having come to rest athwart the intermatte or having
resisted the growth of the plants with their sterile mass.

The excavation of such a wreck is, at first, arduous and slow.
The plants are firmly rooted in the soil, and you have to use a
gardener's claw to pull them up a few at a time. Then you come
up against an unyielding mixture of sand and roots that resists
your tools like the trunk of a palm tree. The sand can be removed

from the roots with a *suceuse* or water gun, but neither instrument is really very effective. The roots seem to stay alive indefinitely, and a great many have grown into the soil during the last two thousand years. My metallic probe sinks easily and deeply into such soil, allowing me to determine the outlines of the site. A wreck found on this kind of bottom is generally very well preserved. The study of such wrecks will make it possible, among other things, to assign a definite date to the growths of posidonia at different points along the coast.

In the vast domain of marine archaeology, the sunken ship is the vestige of human activity with the most specific link to the sea, and, for that very reason, it is difficult to locate. Ancient cities, leveled by their collapse, have been covered with dust by the wind and with the humus from layers of new vegetation. Many of them have disappeared. In our attempts to find them we are often helped by texts in which they are mentioned. When it comes to looking for a necropolis, we can fall back on the analogy with modern cities and the locations chosen for their cemeteries. An expert can get an idea of the archaeological possibilities of a landscape just from looking at it, for human constructions—cities, tombs, or palaces—are linked to the soil by the choice of a favorable location, which is made according to certain rules or customs. In our search for sunken ships we don't have anything to guide us, because a shipwreck is accidental and no human agency has presided over the relations between the ship and the soil.

If each shipwreck is a product of chance, their general distribution obeys a certain logic. Sunken ships are concentrated around hazards to navigation—reefs, obscure islets, and prominent capes—that lie along the principal maritime routes.

23

The PRESERVATION of MATERIALS

THE SOIL UNDER THE SEA preserves the relics of the past relatively well, and while some of them disappear, many of them remain entirely, or at least externally, unchanged. Their state of preservation varies considerably, depending on the physical and chemical properties of the sediment and the microorganisms that it might contain. In particular, the microorganisms associated with the decomposition of organic matter produce compounds that corrode certain metals. A bottom that consists only of sand won't have the same effects as one that consists of mud.

Over the course of two thousand years, the materials of a wreck have been modified by physical, biological, chemical, and electrochemical forces; they have reached the point where they are almost stable and in equilibrium with their environment.

An excavation changes the environment by exposing to the action of the sea materials that have been protected by several yards of sediment. It is dangerous, for example, to leave a hull uncovered for any length of time.

Many of the materials on a wreck, if they are exposed to the air, undergo substantial changes. The evaporation of water from the wood causes it to warp and crumble; salts crystallize to break the surface of glazed pottery and metals that have become friable. The influx of oxygen from the air precipitates a new phase of corrosion.

An object removed from the sea should, as a precaution, be immediately put to soak in fresh water and kept there until its fate has been decided. It can be transported in a plastic bag to prevent evaporation.

The wood on ancient wrecks, protected by the cargo and the sediment, still looks surprisingly new. You can easily distinguish the pine from the hardwood. Many pieces show marks from the tools—saws, chisels, and adzes—that were used to shape them. The joints of the hulls are still perfect and sometimes indiscernible.

But these appearances are deceptive. The pine is soft, and the planks break under the slightest pressure. Only the inner core of the hardwood will be unaltered.

If the wood is taken out of the water and allowed to dry, its appearance changes quite rapidly, with each species behaving in a different way. They all shrink; and while some retain their shape, others twist, crack, peel, or get flaky.

The chemical composition and microstructure of the wood will have been greatly modified. It will be waterlogged and decomposed and will have lost some of its tissue.

The preservation of wood that has spent centuries under the sea is one of the major problems of marine archaeology. The search for a solution has taken two different paths. One method consists of replacing the water contained in the structure of the wood with a series of liquids, the last of which forms a solid. Another approach is to consolidate the subsisting ligneous tissue and give it enough rigidity so that it won't break down as it dries.

Wood isn't the only organic matter preserved on a wreck. Among the ingots on the wreck from the Bronze Age, which was more than three thousand years old, we found the bottom of a basket preserved, no doubt, by copper oxide. We also picked up a few olive pits and some fish bones, which are often found in amphoras from the Roman era. On the *Slava Rossii* I came across two leather saber cases from which the steel blades had disappeared. Many shipwrecks have claimed human lives, but drowning men struggle to survive and their bodies sink slowly; few remain on the ship unless they get trapped inside. The Italians, however, did find a human skull bearing traces of a helmet on the wreck at Spargi, which dated from 120 to 100 B.C. Among the marble balls and long or short cannons on a wreck from the sixteenth century, I gathered up the skulls and broken bones of several sailors, which had been mixed in with the sand, broken pottery, and silver coins scattered about or lumped together. In the soil near the remains of these men, you could see the outlines of their large iron swords. The copper kitchen utensils were crumpled up like old newspapers. After the shipwreck, the cannons, huge powder cases, balls, and lead plate rollers, trapped on the between decks and knocked together by stormy seas, had ground up the pottery and the bones of the dead sailors.

Metals are rarely found in the earth in their pure state. They are usually encountered in the form of ore, i.e., combined with nonmetallic elements. Mineral ore is the metal's natural, permanent state, and when a metal obtained from this ore by chemical processes returns to nature by falling into the sea, it tends to revert to this stable form through corrosion.

Most metals are subject to corrosion, but it can be slow or rapid, depending on the nature of the metal and of the environment.

Electrochemical phenomena play an important role in corrosion.

They are caused by a difference in potential created when two different metals come into contact or close proximity while submerged in an electrolyte, which in this case is the water of the sea. The baser metal becomes corroded, while the other is protected. Alloys are generally more susceptible than pure metal. Electrochemical reactions can also take place on a metal that is submerged by itself, due to foreign particles embedded in its surface, differences in its porosity, or variations in the oxygen content of the seawater.

An iron object buried in the soil at the bottom of the sea will cause the sand around it to get hard, and will often form a thick, very solid block of concretions. When iron is exposed to the water, it almost always gets heavily concreted. Under its matrix of stone, the surface of an iron cannon that has been in the sea for several centuries will, surprisingly enough, be more or less unchanged, with its ornaments and inscriptions intact; but the material will have the look and consistency of chocolate. On a heavy object there will continue to be an inner core of solid metal long after the surface has deteriorated to the point where it can be penetrated with a knife. After a certain number of centuries, the inner core will also disappear, but the shape and surface of the object will remain unaffected. Some isolated iron objects have totally disintegrated, leaving behind just a black liquid in a mold of stone. A plaster cast made from this natural mold will show all the details of the original object. The iron bars from the Roman era found on the wreck at Hyères formed a large, compact mass covered with a layer of hard concretions. Underneath the concretions the metal was black, spongy, and friable, but the outline of each bar was quite distinct.

I live near the sea, and the salt air penetrates the poorly made cement of my house, causing the iron bars embedded in it to expand and crack the foundation. In the sea, the iron filters harmlessly through the matrix of stone.

On a freighter that had been in the water for sixty years, I came upon a bronze porthole with an iron frame. It was still attached to a piece of planking that, protected by the proximity of the metals, had endured while the rest of the wood rotted away. A rust-filled concretion formed a rim around the bronze porthole. Under the porthole the iron frame, with its coat of blue paint, appeared to be intact, but it had the consistency of chocolate. An electrochemical reaction had caused the iron to migrate through the paint.

Copper and its alloys, bronze and brass, although subject to a certain amount of corrosion, are quite durable. The famous bronze statues from Greece had, when they were brought up from the sea, a surface that was rough and occasionally pitted. Restoration has given them a better appearance. In the sand at La Chrétienne I found a bronze bracelet on which there wasn't even a patina. The bronze coin that had been placed under the mast of the wreck was slightly eroded and covered with a layer of concretions. Once the coin had been cleaned you could see a woman's head quite clearly. On the other hand, the bronze coin on the wreck at Port-Vendres had been reduced to just a crust of stone that bore perfect imprints of the two faces.

Fortunately for us, it often happens that the surface of a metal object immersed in the sea will be preserved in spite of the transformations that take place in the rest of it. This phenomenon, moreover, is not peculiar to metals. Near my house, on a high, vertical cliff of smooth, white rock, there are some dinosaur footprints that have never been anything but a surface.

Around the wreck from the Bronze Age, in Turkey, we found several perfectly preserved ingots of copper. The same kind of ingot, in the midst of several hundred pounds of various alloys, had become friable from the effects of electrochemical reactions. The same thing had happened to the small bronze objects, whether isolated or embedded in the mass of the cargo. At Agde, Bouscaras had already, in 1965, recovered eleven hundred different bronze and copper objects from the cargo of a Bronze Age ship whose remains had been scattered by the sea over an area where the depth of the water varies from twenty-six to thirty-three feet. All the objects were in good condition, and some were scarcely tarnished. Certain of them had been worn and polished from continuous exposure to the movements of the sand.

Copper nails that have remained in place in the wood of ancient ships have been reduced to oxide, whereas those that have fallen out of rotted wood have been kept almost intact by the sand. Some of them have retained a coat of wood preserved by oxide. The extent of their corrosion seems to depend on the length of time spent in the wood. After more than two thousand years, the little brass ingots found near the lighthouse at Les Magnons had only a fine patina under which the metal was sound. On a freighter that had sunk a few decades before, I took a brass compass binnacle with two small lanterns. The metal had crystallized and could be easily broken by hand. A freighter, being a vast assemblage of different metals, is almost made to order for electrochemical reactions.

Lead is highly durable, and pewter even more so. Several pewter bowls and jugs have been found perfectly intact on wrecks from the sixteenth century, as were the pewter plates bearing the arms of Imperial Russia on the *Slava Rossii.*

The leaden stocks and crosspieces from antique anchors, as well as rings and other parts of the rigging made from lead, are usually rough on the surface, but shine when scratched. Leaden hull plate, made to a thickness of about half an inch, is still in a metallic state. The inscriptions on the lead ingots at Les Magnons remained perfectly legible.

Silver that is isolated on a wreck will get thoroughly corroded and covered with a thin layer of concretions peculiar to that particular metal. The silver coins that I found all by themselves on a wreck from the first half of the sixteenth century were friable, but the covering of stone bore the imprint of their faces. I later brought up, without being aware of it, a block containing a hundred twenty-seven of these coins from the doges of Genoa. I had to separate it from a heavy powder case in order to take it to the Cabinet des Médailles. When I broke it, a handful of shiny coins tumbled out. On Benoit's desk I saw the silver coins that had been found on the wreck of a Roman ship near Cap Sicié. They had been cleaned and were shiny. I suspect that they also formed a block.

The gold coins found at the bottom of the sea were intact.

Marble objects like statues, sarcophagi, and capitals weather the sea very well when they are buried in the soil of the bottom. Those that have been exposed to the water have been devoured by the date mussel, or *lithophaga*. I have often gone into the sea with a sledgehammer to break up the rocks on a certain jetty in order to get at these delicious shellfish. Date mussels live in calcareous stone, which is their only protection. Their long, narrow, oval, and bright maroon shell is thin and fragile. The specimens in the rocks of the jetty grow to a length equal to that of a large mussel. On the coast, where the water isn't as rich, they don't get so big. The holes on the surface of the rocks are much more narrow than the dates themselves, which means that they can't get out. The tunnels, like their creators, are cylindrical, with smooth, highly polished sides. Date mussels are said to dig by spinning around while giving off an acid secretion. They distribute their homes more or less at random, but make maximum use of their space, sometimes digging so close to one another that their tunnels meet and the water can circulate through them. After the first layer of tunnels there is another further on in the rock. That is as far as my gastronomic investigations have taken me.

Smaller animals also attack calcareous stone, leaving it marked with a multitude of canals and little cavities.

Other kinds of rock aren't affected, and divers often bring up well-preserved primitive stone anchors. Stone is a natural element.

Pottery will survive a long time if it is protected by sand or mud, but if it is out in the water it will get covered with concretions that can alter its surface, or it will be eroded.

Some amphoras, if they're left in the sun after being taken out of the water, will crack. The sun warms and dries the exterior before the interior, and the whole of the outer side before the side in the shade, thereby creating internal tensions that can cause ruptures.

Ancient or modern china and antique pottery with black varnish that have been preserved by the soil on the bottom of the sea will, if simply left on a shelf, dry out, and the salts will crystallize, causing the enamel or varnish to crack. After a while you have nothing but an earthenware form surrounded by a pile of dust. This kind of pottery has to be soaked for months in frequently changed fresh water and then allowed to dry out slowly.

24

PILLAGE

MORE THAN TWENTY-FIVE YEARS ago the aqualung made the sea accessible to everyone.

For the first divers it was enough that they could enjoy the mystery that seems to surround the sea, the beauty of the underwater landscapes, the pride associated with participation in what was then still an adventure, and the sensation of floating weightlessly in space, which was something they had always dreamed about. Some of them got interested in spearfishing, with the result that fish became scarce and timid. Then they turned to gathering up lobsters, sponges, and red coral, which, although it comes in a multitude of different shapes, seldom forms the highly coveted cross.

In spite of its appeal, diving was then a rather rugged sport; there were no rubber suits, and only a diver's fanaticism could make him forget the cold.

Many of us were obsessed with the thought of sunken treasures. There are no doubt some fabulous treasures to be found, but, as we soon learned, the sea is immense and has great powers of dissimulation.

Along the jagged coasts of the Mediterranean, divers encountered a wide assortment of antiques, including leaden anchor stocks, broken pottery, and the buried cargoes of amphora ships. As the initially small fraternity of divers grew larger, the members kept in touch with one another. The excitement created by the first archaeological discoveries sent everyone off looking for artifacts, and the goal of the diver became the collection of souvenirs.

Only a saint, and one endowed with considerable scientific knowledge, could have resisted the temptation to lay hands on the elegant amphoras decorated with concretions in bright, if ephemeral, colors.

Amphoras became fashionable. When, in the spring, flowers were abundant and selling poorly, there would be huge amphoras full of flowers on the floats in the carnival at Nice. Every tourist restaurant, every nightclub, and some of the more expensive stores displayed amphoras as symbols of the pleasure to be derived from living close to the sea. For the diver, the amphora was a sort of trophy crowning a successful vacation. The passion for amphoras spread to the general public and a black market, supplied by professionals, sprang up. An amphora with a respectable growth of concretions sold, in the beginning, for thirty thousand *anciens francs** in Marseilles and for fifty thousand in Cannes. The prices have risen steadily since then.

Some archaeologists accuse us of having opened a Pandora's box in making the bottom of the sea accessible to everyone. It's true that, in the domain of archaeology, free diving has proven to be a much better tool for pillage than for scientific work.

But this is not entirely the fault of divers. Oceanographers, biologists, and geologists were quick to see the advantage of going down themselves to inspect and work on the bottom, which they had been studying for so long from above by means of instruments lowered on the end of a rope. Archaeologists have not followed suit, probably because they have lacked the necessary funds. The other scientists, however, had the advantage, not enjoyed by archaeologists, of being able to contemplate the future without apprehension. The objects of their study weren't subject to pilferage by divers and are not, like ancient relics, disappearing at a constantly accelerating rate.

---

* $60.00.

The looting of archaeological sites in the sea is merely a new phase of the pillage of souvenirs from the past. There has always been a flourishing trade in artifacts taken from the soil. In Greece, despite the protection of stringent laws, numerous painted vases and a few marble statues are smuggled out of the country every year. Etruscan tombs are invaded at night by unsuperstitious thieves who remove the bronze statuettes and black vases placed there as offerings to the dead. Egyptian sepulchers had already been pillaged at the time of the Pharoahs, in spite of the ingenuity that had been employed to make them secret and inaccessible.

From this point of view the sea differs from the land in that it was for thousands of years an obstacle to looting. The famous dives reported in all the historical accounts of man's penetration of the sea were dubious, isolated instances of little consequence. Even if it is admitted that Alexander the Great descended into the sea, he wasn't looking for amphoras.

On the coasts of France there are anchorage areas that are becoming impossible to find and wrecks that can, in a single season, lose their entire upper layer, which is poorly preserved and all the more important because it can contain elements that we won't see elsewhere. On many wrecks the divers have arrived at the wood of the hull. But there are also numerous unspoiled wrecks on coasts where there has yet to be any looting, that is to say on almost all the shores of the Mediterranean and its islands exclusive of France, Italy, Spain, and part of North Africa. There are also a great many wrecks far from the coasts, where they're safe from divers.

A diver looking for amphoras works in the midst of a cloud of mud raised by his movements. He feels around for the jars with his hands, neglecting anything else he might come in contact with. Surveillance of wrecks being pillaged would have saved many an important artifact. I have sometimes visited such wrecks and recovered amphora stoppers, necks with markings, and whetstones, which were varied and numerous among ancient sailors due to the inferior quality of their knives.

The amateur, because he has to worry about the police, can't dig very deeply into the soil at the bottom of the sea. Routine surveillance can prevent the use of a *suceuse* or water gun, both of which are cumbersome and create a highly visible wake on the surface of the water. The soil that the amateurs can't remove with their hands conceals the delicate and fascinating part of the wreck, which is the ship itself.

Archaeology is the art of learning from the remains and traces of antique objects by studying their general and reciprocal relationships. The archaeologist tries, from his examination of a wreck, to trace its history and to reconstruct the daily lives of its crew from minute details that are significant to him only because of his long training. His task is difficult, but not hopeless, especially when you compare it to that of the prehistorian, who, in his search for the first manifestations of human intelligence through physical or cultural activity, has to rely on debris that has fallen or been abandoned, thrown, or lost in different geological strata. It should also be noted that, while the land-based archaeologist is, more and more, required to devote himself to obscure labors which rarely yield any surprising results, the archaeologist who explores the bottom of the sea can begin each day with the expectation of making important or spectacular discoveries.

All divers pick up things on the bottom of the sea. Many of them, with the best of intentions, take their little treasures to archaeologists and, thinking that they have done a good thing, are surprised when the scientists greet them with a frown.

Someday there will be systematic excavations conducted by archaeologists capable of going down to work under the water. When that day comes, divers, seeing competent scientists at work, will understand the historical importance of such sites and will of themselves make a better contribution. The rigors of diving are the same for the looter and the scientist, and I'm not sure that they're not both motivated by the same thing—the passion for exploration and discovery. If their ultimate goals are different, they're not irreconcilable. The scientist, once he has studied an object in his laboratory, doesn't particularly care whether it winds up in a museum or in a private collection. Many divers, if they understood the dedication with which the scientist conducts his inquiry, would see that as an added incentive for indulging their penchant for exploration and would render great service while pursuing their pleasure.

Divers should realize that the salvage of antique objects doesn't make you an archaeologist.

If, every year, you take twenty anchor stocks to a museum, the quantity of lead bequeathed to the French nation will not particularly add to its wealth; but opportunities to learn about methods of navigation and shipping routes through the study of anchorage areas will have been lost.

If a well-intentioned police officer were to put everything contained in the room where a crime had been committed into a truck and take it to the detective in charge of the case, no one would be surprised to see the detective go into a fit of anger.

25

The FUTURE of UNDERWATER ARCHÆOLOGY

THE FIELD OF INVESTIGATION for the underwater archaeologist includes rivers, streams, lakes, ponds, pits, and fountains, all of which conceal traces of our past under their mass of fresh water.

The mouths of rivers, having served throughout history as natural shelters, are repositories for all the odds and ends that accumulate in the sea near a port, a list of which would be much too tedious. Sailors live in cramped quarters and are quick to throw anything they don't need over the side.

Rivers have been used for shipping since the most ancient times and are, like the sea, graveyards for sunken ships. They have served as dumps for the cities they pass through, and their beds are littered with debris from the monuments on their banks, for the history of every city consists of a series of demolitions. The divers who have been excavating the bed of the Hérault, in Agde, have filled a museum that would be the envy of many a city.

In South America there are lakes, wells, and fountains where pre-Columbian peoples deposited offerings, sacrifices, and, perhaps, treasures that they wanted to keep from falling into the hands of approaching invaders. Works of art and everyday objects have already been found in such places.

Cities, villas, temples, and ports have been buried by earthquakes, while others have slid gradually into the sea. The folklore of maritime countries abounds in sunken cities of which one can still hear the bells, and where we would like to exercise our talents as divers along streets occupied by fish, algae, and sponges. Unfortunately, these devastated cities have fallen into vast, monotonous heaps that the rapid sedimentation of the coasts has covered with a thick carpet of sand. Inhabited cities built on a slight incline have slowly lost everything but their foundations.

There are many famous cities of antiquity, especially in Turkey, that are still overrun with underbrush and would be much easier to excavate than a city at the bottom of the sea. I would readily agree that the excavation of sunken cities should be considered as an extension of land archaeology.

Along the rocky coasts of Greece and Turkey there are ancient cities right on the sea that were repeatedly pillaged and destroyed, and many objets d'art were thrown down from the heights of their cliffs. Where the bottom is rocky, the objects will be visible but corroded and decomposed. If they're in sand, they will be covered by a heavy layer of sediment and will be well preserved.

The study of ancient ports, although relatively easy, is nevertheless only in an early stage of development; it will eventually provide us with much valuable information about this still obscure aspect of maritime activity.

The study of shipping lanes and methods of navigation through objects discarded or lost along the way would have to be pursued for quite some time before it yielded any results, and may never be undertaken on a systematic basis.

From my observation of the numerous antique anchors lost in places where there was no shelter from the bad weather, I have been able to get an idea of the manner in which the ancients sailed along the coasts of France. When the weather in the Mediterranean is good there are light, variable, and irregular breezes. In the morning there is a gentle breeze from the east, but during the course of the day it turns to follow the path of the sun, and by late afternoon it's blowing in from the west. Ancient ships couldn't make any headway against these winds and had to stop and wait if they were blowing in the direction opposite to their destination. But on the majority of rocky coasts the depth of the water makes it impossible to moor a ship far enough from the shore so that it can get under way again without danger. That is why ancient sailors liked reefs, the underwater extensions of capes, and isolated shoals, all of which have the advantage of shallow water and enough space to maneuver under any circumstances.

Sites of a new type will be discovered under the water—fishing areas marked by anchors from small boats and lost equipment; places where offerings to the sea were made; prehistoric grottoes now submerged; battle sites where stricken galleys sank and arms fell with the dead in combat; and many other sites whose existence is still unsuspected.

The layman, seeing the fantastic technology employed in the conquest of space, might think that underwater archaeologists are similarly well equipped. Unfortunately, however, excavations in the sea are expensive and archaeologists have only modest sums of money at their disposal. The task of the archaeologist, which is slow and time-consuming on land, is even more complicated in the water, where our possibilities are limited and where ideal conditions are rarely achieved, due to the lack of financial resources. The archaeologist often has to be content with small subsidies, and I'm persuaded that he will do a good job. It takes a great deal of money to conduct a full-scale excavation, but a large budget is not indispensable for a project with a limited objective, as long as there is sufficient time.

The first underwater excavations were little more than salvage operations. But archaeology on land was for a long time conducted on the same unscientific basis. People dug holes to find relics. At the end of the last century Lieutenant General Pitt-Rivers, acting on his own, inaugurated the scientific method, which was later, around 1920, perfected by another Englishman, Sir Mortimer Wheeler.

The surprising results of the first underwater excavations, which were conducted by divers without any training in archaeology, impressed the scientists. They are now learning to dive and are trying to apply all the methods that they have used successfully on land. They will learn from their experience, which will sometimes be disillusioning, and it's hard to predict how long this second phase will last. In a third phase, archaeologists will be led to modify their techniques in order to adapt them to the very different underwater environment. After having attempted to sketch everything, they will make use of photogrammetry; after having tried to dissect everything, they may decide to employ salvage contractors to build cofferdams or to raise large masses of material.

As the problems created by the water become more sharply defined, new tools will be devised to solve them, and this will lead to a reevaluation of the standard methods. Following the example of their colleagues who work on land, the underwater archaeologists will utilize electronic devices that will be more and more sensitive to an increasingly wide range of phenomena. Many of these devices can be used only by the person who has designed them, and, the competition in this new area being what it is, some archaeologists will perhaps conceal their disillusionment or failure. With such overly optimistic reports, it will take more time to learn the truth about the new devices. But underwater archaeology can't be a failure; there is too much new information about the cultural and economic relations of the past waiting for us under the sea.

On the practical level, underwater archaeology is directly linked to progress in the technical aspects of diving.

Air is composed of about eighty percent nitrogen and twenty percent oxygen. A diver breathes air under pressure and risks being affected by two particularly important physiological phenomena: the dissolution of nitrogen in the body by pressure and the narcotic effect of this gas in very deep water.

When a diver is under the water, the nitrogen from his air supply, as soon as it reaches his lungs, dissolves in his blood, which spreads and stores it throughout his body. If, after remaining for a long period of time at a considerable depth, the diver returns rapidly to the surface, the nitrogen will expand and form bubbles in his blood or even in the other tissues of his body. The gas creates strings of cylindrical bubbles that obstruct the veins and arteries, causing tissual asphyxiation. Such accidents can result in anything from local pain to paralysis, and even death.

In order to let the nitrogen pass out of his body the way it came in, i.e., through the lungs, the diver has to make his ascent at an ever-decreasing rate of speed. This kind of ideal ascent is difficult to achieve and to verify. In practice, the diver, once he gets to within a certain distance of the surface, proceeds by stages; the depth at which these stages begin and the length of time spent in each one are directly proportional to the depth and duration of his dive.

A diver returning from an extended stay in deep waters has to make such long stops at the various stages that the dive turns out to be almost a waste of time.

It takes about twelve hours for the body to become saturated with dissolved nitrogen. After that the diver can remain on the bottom without aggravating his condition, because the quantity of dissolved nitrogen doesn't increase. His ascent will obviously be quite prolonged, but it will be theoretically the same no matter how much time he spends on the bottom.

This fact has made it possible for divers to live under the sea in dwellings which, because the pressure inside is equal to that of the water, they can enter and leave at will. They can even go down to work at a depth thirty percent lower than that at which they are living and return to their dwelling without taking any precautions. When their work under the sea is finished, they return to the surface inside the dwelling, which is hauled up, and remain there to undergo decompression while enjoying all the comforts of home.

Man cannot live for long periods of time in compressed air, and it severely retards his mental processes. The brain begins to get sluggish well in advance of a hundred thirty feet, becoming practically useless beyond that depth. This phenomenon has been attributed to the density of the air; it has therefore become the practice to lighten the air breathed by the diver and that of the undersea dwellings by diluting it with helium in amounts directly proportional to the depth of the water around them. This influx of light gas, by some only partially understood process, makes the atmosphere suitable for human beings and eliminates the impairment of their mental function. Oxygen, on the other hand, beyond a certain multiple of the partial pressure at which we ordinarily breathe it, becomes toxic and produces very harmful effects. As the depth of the water increases, the percentage of oxygen in the gaseous mixture fed to the diver or into the dwelling should be diminished, so that the quantity of oxygen inside remains about the same as it would be at atmospheric pressure. When an undersea dwelling is stationed in very deep water, the atmosphere inside consists almost entirely of helium, with a very low percentage of oxygen.

The preceding is a very summary theoretical exposition of the question. Experiments in this area have brought up a number of fundamental or subsidiary problems which it will take long, hard work to resolve.

Not too long ago I witnessed from up on the surface a marvelous experiment conducted by Cousteau, during the course of which six men lived comfortably for twenty-six days, ten hours, and fifty minutes under a pressure of a hundred twenty pounds per square inch, of which twenty days, sixteen hours, and forty minutes were spent more than three hundred feet down in the sea. The results encouraged us to be very optimistic about the possibilities of underwater dwellings, the limitations of which have yet to be determined.

I was able to watch my friends the oceanauts on the television screen installed at the project base that had been established in the lighthouse on Cap Ferrat, where there was also a great variety of other electronic equipment for communication with and observation of the men below. My respect for their courage and my admiration for the great experiment they were participating in were almost enough to make me forget the nasal quality of their voices, which were so distorted that they would have made Donald Duck sound like a teacher of elocution. A few specially gifted individuals claimed to be experts in the translation of this extraterrestrial language, but I couldn't understand a word of it. When Cousteau telephoned to his son, who was one of the six oceanauts, Philippe appeared before the television camera and moved his lips, but all we heard were some unintelligible groans. Although he could hear his father quite well, Philippe couldn't get through to us, so he finally gave up and simply wrote his message on a piece of cardboard—he had been trying to say that the film in his camera was broken. This effect of helium is one of those annoying little problems that will eventually, like so many others, be solved.

The underwater dwelling would be ideal for an excavation, because it would allow scientists whose presence on the site is indispensable to remain below throughout the working day. But I wouldn't want archaeologists to get their hopes up. Underwater dwellings are extremely expensive to own and to operate; at the present time only the petroleum industry has enough capital to finance any extensive use of such equipment.

Specialists from several disciplines have shown interest in the possibilities offered by underwater dwellings, and we will just have to hope that some group of scientists, of which archaeologists would form a part, will take it upon themselves to try this new approach.

The future of underwater archaeology will also be influenced by the development of new tools for the exploration of the sea.

Exploration by divers, which is a method devised for operating in murky waters and which is used by navies to locate mines, has become the standard practice; but it requires plenty of time and large numbers of men and is suitable for archaeological purposes only in a few special cases.

Professional fishermen and sponge divers have accumulated and passed from one generation to another a considerable fund of knowledge about the bottom of the sea. They can furnish the archaeologist with valuable information, but to verify it through exploration by divers involves long hours of demanding work.

A new approach, based on an old principle, is now being developed. Miniature submarines designed for exploration, with space for only one or two persons, are cropping up just about everywhere. Advertisements printed in the United States give the impression that you can buy these subs at any large store.

There have been several accidents, one of which took the life of our colleague Boissy. The experiments that occasioned these misfortunes were the first tentative steps toward the development of this new method of exploration, for which it was difficult to extrapolate from regular submarines to the smaller model. But it seems to me to be an excellent idea, and I believe in its future.

In the warmth and comfort of such an underwater chamber, the archaeologist will be able to explore promising sites with a clear head. He will have a tape recorder for making notes and a battery of photographic equipment to register what he sees. Once the minisub has been equipped to navigate with accuracy, which shouldn't be too difficult to accomplish, the man at the controls will be able to make topographical measurements in much less time than it takes a diver. He will utilize stereoscopic photography, a technique used by aviators to get an exact reproduction of the terrain. He will have special sounding devices that will give a picture of the various layers of soil on the bottom and of hidden obstacles, natural or artificial.

Man's perception of his environment is much less acute under the water; his vision is particularly limited, and he is often unable to see more than a few yards in any direction. To complement the vehicles that have been invented to enable us to move more rapidly under the water, there is a whole array of electronic equipment—sounding devices and detectors—being developed. Many of these instruments are too cumbersome to be adapted without restrictions for use by divers. They can, on the other hand, be utilized on board miniature submarines.

While the underwater dwelling has no means of propulsion, the submarine can't be used to do any work on the bottom. Some of them have jointed arms, but it's hard to get the craft itself precisely where it has to be in order to get anything done. The two approaches are on the point of being combined. Attempts are being made to create a submarine of which one compartment will be an underwater dwelling. The crew will live under atmospheric pressure. If the divers are going to work for only a short time, they can go out and then undergo decompression in the living compartment. If they are going to work below for several days, they can live under pressure equal to that of the water, entering and leaving the compartment as the need arises; and, if their task makes it necessary, the submarine can move rapidly over short or extended distances. This new tool should make man the master of the ocean floor.

In the realm of diving and underwater exploration the age of the amateur and of individual exploits is over. The power of industry has allied itself with scientific research and has set out to conquer the world that lies under the sea.

If my colleagues from the *Calypso* have had the courage to read as far as that last sentence, which is a bit inflated, they will no doubt accuse me of being corny. But they believe it.

Bibliography

There is an excellent bibliography, which it would be super-fluous to reproduce here, in *Marine Archeology*, by Joan du Plat Taylor, Hutchinson, London, 1965.

The numerous publications of Fernand Benoit and of Nino Lamboglia constitute the most important record of the achievements of underwater archaeology.

The *Rapport du premier congrès international d'archéologie sous-marine*, Club alpin sous-marin, Cannes, 1955; and the *Actes du II*e *congrès international d'archéologie sous-marine*, Institut International d'Etudes Ligures, musée Bicknell, Bordighera, 1961, are two very useful publications full of ideas and facts.

The basic text for the study of ancient ships is still: Ucelli, *Le Navi Di Nemi*, Libreria dello stato, Roma, 1950.

One of the best books on the knowledge of ancient ships through texts and iconography is *Ancient Ships*, by Cecil Torr, Cambridge University Press, 1894.

For the custom of the luck coin under the mast, see: Peter R. V.

Marsden, "The Blackfriar's Ship" and "The Luck Coin in Ships," *The Mariner's Mirror,* 1965, vol. 51, no. 1, pp. 33 and 59.

In *Archeology Under Water,* Glyn Daniel, Thames and Hudson, London (which is also available as a paperback from Penguin Books, Baltimore, Maryland), George F. Bass gives an excellent analytical account of the work done by archaeologists under water and of the methods they have employed.

I also want to mention *History Under the Sea,* by Alexander McKee, Hutchinson, London, 1968. The author is a journalist, rather than a scientist, but he has collected a great deal of information.

The reader may want to consult as well the following articles that have appeared in the *National Geographic Magazine:*

"Fish Men Explore a New World Undersea," by Jacques-Yves Cousteau, October 1952.

"Fish Men Discover a 2,200-year-old Greek Ship," by Jacques-Yves Cousteau, January 1954. The wreck at Grand Congloué.

"Thirty-Three Centuries Under the Sea," by Peter Throckmorton, May 1960. The wreck from the Bronze Age.

"Ghost From the Depths: the Warship *Vasa,*" by Anders Franzen, January 1962.

"Oldest Known Shipwreck Yields Bronze Age Cargo," by Peter Throckmorton, May 1962. More about the wreck from the Bronze Age.

"Underwater Archeology: Key to History's Warehouse," by George F. Bass, July 1963.

"New Tools for Undersea Archeology," by George F. Bass, September 1968.

"Ancient Shipwreck Yields New Facts—And a Strange Cargo," by Peter Throckmorton, February 1969.

"Resurrecting the Oldest Known Greek Ship," by Michael Katzev, June 1970.

"Last Harbor for the Oldest Ship," by Susan W. and Michael L. Katzev, November 1974.

Index

Alifuri (island), 169
Alinat, Lieutenant Commander, 8–10,
    12–13, 70, 72, 74–75
Amphoras, 179–80
    Carthaginian, 60
    formation of, 179
    Greek, 44
    inscriptions on, 19, 38
    Ionian, 5
    Italian, 19, 44
    at La Chrétienne, 16–20
    pillaging of, 200
    at Port Cros, 4–5
    storage of, 179
    uses of, 180
    made watertight, 180
    wreck analysis using, 182
Ancient ships, 172–78. See also Construc-
    tion of ships, ancient; Lead on ancient
    ships; Shipwrecks
Antikythera, 48–60
    pottery at, 57
Archaeologist, function of, 132
Archaeology, underwater, future of, 202,
    204–11

Bargiarelli (diver), 116
Barnier (diver), 118
Baskakov, Lieutenant Capt. Jean, 114
Bass, George F., 78–79, 82, 88, 90, 93–95,
    98–99, 101–5, 107–9, 176
Baths on ships, 132–38
    slipper, 132–33
Bébert. See Falco, Albert
Bends, cause of, 14–15
Benoit, Fernand, 22–24, 26–27, 29, 32–33,
    35, 38–39, 44, 69, 74, 122, 133–34,
    139, 141, 146, 164, 176
Beuchat (diver), 111
Bey, Akki, 84–85, 88, 99–100
Bézaudin (diver), 20, 64
Bilge pump, 152–67
Boissy (diver), 210
Bonnici (diver), 155, 158
Bottles. See Amphoras
Bowls, 136–38
Bronze Age
    artifacts from, 109–10
    ingots of, 95
    wreck from, 77–110
Broussard (diver), 16

214

Byzantine
    artifacts, 150–51
    wrecks, 78

Caesar, Julius, 47
Calypso, 21, 25, 35, 38–41, 48, 50, 53,
    59–60, 143–44, 146–47, 168–69
Campanian pottery, 24, 27, 45
Cannons
    on Italian wreck, 117
    on *Slava Rossii*, 115–16
Canoé (diver), 150, 155
Cargoes of wrecks, 174–75
Carthage, search for Roman port of, 6–15
Carthaginian amphoras, 60
Catherine the Great, 113
Ceramics. *See* Amphoras; Pottery
Chevalier (diver), 123–24, 152–55, 166
Christianini (diver), 22
Clock, astronomical, 57
Coins, 121–24
Coll, Raymond, 155, 158, 165
Construction of ships
    ancient, 169–70, 175–78
    of Maldive Islands, 170–71
    modern, 169
Core sampler, 78
"Coup de reins," 2
Cousteau, Jacques-Yves
    at Antikythera, 51–54
    at Cape Dramont, 69–70
    films of, 3, 14, 48
    at Grand Congloué, 21–25, 27–31,
        34–36, 39–40
    at La Chrétienne, 16
    at Mahdia, 5–10, 12, 14
    as naval officer, 3
    at Navarino, 60
    submarine development of, 155
    underwater dwelling experiment of, 209
Cousteau, Philippe, 54, 209
Cousteau, Simone, 144
Cutty Sark, 178

Davin, Capt., 113
Delattre, Robert, 152, 155, 157, 161, 163
Delos, ruins at, 54
Dénéréaz (diver), 16
Devilla (doctor and diver), 16–17, 20
Divanli, Rasim, 81
Divers
    air and, 207
    efficiency of, 128
    helium and, 209

nitrogen and, 207–8
    See also specific divers
Diving, origins of, 199
Dolium, 133
Doria, Andrea, wreck from fleet of, 117
Dramont, 66, 68–76, 177
Duthuit, Claude, 78–79, 89, 93
Dwellings, underwater, 209–11

Earthenware vessel. *See* Amphoras
Edgerton, Harold, 48, 157
Egyptian scarabs, 107
Elie Monnier, 6, 16, 62–63, 114–15, 132,
    136
Espadon, 69–70, 73–74, 154–55, 157, 164

Falco, Albert (Bébert), 29, 35, 41–42, 45,
    51–55, 59, 144, 146, 150, 155–60
Films
    Cousteau's first color, 14
    on underwater hunting, 3
    See also specific films
French navy, 6–7
French shipwreck, 65
Fresnel, 30–31, 36–37
Frost, Honor, 78–79, 81, 83, 94, 97, 99–
    100, 102, 107, 120

Girault (diver), 43, 51
Glory of Russia. *See Slava Rossii*
Golerne (diver), 30–31
Grace, Virginia, 44, 79–80, 180
Grand Congloué, 21–48, 80
Grande Sultane, 59
Greek amphoras, 44
Grier, Herb, 88, 93, 98, 107

Helium, divers and, 209
Hodges (diver), 17
Hounot (crew), 16
Huston, John, 77
Hydrographic circle, 8
Hyères, wreck at, 153–55
Hygeia, 45

Illing, Waldemar, 101, 107–8
Ingots, 139–42
    Bronze Age, 95
    inscriptions on, 141, 165–66
    at Les Magnons, 139–42
    oxhide-shaped, 95, 108
Ionian amphora, 5
Isis, 178
Issaverdens, Jack, 118, 128–29, 131,
    133–34

Issaverdens, Jane, 118, 128, 133–35
Italian amphoras, 19, 44

Jeres, Capt., 30–31, 36
Junier, François, 24–25, 30

Kapkin, Mustapha, 81
Kasim (crew), 83, 99
Kemal, Capt., 83, 87–89, 91, 99, 104
Kiki (diver), 150
Kirk (diver), 101–2

Labat (diver), 28, 33
La Chrétienne
    amphora field at, 16–20
    wreck at, 18, 20, 118–32
Lallemand (archaeologist and diver), 5,
    25–26, 32–34, 51
Lassius, Marcus et Caius, 19
La vente, 121
Lead on ancient ships, 46
Le Corbusier, 41
Les Magnons (island), 1–5, 139–42
Looting. See Pillaging
Louis XVI, 113
Lucky coin, 121–24
Lufti Gelil, 83, 89–91, 93–94, 98–99
Lugagne (factory owner), 150–51

Mahdia, wreck at, 6–15, 20
Maldive Islands, 168–71
Malle, Louis, 48
Malville (diver), 36
Mandalinci, 83, 89, 91, 97, 104
Marsden, Peter R. V., 122
Médan (diver), 33
Medeon, dives at, 147–51
Mediterranean Sea, 127
Messenger, 29
Mollat (professor), 122
Monde sans soleil, Le (film), 143

Navarino, diving at, 59
Naxos, diving at, 58
Nemi, Lake, 46, 178
Nitrogen, divers and, 207–8
Noria, 160–61

Omer (diver), 155, 159
Ortolan, Capt., 62, 64–66
Oscan inscription on amphora, 19
Oxhide-shaped ingots, 95, 108

Panama, 61–67, 184
Perga, ruins at, 100–101

Phoenician
    glass beads, 101
    inscription on coin, 122
Pic (Robert; Picassou), 36–37
Pillaging, 199–203
Pitt-Rivers, Lt. Gen., 206
Podevin (diver), 18–19
Poider, Father, 6–10
Pointe de Russe. See Russian Point
Pomègues, wreck at, 111–12
Pori (island), 53
Port Cros amphora, 4–5
Posidonia (aquatic plant), 3
Pottery
    from Antikythera, 57
    Campanian, 24, 27, 45
    Roman, 27
    See also Bowls
Preservation, 192–98
    of bones, 194
    of gold, 197
    of marble, 197
    of metals in general, 194–96
    of organic matter, 193
    of pottery, 198
    of silver, 197
    of skulls, 194
    of stone, 197
    of wood, 193
    of wrecks, 189
Price, Derek, 57
Pump, bilge, 152–67

Raibaldi (diver), 136–37
Raud (crew), 25, 29, 32, 36
Red Sea, 143–46
Riquet (diver), 74–75
Robbery. See Pillaging
Roman baths on ships, 132–35
Roman inscriptions on amphoras, 19
Roman port of Carthage, search for, 6–15
Roman pottery, 27
Roman ships
    baths on, 132–35
    deterioration of, 184
    in Red Sea, 145
    size of, 130, 157
    wrecked at La Chrétienne, 118–32
    wrecked in Thames River, 122
Roman theatre, ruins of, 99
Rossignol (U.R.G. commander), 16
Rotting. See Shipwrecks, deterioration of
Ruins
    at Delos, 54

at Mahdia, 10
at Perga, 100–101
Roman theatre, 98
at Side, 100
at Xanthos, 84
Russian Point, wreck at, 113
Russian ship. *See Slava Rossii*

Saint-Aignon, M. de, 114
Salammbo, Carthage site of, 8
Salvatori (diver), 155, 161, 163–64
Sanary, Bay of, 1
Sand, source of, 145
Santa Maria, 178
Santamaria (diver), 68–69
Saout, Capt., 52
Scarabs, Egyptian, 107
Sentinaculum, 160
Sestius, Marcus (Sestios, Marcus), 38,
    44–45
villa of, 54
Shab Rumi, wreck at, 143–46
Ships
  ancient. *See* Ancient ships
  construction of. *See* Construction of
    ships
  modern. *See Calypso;* Construction of
    ships, modern; *Elie Monnier;
    Espadon; Fresnel; Lufti Gelil;
    Mandalinci*
  sinking of, 183–84
Shipwrecks
  from Bronze Age, 77–110
  from Byzantine era, 78
  cargoes of, 174–75
  cause of, 182–83
  of *Cutty Sark*, 178
  deterioration of, 67, 184–86
  of *Dramont*, 66, 68–76, 177
  exposure to air of, 192–93
  formation of, 181–91
  of *Grande Sultane*, 59
  at Hyères, 153–55
  at La Chrétienne, 118–32
  at Lake Nemi, 46, 178
  locating, 191

at Mahdia, 6–15, 20
of the *Panama*, 61–67, 184
at Pomegéus, 111–12
preservation of, 189, 193
Roman, 119, 122
of *Slava Rossii*, 113–32, 184
at Sou Ada, 86
of the *Vasa*, 178
of the *Victory*, 178
Side, ruins of, 100
Silent World, The (film), 48
Sivirine (writer), 76
Slava Rossii, 113–32, 184
Slipper bath, 132–33
Sou Ada, wreck at, 86
Sponge trawl, 81
Statues, 55–56
Submarines, miniature, development of,
    155, 210–11
Suceuse (suction hose), construction and
    operation of, 17

Tailliez, Philippe, 3, 6, 10–11, 16, 20, 61,
    117
Taylor, Joan du Plat, 78–79, 81, 83, 94,
    96–97, 99, 102, 108
Throckmorton, Peter, 77, 79, 82, 84–89,
    93–95, 99, 102–4, 160
Tiles, 111–12
Turkey, 77–110

Ucelli (author and diver), 160
Undersea Research Group, 6, 16
Underwater archaeology, future of,
    204–11
Underwater dwellings, 209–10

Vasa, 178
Vases. *See* Amphoras
Vessels. *See* Amphoras; Doliums
Victory, 178

Wheeler, Sir Mortimer, 206
Wrecks. *See* Shipwrecks

Xanthos, ruins at, 84